Ageing, Health, and Productivity

Reports for the Fondazione Rodolfo DeBenedetti

Ageing, Health, and Productivity

The Economics of Increased Life Expectancy

Edited by

Pietro Garibaldi,
Joaquim Oliveira Martins,
and Jan van Ours

With

Axel Börsch-Supan, Brigitte Dormont, Vincenzo Galasso,
Pekka Ilmakunnas, Enrico Moretti, Florian Pelgrin,
Vegard Skirbekk, Marc Suhrcke, Etienne Wasmer,
and Matthias Weiss

OXFORD
UNIVERSITY PRESS

OXFORD
UNIVERSITY PRESS

Great Clarendon Street, Oxford OX2 6DP

Oxford University Press is a department of the University of Oxford.
It furthers the University's objective of excellence in research, scholarship,
and education by publishing worldwide in

Oxford New York

Auckland Cape Town Dar es Salaam Hong Kong Karachi
Kuala Lumpur Madrid Melbourne Mexico City Nairobi
New Delhi Shanghai Taipei Toronto

With offices in

Argentina Austria Brazil Chile Czech Republic France Greece
Guatemala Hungary Italy Japan Poland Portugal Singapore
South Korea Switzerland Thailand Turkey Ukraine Vietnam

Oxford is a registered trade mark of Oxford University Press
in the UK and in certain other countries

Published in the United States
by Oxford University Press Inc., New York

British Library Cataloguing in Publication Data
Data available

Library of Congress Cataloging in Publication Data
Data available

Typeset by SPI Publisher Services, Pondicherry, India
Printed in Great Britain
on acid-free paper by
MPG Books Group, Bodmin and King's Lynn

ISBN 978–0–19–958713–1

10 9 8 7 6 5 4 3 2 1

Contents

Contents

Part II: *Age and Productivity*
Pekka Ilmakunnas, Jan van Ours, Vegard Skirbekk,
and Matthias Weiss

Contents

List of Figures

List of Tables

List of Contributors

Axel Börsch-Supan, Mannheim Research Institute for the Economics of Aging, University of Mannheim, Germany

Brigitte Dormont, University of Paris Dauphine and CEPREMAP, Paris, France

Pietro Garibaldi, Fondazione RDB, University of Turin and Collegio Carlo Alberto, Italy

Vincenzo Galasso, Bocconi University and IGIER, Italy

Pekka Ilmakunnas, Helsinki School of Economics, Finland

Enrico Moretti, University of Berkeley, California, USA

Joaquim Oliveira Martins, OECD and Sciences-Po, Paris, France

Florian Pelgrin, DEEP University Lausanne-HEC, CIRANO, IEMS, Switzerland

Vegard Skirbekk, IIASA-Institute for Applied Systems Analysis, Austria

Marc Suhrcke, Health Economics Group, University of East Anglia, UK

Jan van Ours, Tilburg University, The Netherlands

Etienne Wasmer, Sciences-Po, Paris, France

Matthias Weiss, Mannheim Research Institute for the Economics of Aging, University of Mannheim, Germany

Introduction

Pietro Garibaldi

The increase in life expectancy is arguably the most remarkable by-product of modern economic growth. In the last 30 years we have been gaining roughly 2.5 years of longevity every decade both in Europe and in the United States. This progress outpaced the most optimistic scenarios and documented that demographic projections are no more reliable than economic forecasts. The progress may also turn out to be resilient in the years to come. The sharp reduction in the number of childbirths per woman, a phenomenon somewhat parallel to the increase in longevity, implies population ageing. Successfully managing ageing and longevity over the next 20 years is one of the major structural challenges faced by policymakers in advanced economies, particularly so in the area of health spending, social security administration, and labour market institutions. This book looks closely into those challenges, raising a few fundamental issues at both the macroeconomic and microeconomic levels. Among these: is it possible to turn the challenges faced by ageing and longevity into a long-term productive opportunity? Can advanced economies engineer a healthy ageing scenario with long-term spillovers in terms of enhanced technological progress and acceleration of long-term growth? What is the microeconomic relationship between ageing and productivity, and how can specific policies postpone any age-related decay in productivity at the firm and individual levels?

Over the last two decades, economic research demonstrated theoretically and empirically that human capital accumulation is a key catalyst for sustained economic growth. In real life economies, a given endowment of human capital can generate the appropriate returns as long as it is embodied in healthy operating individuals. In this respect, the average health conditions of an ageing population play a first-order effect in a macroeconomic perspective, and will represent a key factor for economic growth in the 21st century. The first half of the book studies the macroeconomic relationships between health spending, technological progress in medical related sectors, economic growth, and welfare state reforms.

In the popular press, longevity and population ageing are typically perceived as a tremendous burden, and the idea of a 'demographic time bomb on advanced economies' is the most picturesque image of this perception. At a more scientific level, the staggering increase in the dependency ratio of the elderly population over the next 50 years is indeed a worrying summary statistics. These projections are nevertheless based on a constant set of policies in the area of labour market and social security. With a proper set of reforms, conversely, advanced economies have the option of transforming the enormous challenge posed by longevity into a long-term opportunity to boost aggregate outcomes. The argument runs as follows. With properly designed market incentives to remain on the job, healthy elderly workers would provide an increase in average labour market participation, with potential positive effects on a country's gross domestic product. Current policies do not provide such incentives. As a result, the basic prerequisite of a healthy ageing scenario is a substantial structural reform in social security and in labour market institutions.

In addition to social security reform, the healthy ageing scenario inevitably requires further improvements in the average health condition of the elderly population, in a way consistent to what happened over the last century. These improvements in health conditions, if biologically feasible, will not come up as a free lunch. Health is indeed very costly, and today most advanced economies already devote some 6–15% of their gross domestic product to finance health expenditures. Since the importance of health is bound to increase, it is crucial to study in detail the determinants of per capita health expenditures. Is health expenditure driven by demographic factors, consumer demand, and/or by technological progress? Health expenditure is largely a normal good, with an elasticity with respect to income not very different from one. However, the key determinants of per capita health expenditures are changes in medical practices: new, more sophisticated, and more costly ways of treating similar diseases. Since these trends will continue over the next 50 years, the book envisages a further increase of health expenditure of at least 5% of GDP.

If the medical sector is going to absorb some 11–20% of gross domestic product, can such expenditure, through its effect on technological progress, be a catalyst for economic growth? This is indeed one of the key questions. New growth theory and models of semi-endogenous growth suggest that is indeed the case. Nevertheless, empirical evidence of the long-run impact of health expenditure on growth is rather limited. The interpretation given in the book is that incentives to retire early in Europe work as an obstacle to the potential growth-enhancing spillovers of health expenditure. This is a key reason for understanding the link between social security reforms and long-run growth. These technological spillovers could generate a *growth* effect in income, a much more powerful instrument than the *level* effect obtained by simply keeping more people in production. Reforms in the goods market are also part of the story, since health expenditure is mainly related to the service sector, an area where Europe's structural rigidity emerges. Overall, the healthy ageing scenario requires a complementary approach to reform in the area of social security, labour market institutions, and product market regulation.

The second part of the book looks closely at the microeconomic relationship between population ageing and productivity, both at the individual and at the firm levels. There is surprisingly little research on such key questions. The book contributes to this debate along two dimensions. First, it presents a detailed analysis of the determinant of productivity, with a focus on both long-run historical evolution and cross-sectional changes. Second, it uses econometric analysis to look into the determinants of the various dimensions of individual productivity.

Individual productivity is a multidimensional phenomenon, and age has a different effect on its physical and its cognitive dimensions. As a result, the relationship between ageing and productivity depends on the relative weights at the job level of the different dimensions of productivity. In as much as jobs require physical effort, productivity is adversely selected by age. Conversely, cognitive ability depreciates more smoothly and appears to have a long-lasting effect on individual productivity. Over the last century, the structure of the representative job has changed dramatically toward the service sector, and thus the relationship between age and productivity has reduced the importance of the physical dimension.

The relationship between age and productivity can be studied with a variety of data, and the book conceptually distinguishes between an extensive and an intensive margin of productivity. The extensive margin can be proxied by absenteeism data. The intensive margin requires some observation (in specific jobs) of individual productivity.

Absenteeism data suggest that younger workers take more days off as sick leave than older workers on average. However, each spell of absence lasts longer for the older worker. The book finds a non-linear relationship between age and productivity: absence due to sickness increases up to the age of 45, and decreases thereafter. In a medium-run perspective, the shift of older workers towards occupations that require less physical effort is likely to reduce absenteeism and boost the extensive margin of individual productivity. This is a very basic but nevertheless important message. Technological progress and structural change in the labour market do work in the right direction.

On very specific cases, one can directly observe a measure of productivity in the workplace, and thus focus on the intensive margin of the relationship. Based on real productivity data on a car manufacturing plant, individual productivity at the workplace is seen to decrease monotonically with age. But the role of experience works in the opposite direction. Since older workers are more experienced on average, the relationship on the intensive margin is thus ambiguous, since it is the result of a composition effect between a pure age effect and an experience effect. In any event, there is clear evidence that human capital investment acts to smooth the adverse pure age effect of productivity. This is yet another piece of evidence on the effects of human capital investment at the microeconomic level.

Individual decisions on how to allocate the human capital across occupation, as well as managerial decisions as to how to optimally exploit the available human capital in the workplace appear to be much more important determinants of individual productivity than demographic trends. This is good news, since there is ample room for various policies to engineer productive longevity. More flexibility in retirement, properly designed personnel policies, flexible wage setting and employment protection legislation can jointly act to boost the productivity of elder workers. In light of the large heterogeneity across workers, flexibility is really the key word, and should be taken seriously by policy-makers. The message seems to be that the complex relationship between population ageing and longevity is not written in stone, and can be modified by properly designed choices.

Part I

Health Expenditures, Longevity, and Growth*

Brigitte Dormont, Joaquim Oliveira Martins,
Florian Pelgrin, and Marc Suhrcke

* Presented at the Ninth Annual Conference of the Fondazione Rodolfo DeBenedetti on Health, Longevity and Productivity, held at Limone sul Garda in May 2007. The authors would like to thank Tito Boeri, Axel Borsch-Supan, Vincenzo Galasso, Pietro Garibaldi, and an anonymous referee for comments and suggestions on earlier versions of this chapter. We also thank Christine de la Maisonneuve for useful remarks and input. The usual disclaimer applies. The views expressed are those of the authors and do not reflect those of the OECD or its member countries.

Introduction

Several arguments contribute to the idea that health matters for growth and productivity. Better health positively impacts labour supply, notably through a longer life expectancy, and healthier individuals can reasonably be assumed to produce more per hour worked. According to human capital theory, a longer life span will also encourage people to acquire more education. Good health results in more educated and productive people. Healthier individuals (or the total population) are more willing to undertake investment, which in turn promotes growth. Finally, a substantial share of health spending being devoted to finance R&D, it contributes to innovation and growth.

Ageing, on the contrary, is expected to induce a drag on potential growth and make social security systems unsustainable in many developed countries. Inspired by the seminal work of Auerbach and Kotlikoff (1987), recent models have quantified such an adverse impact from the projected change in population structure, the subsequent decline in the labour force, and different reform scenarios in pensions systems and labour markets (e.g. Ingenue, 2001; Börsch-Supan *et al.*, 2002, 2006). Their broad conclusion is that ageing trends are unlikely to be fully compensated by economic factors, like higher capital intensity, migration, or productivity.

Nonetheless, this literature had mostly addressed the impact of the fall in fertility rates from post-World War II levels. Less attention has been devoted to the issue of *longevity without incapacity* and how to benefit from it. Contrary to common views about ageing, healthy longevity should not be perceived as a negative shock. Rather, it is good news about individuals able to live and work longer, provided they are not hampered by a premature retirement decision. Several studies (e.g. Duval, 2003; Börsch-Supan, *et al.*, 2005) have shown that the decision in favour of early retirement is much less a matter of individual preferences for leisure than the result of perverse incentives created by current institutional arrangements in pension systems and labour markets.

Therefore, there could be a possible path taking advantage of both the improved health status of the population and the extended duration of active life, which could promote the growth potential of economies faced by ageing trends. Such active 'healthy ageing' scenario would critically depend on political support of mechanisms linking the duration of active lives to longevity gains (see Galasso, 2006). In this scenario, the growth potential could dramatically improve compared with a situation where a large amount of labour resources are 'wasted' by a premature exit from an active life, notably in European economies (see Oliveira Martins *et al.*, 2005).

Against this background, this part aims to understand the links between health spending, medical innovation, health status, growth, and welfare.[1] The objective is to identify the conditions under which a healthy ageing regime could develop and what its impacts on the economy might be. The different links are illustrated in Figure 1. Health spending is supposed to trigger technological progress in the health sector, which in turn impacts on expenditures. Both health spending and technological progress are a potential source of better welfare outcomes in terms of longevity and health status at every age. The latter has a feedback on expenditures and is an indirect source of growth through an improvement in human capital. This contributes to gross domestic product (GDP) per capita, mainly through higher participation of the population in the labour force and higher labour productivity levels. Growth GDP also benefits from innovation in health services and bio-tech industries. Closing the loop between health and growth, more aggregate income induces an increase in health expenditures, as richer countries tend to have a higher share of health goods and services in GDP.

A key policy driver for the analysis presented here relates to the sustainability of health expenditure growth. As a share of GDP, total spending on health care[2] has risen steadily over the past 30 years and has roughly doubled since the early 1970s (Figure 2). Policy-makers are rightly concerned that ongoing population ageing may exacerbate these

---

[1] Data and empirical evidence covered here focus on three main developed regions: the US, European Union (EU) (mostly the EU-15), and Japan.

[2] Note that for data availability reasons, total health spending displayed in the figure includes both health and long-term care expenditures. But given the still low share of long-term care in total spending (on average below 1% by 2005 for OECD countries), the qualitative picture is not changed by this approximation.

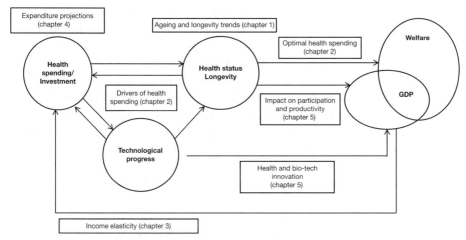

Figure 1. Links between health spending, technological progress, longevity, and GDP

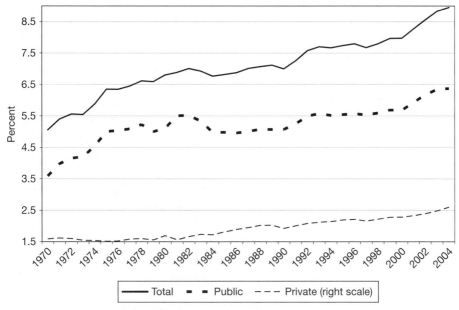

Figure 2. Evolution of total, public, and private OECD health spending (in % of GDP)

Note: Unweighted average of available OECD countries, including long-term care expenditure.

Source: OECD Health Database (2005a)

expenditure trends. Notably, as they cumulate with other social spending, such as pensions, as well as exceptional pressures on public debts in the context of the 2008 financial crisis.

However, both micro- and macro-level evidence presented below shows that the impact of ageing *per se* on health care is small. In contrast, the role of preferences and technology are crucial. Confirming other studies, we provide empirical evidence that health expenditures tend to grow roughly in line with aggregate income. On top of this income effect, the diffusion of new medical technology explains the growing share of health spending relative to GDP. Drawing on this analysis, we carry out several projection exercises suggesting a substantial increase in health expenditure shares by 2050.

Although increased health spending, through a better health status, is expected to positively influence aggregate productivity and growth, evidence on this link is somewhat inconclusive, at least for high-income countries. While we discuss the reasons for this puzzling result, we also analyse the growth potential related to health research and development (R&D) and innovation activities.

To simplify what is an already complex web of interrelated factors, we decided not to include long-term care in the picture.[3] Indeed, in contrast to health care, long-term care corresponds to rather low-productivity basic services and spending is mainly related to demographic developments, in particular the growing share of very old and frail individuals in the total population. Long-term care will certainly contribute to public expenditure pressures over the next decades, but can hardly enhance growth prospects.

The policy implications of the analysis are manifold. Over the next decades, pressures for public expenditure are likely to be large in health systems. These challenges require an integrated and complementary package of policies. Reforms in pension systems, the health sector, labour, product and financial markets are deeply interrelated. While only a subset of these policy linkages are dealt with in this part, to our knowledge, it is one of the first comprehensive attempts to cover these links. Further research in this area is much needed.

Figure 1 provides a reader's guide to the mapping between the different links analysed in the chapters in this part of the book. The first chapter deals with demographic facts. Chapter 2 analyses the links between health-care expenditures, technology, and health status from a micro-level

---

[3] For a comprehensive discussion on long-term care, see e.g. Norton (2000) and OECD (2005b).

perspective. Chapter 3 investigates the relationship between GDP growth and health expenditures empirically. Chapter 4 develops a projection method to assess the size of aggregate expenditures (both public and private) that could be channelled to the health sector. In Chapter 5, we assess the impact of health expenditures and better health status on potential growth and productivity. We carry out some 'thought experiments' on the indexation of active life on longevity and the impact of ageing on aggregate productivity. Chapter 6 summarizes and draws policy conclusions.

1

Transitory vs. Permanent Demographic Shocks: From Ageing to Longevity

Ageing trends are the result of two different and contrasted phenomena: the change from a high to a low fertility regime and the increase in longevity. The baby boom and subsequent fertility bust was a massive, but *transitory*, shock. In contrast, the smooth and steady increase in longevity does look like a *permanent* shock (Oeppen and Vaupel, 2002; EC, 2003; Barbi, 2003). Supporting this hypothesis, the frontier of longevity in different countries has increased almost linearly by 2.4 years per decade over the past century and a half (Figure 1.1). A similar trend was observed on average for the United States, Europe, and Japan over the past 40 years (Table 1.1), though with a wide cross-country dispersion.

During the 20th century, increased longevity has resulted from uneven developments in mortality rates across age groups. The first half of the century mainly experienced a reduction in child mortality. In the second half, the reductions in mortality were located in prime and old age groups. The role of health care was also different in the two periods (Vaupel, 2002; Yashin, 2003; Lichtenberg, 2003). The development of mass vaccination and antibiotics, together with improved hygiene and life style, helped eradicate infectious diseases (tuberculosis, pneumonia, flu, etc.). The latter were the main cause of mortality in the early 20th century, affecting in particular young children. But since then, the reductions in mortality have been associated with distinct factors, notably the treatment of cardiovascular diseases and cancer. The prevalence of these diseases is increasing in age and their treatment has triggered the development of medical innovation, as will be discussed below.

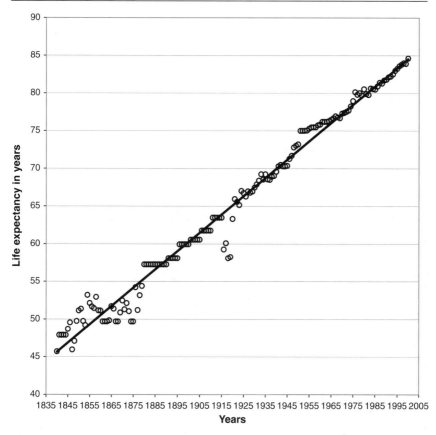

Figure 1.1. Historical trends in female life expectancy, 1840–2000[1]
Note: [1]Country with the highest life expectancy. The linear trend: slope = 2.43 and R^2 = 0.98.
Source: Oeppen and Vaupel (2002).

Accordingly, Oeppen and Vaupel (2002) argued that population projections need to take into account a steady progression of longevity gains.
Notably, Cheung and Robine (2007) provided empirical evidence of a shift
of the modal age of death in Japan, suggesting that currently there is no
evidence that we are approaching an upper limit in human longevity.
However, Olshansky *et al.* (2005) have put forward an opposite view.
They noted that extrapolation of past trends cannot provide a good basis
for long-term projections because longevity gains have been driven by
improvements in environmental, economic, and social factors that may
not last in the future. In particular, widespread obesity trends in many

Table 1.1. Increases in life expectancy for different age groups. Change in years over the last 40 years[1]

	Females					Males				
	at birth	at age 40	at age 60	at age 65	at age 80	at birth	at age 40	at age 60	at age 65	at age 80
United States	6.4	4.5	3.6	3.4	2.3	7.5	5.5	4.1	3.5	1.6
Europe										
Austria	9.3	6.1	5.3	4.9	2.5	10.0	6.1	5.0	4.2	2.2
Belgium	7.3	5.7	5.1	4.7	2.3	6.9	4.9	3.8	3.1	1.4
Czech Republic	5.0	3.4	2.8	2.6	1.4	3.8	1.4	1.4	1.2	0.5
Denmark	4.9	3.3	3.0	3.0	n.a	4.1	2.2	1.8	1.5	n.a.
Finland	8.5	7.0	6.1	5.6	2.6	8.7	6.4	4.8	4.0	1.6
France	9.1	6.4	5.8	5.3	3.0	8.2	5.3	4.6	4.0	2.3
Germany	8.3	5.7	4.9	4.6	2.4	7.8	4.5	3.7	3.1	1.6
Greece	8.2	5.7	4.6	4.1	1.2	8.2	3.5	3.2	2.9	1.4
Hungary	5.6	2.3	2.6	2.5	1.5	1.3	-2.6	-0.3	0.3	0.9
Ireland	7.3	5.0	3.8	3.3	n.a.	6.1	3.7	2.5	2.0	n.a
Italy	10.1	n.a.	n.a.	n.a.	n.a.	9.1	n.a.	n.a.	n.a.	n.a.
Luxembourg	9.1	6.6	5.8	5.3	3.4	8.4	5.0	3.8	3.1	1.5
Netherlands	5.1	4.4	4.1	3.9	2.1	4.0	2.7	1.8	1.4	0.7
Poland	7.3	3.0	2.7	2.4	1.2	4.8	0.1	0.8	0.9	0.9
Portugal	12.9	4.4	3.5	3.0	n.a	11.5	3.2	2.3	1.7	n.a.
Slovak Republic	4.7	n.a	2.2	1.9	n.a	0.8	n.a.	-0.7	-0.3	n.a.
Spain	10.5	6.4	5.3	4.8	2.0	8.1	4.0	3.3	3.0	1.3
Sweden	7.1	5.6	5.0	n.a	2.6	6.2	4.2	3.4	n.a.	1.4
United Kingdom	6.5	4.9	4.1	3.8	2.3	7.5	5.7	4.4	3.7	1.7
EU-15 average	*8.3*	*5.5*	*4.7*	*4.3*	*2.4*	*7.7*	*4.4*	*3.5*	*2.9*	*1.6*
Japan	14.4	10.6	9.1	8.3	4.7	12.4	8.1	6.6	5.9	3.1
OECD average	*9.1*	*5.3*	*4.4*	*4.0*	*2.3*	*8.2*	*4.2*	*3.2*	*2.6*	*1.5*

Note: [1] 1960 (or 1961) to 2000 (or 1999).

Source: OECD Health Data.

developed countries would contribute to a deterioration of the health status of the population, which *in fine* will reduce life expectancy.[1]

The critical condition for these potential longevity gains to materialize in longer working lives is a dynamic equilibrium between the increase in life expectancy and the number of years of good health (the so-called 'healthy ageing' regime). Achieving this virtuous cycle may require large investments in health care, which to be sustainable may require in turn a careful design of insurance mechanisms and use of technological progress. Understanding these mechanisms is the aim of the next chapter.

---

[1] The population projections (2005–50) used in this study are derived from the OECD Population Projections Database. They are based on national data and embody a certain slowdown in longevity gains at the horizon of 2050 compared with past trends. For a discussion see Oliveira Martins *et al.* (2005).

2

The Growth of Health Expenditures: Ageing vs. Technological Progress

2.1 How can we Explain the Rise of Health Expenditures as a Share of GDP?

A conventional explanation for the rising share of health spending in GDP, noted in the introduction, is that transfer programmes, such as Medicare and Medicaid in the US or comprehensive health insurance in Europe, by increasing coverage also boosted aggregate health spending. However, the latter does not explain why the demand for health care, as well as the demand for comprehensive insurance, has increased so rapidly. Another explanation is related to a 'cost disease' effect (Baumol, 1967, 1993). Health, like other care services, uses labour intensively and hence may display low productivity growth. As a result, the relative price of health care tends to rise over time and, depending on preferences, this leads to a rising expenditure share. Along these lines, Triplett and Bosworth (2000) argued that labour productivity growth in the health sector was negative between 1987 and 1997, while at the same time the medical care component of the consumer price index (CPI) has increased faster than the overall CPI. An alternative, and somewhat opposite explanation, is that the bulk of the expenditure increase is attributable to technological change (Newhouse, 1992). This explanation, which has received increasing attention in the literature (e.g. Fuchs, 1984; Okunade and Murthy, 2002; Cutler, 2004; Jones, 2004), will be the focus of our analysis.

In the course of the 1980s, governments started to react to these spending trends by putting in place a number of cost-containment policies (see Docteur and Oxley, 2003), resulting in a stabilization of public health-care expenditures in the OECD from the mid-1980s to the late 1990s. Concomitantly, private health spending accelerated. As public cost-containment policies acted mainly through macroeconomic mechanisms (e.g. wage moderation, price controls, or postponement of investments), they could not be sustained forever.[1] Thus, after a long period of cost containment, since 2000 the share of public expenditures to GDP has been increasing at a rate of over 3% per year for the OECD as a whole. In this context, it is crucial to identify the drivers of these expenditure trends. Are they related to demography or to other factors?

2.2 The Main Drivers of Health Expenditure Growth

The combined effects of the projected ageing of the population (Figure 2.1) and the fact that health-care expenditures increase with age (Figure 2.2) are often seen as a major determinant of future health-care expenditures. These two phenomena are illustrated at this stage for the particular case of France, but wider cross-country evidence will be provided in Chapter 4. By applying demographic projections to a static expenditure profile by age, the *demographic* impact on future health-care expenditures could in principle be simulated.

However, the profile of expenditures by age group changes over time. Again using French data, for which this calculation was possible, a sizeable upward drift can be observed for each age group between 1992 and 2000 (Figure 2.3). As we will see below, the drift is not due to a deterioration of patients' health status. This drift is rather related to changes over time in patients' behaviour, physicians' practices, as well as to the effect of technological progress. Therefore, it is a *non-demographic* effect. As we will see below, the upward drift of the expenditure profile displayed in Figure 2.3 is actually the main driver of expenditure growth. Ageing plays only a relatively minor role.

2.2.1 *The Role of the Proximity of Death*

Estimates on cross-sectional or panel data for OECD countries suggest a very small or non-significant influence of age on health expenditures. In

---

[1] Indeed, it is difficult to contain wages and, at the same time, attract young and skilled workers in the health-care sector. Controlling prices is not easy when technical progress is permanently creating new products and treatments. Equipments also need to be renovated, especially in the presence of rapid technical progress.

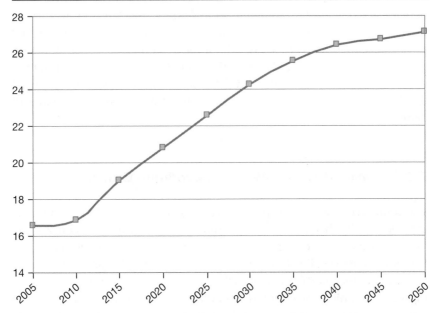

Figure 2.1. Proportion of people aged 65 and over (demographic effect), France (in % of total population)
Source: OECD.

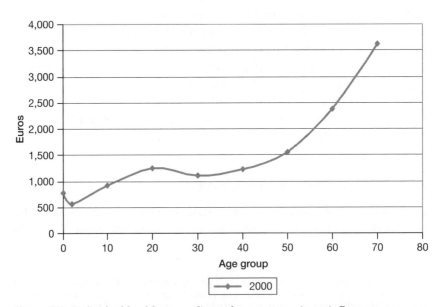

Figure 2.2. Individual health expenditures by age group (euros), France
Source: Dormont *et al.* (2006).

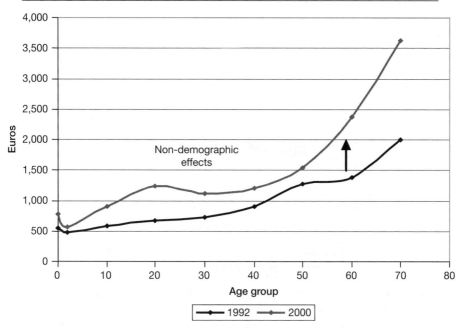

Figure 2.3. Drift in health expenditures by age group, 1992 and 2000, France

Note: The upward shift of the expenditure curve illustrates the effect of non-demographic drivers (income, technology, etc.).

Source: Dormont *et al.* (2006).

contrast, GDP has a sizeable and highly significant impact (Getzen, 1992; Gerdtham *et al.*, 1992, 1998; Hitiris and Posnett, 1992; Leu, 1986; O'Connell, 1996; OECD, 1987). Zweifel *et al.* (1999) put forward a plausible explanation for the small impact of age on expenditure. They follow Lubitz and Riley (1993), who pointed out that yearly payments per person for people dying within the year were 7.1 times larger than for survivors (based on US Medicare beneficiaries in 1988). In other words, health expenditures appear to be increasing with age just because health-care costs increase in proximity to death and the probability of dying increases with age. Zweifel *et al.* (1999) used micro-econometric estimates on Swiss data to support this finding. Once proximity to death is controlled for, age *per se* does not influence health expenditures.

Subsequently, other papers have investigated the respective influences of time to death and age on health expenditures (Seshamani and Gray, 2004a, 2004b; Stearns and Norton, 2004; Zweifel *et al.*, 2004; Werblow *et al.*, 2007). A very enlightening article written by Yang, Norton, and Stearns (2003)

19

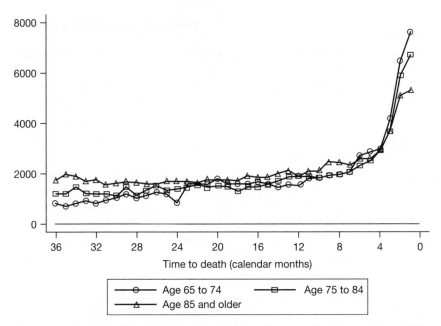

Figure 2.4. Individual health expenditure ($) in relation to death proximity, Medicare beneficiaries (USA)

Source: Z. Yang, E. C. Norton, and S. C. Stearns (2003), 'Longevity and Health Care Expenditures: The Real Reasons Older People Spend More', *Journal of Gerontology B, Psychol Soc Sci* (2003), 58(1), S2–S10. Reproduced by kind permission of the authors and Oxford University Press.

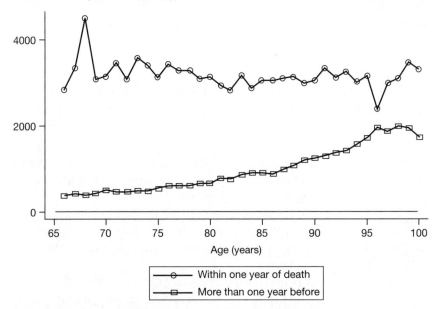

Figure 2.5. Individual health expenditure ($) by age-group decedents versus survivors, Medicare beneficiaries (USA)

Source: Z. Yang, E. C. Norton, and S. C. Stearns (2003), 'Longevity and Health Care Expenditures: The Real Reasons Older People Spend More', *Journal of Gerontology B, Psychol Soc Sci* (2003), 58 (1), S2–S10. Reproduced by kind permission.

makes it possible to understand the mechanisms at stake. The authors conduct a graphical analysis of person-month data for 25,994 Medicare beneficiaries. Figure 2.4 displays the individual health expenditure in relation to death proximity for three age groups (65 to 74, 75 to 84, and 85 and older). The curves for each age group are very close. Their main characteristic is the dramatic increase in health expenditures around four months before death, from $2,000 twelve months before death, to $8,000 in the last months. Figure 2.5 displays the average health expenditure by age, distinguishing between decedents (people dying in the year) from survivors. Large differences emerge between the two groups, supporting the role of proximity to death. Interestingly, however, we observe that the curve relative to survivors is increasing with age. Thus, time to death is not the only factor. For survivors, who account for the bulk of aggregate expenditures, health expenditures are still increasing with age.

To sum up, the empirical evidence suggests that both age and time to death have an influence on health expenditures. Therefore, health expenditure projections have to include the time to death. If it is death proximity, rather than age, that influences expenditures, increased longevity could actually slow down expenditure growth. Using US projected life tables for 2020, Stearns and Norton (2004) show that omitting time to death leads to an overstatement of around 15% for health expenditures. This downward correction is due to the fact that an increase in longevity is expected in the future.

2.2.2 *The Predominant Impact of Changes in Medical Practices*

While the discussions about the role of time to death focus on the interpretation of the profile of health expenditure by age (Figure 2.2), they omit to consider the main driver of expenditure growth: the upward drift of the age-profile of health expenditures over time (Figure 2.3). In other words, the predictions about future expenditures assume a constant level of technology, overlooking the role of changes in medical practices. Dormont, Grignon, and Huber (2006) have proposed a micro-simulation method for analysing changes over time in the age-profile that makes it possible to disentangle changes in morbidity, on the one hand, and changes in practices, on the other hand. The authors consider changes over time in the prevalence of chronic illnesses and disability indicators by age. This enables them to compute the resulting impact of those changes on expenditures by age.

More precisely, for a given morbidity level, the changes in practices between 1992 and 2000 are captured by changes in the coefficients which measure the impact of morbidity on health-care demand. These changes may be due to changes in patients' preferences, in physicians' behaviour, and/or to technological progress (innovative procedures or drugs).

Dormont *et al.* (2006) use a representative sample of 3,441 and 5,003 French individuals, in 1992 and 2000 respectively.[2] Their micro-simulation approach identifies the components of the drift observed between 1992 and 2000 in the age-profile of health expenditures. To give an illustration, the observed drift in pharmaceutical expenditures is displayed in Figure 2.6. A large upward drift is observed for the age-profile of individual expenditure between 1992 and 2000 (age-profiles 1 and 4, respectively). The simulations show that this large upward drift is entirely due to changes in practices for a given level of morbidity (profile 1 to 2). For the same morbidity level experienced in 1992, individuals have spent more in 2000 than they would have spent in 1990, irrespective of their age. In contrast, the changes in morbidity (or a better health status) induce a downward drift (profile 2 to 3) for all age groups (except 70+). Thus, changes in health status have *ceteris paribus* led to lower spending.

Applying the simulated profiles to the structure by age of the French population enables us to assess the relative effects of the demographic change and expenditure profile drifts for the period 1992–2000 at the aggregate level. The results for pharmaceutical and total expenditures are provided in Table 2.1. Overall, pharmaceutical expenditure increased by around 67%. The changes in practices contributed to 52 percentage points of this increase. Comparatively, the effect of changes in the age structure appears to be very small (only 4.6 percentage points). For total expenditures, the changes in practices explain 13 percentage points, while 3.4 percentage points are due to changes in the age structure. For total expenditures, other factors, such as income, explain a large amount of the variation (around 46 percentage points). Most importantly, the aggregate effect of changes in morbidity is negative for both pharmaceuticals and total

---

[2] The database used by Dormont *et al.* (2006) has the advantage of providing detailed information about morbidity and health expenditures at the micro-level and for rather a long period. This makes it possible to: (i) provide empirical evidence of global health improvement; and (ii) evaluate the savings due to changes in morbidity. Such databases are rare in other countries. The Survey of Health, Aging and Retirement in Europe (SHARE) collects the same kind of information, but only beginning in 2004. The second wave concerns 2006. In the future, this survey will provide precious information for several European countries. However, it is currently too early to use it for an evaluation of changes that have occurred over time in morbidity and in medical practices.

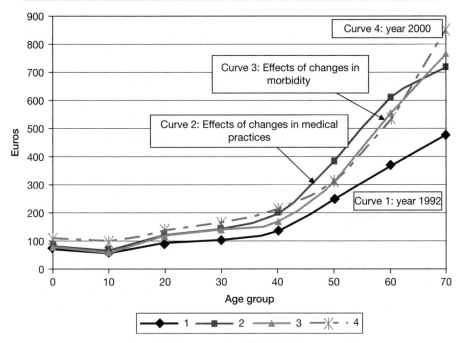

Figure 2.6. Decomposition of the drift of the age-profile of individual pharmaceutical expenditures, France (micro-simulations), 1992–2000

Note: The decomposition method enables the effect of changes in medical practices to be disentangled from the changes in morbidity, explaining the drift in the expenditure curve between 1992 and 2006.

Source: Dormont *et al* (2006).

Table 2.1. Explaining health expenditure growth, France

Variation 1992–2000 (%)	Pharmaceutical Expenditures	Total expenditures
Total demographic change of which:	7.63	6.35
part of structural change	*4.61*	*3.36*
part of growing size of population	*3.02*	*2.99*
Changes in practices for a given morbidity	52.24	12.87
Changes in morbidity	−9.24	−9.74
Changes in age dummies	14.11	−1.55
Other changes	2.53	45.95
Total variation	67.27	53.89

Source: Dormont *et al* (2006).

expenditures (above 9 percentage points), reflecting the impact of health improvements. These more than compensate the increase in costs related to pure ageing effects.

The question now is what these changes in practices are made of. Evidence shows that changes in practices are mainly induced by technological changes: for given age and morbidity, more treatments are provided, leading to higher costs and better outcomes. It is therefore crucial to examine thoroughly the dynamics of technological change in health care.

2.3 Technological Change and its Impact on Health Status and Spending

2.3.1 *The Pattern of Innovation and Product Diffusion in Health Care*

The fact that technological change could be the main driver of health expenditure growth appears to contradict the conventional wisdom, according to which innovation is expected to increase productivity and reduce unit costs.[3] Gelijns and Rosenberg (1994) criticize a 'linear conceptualization' of medical progress, where 'new ideas' of the biomedical scientists would go from laboratory to animal testing and then to patients. The research leading to medical innovation does not necessarily take place in the biomedical sector: lasers, ultrasounds, magnetic resonance imaging, computer, nanotechnology have their origin in more general-purpose research and innovations. Moreover, product development does not end with the adoption of an innovation. Adoption is generally the beginning of a long process of redesigning the medical product based on feedback from users. These incremental improvements after initial adoption play a crucial role in the development of pharmaceutical drugs and medical devices.

Medical technological change entails two basic mechanisms: (i) the substitution of old treatments by new ones, this generally induces a gain in efficiency; and (ii) the extension of new treatments. The first substitution effect leads to a gain in productivity and often lowers unit costs, in accor-

---

[3] Quoting Gelijns and Rosenberg (1994): '...*Outside of medicine, technological change is identified as the primary driving force behind improved productivity and economic growth. One of the most decisive effects of technological change is that it makes it possible to produce a given volume of output with a smaller volume of inputs. Why, then, when considering medicine, is technological change deemed responsible for rising costs?*'.

dance with the standard view of the impact of technological progress. The rising costs in health-care spending are mainly due to the expansion treatments, that is, related to a potential demand for new goods and services.

Available statistics from the TECH network[4] on heart attack treatments allow this discussion to be made more concrete. Heart attacks are both the most common cause of death in most developed countries and an area where many innovations have occurred over the past 15 years (see Box 2.1). Cutler and McClellan (2001) and TECH Research Network (2001) show that there was a rising number of innovative procedures for heart attack treatments in the US and seven countries participating in the TECH network. Other indicators taken from the OECD health database (Figure 2.7) also show the increasing use of new medical procedures, such as cataract surgery, hip replacement, and knee replacement.

Cutler and McClellan (1996) showed that growth in treatment costs for heart attack in the US has resulted entirely from diffusion of innovative procedures, as prices paid for a given level of technology are fairly constant over time. In the US, by 1998, more than half of heart attack patients

---

Box 2.1 MEDICAL INNOVATIONS IN HEART ATTACK TREATMENT

A heart attack is an acute event characterized by the occlusion of the arteries that supply blood to the heart. Together with drug therapy (aspirin, beta blockers, etc.), patients can receive various treatments such as thrombolytic drugs, cardiac catheterization, percutaneous transluminal coronary angioplasty, and bypass surgery. Catheterization is a procedure used to view the blood flow to the heart to improve the diagnosis. Developed in the late 1970s, angioplasty appeared more recently than bypass surgery, which was developed in the late 1960s. It is an alternative, less invasive procedure for improving blood flow in a blocked artery by inflating a balloon to create a channel through the blockage. This innovative procedure is less costly and more respectful of patients' quality of life than bypass surgery. Angioplasty can replace bypass surgery in some cases. However, the use of angioplasty is spreading above and beyond this type of substitution. Since the mid-1990s, it has increasingly been performed with the implantation of one or more stents (small mesh tubes that hold open the coronary artery) to improve outcomes.

---

[4] The Technological Change in Health Care (TECH) Research network set up by Mark McClellan and Daniel Kessler has brought together investigators in clinical medicine, economics and epidemiology from sixteen countries to carry out international comparisons of technological change in the treatment of heart attack.

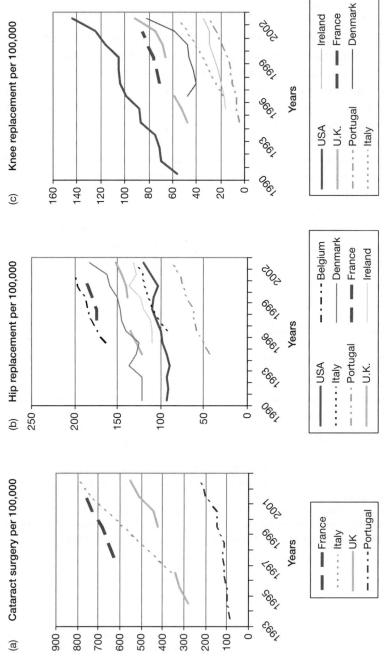

Figure 2.7. Use of cataract surgery, hip, and knee replacement in OECD countries

received catheterization and usually another procedure, instead of only 10% of heart attack patients in 1984.

Turning to other areas, the introduction of new medications such as selective serotonin reuptake inhibitors (SSRIs), including Prozac and similar medications, changed the treatment of depression completely. In the mid-1980s, treatments with psychotherapy or tricyclic anti-depressors were the norm. Berndt *et al.* (2000), and Cutler and McClellan (2001) show that the introduction of SSRIs was followed by a demand boom in the US. In 1991, 30% of depressed patients were treated with an SSRI; this proportion rises to nearly 50% by 1996. Berndt *et al.* (2000) show that this substitution effect led to a gain in efficiency. The spending per incremental remission probability was reduced by about 20%. Therefore, costs have been rising because of treatment expansion: diagnosis and treatments for depression doubled over the 1990s. The latter may have resulted from supply-induced demand encouraged by manufacturers of SSRIs providing incentives to doctors to watch out for depression. However, the supply of these new products meets demand needs that were not previously satisfied. Indeed, many studies in the 1980s suggested that half of depressed persons were not appropriately diagnosed and treated.

For cataract, the substitution of newer for older technologies led to obvious gains in efficiency (Shapiro *et al.*, 2001). There was no increase in the cost of a cataract operation between the late 1960s and the late 1990s, while health outcomes have increased: better visual quality and a reduction in complication rates. As operations are safer and more effective, there has been a treatment expansion: a larger number of patients are operated on (Figure 2.7(a)), including those with less severe visual acuity problems.

Nonetheless, technological progress in health care is likely to have had an impact on the price of health care relative to other goods in the economy. Non-adjusted official medical price indices have generally increased more rapidly than prices in the rest of the economy. For example, in the US, the medical-care CPI increased by 1.8 percentage points annually above the growth rate of the aggregate CPI between 1960 and 1999 (Cutler and McClellan, 2001). But these indices are poorly adjusted for quality changes and include as a price change many factors that should be counted as quantity increases resulting from medical innovations. When they are adjusted for quality it is possible that 'true' price indexes have actually declined. Adjusting prices for the variety of products can lead to a similar decrease in the true relative price of health-care goods (Box 2.2).

27

Box 2.2 TECHNICAL PROGRESS AND QUALITY/VARIETY-ADJUSTED MEDICAL
PRICES

A way to measure the benefit of health care is to focus on consumers' utility and
consider price effects adjusted for quality. When a consumer's marginal valuation of
the good equals its costs, it is possible to link costs and value using a hedonic analysis
(Griliches, 1971). As regards health care, the fact that patients are insured, together
with the asymmetry of information between patient and care providers, do not allow
us to assume that the marginal value of care equals its costs. One has to use direct
evidence on the expected value of health improvements to assess the benefit of
medical care. Accordingly, Cutler *et al.* (1998) build a Cost of Living (COL) Index to
measure how much consumers would be willing to pay for changes in medical
treatments and prices over time (Fisher and Shell, 1972). Applying this method to
the price of heart attack treatments, they estimated the COL Index relative to the
GDP deflator to have actually fallen by about 1% annually. This result was subsequently confirmed by Cutler and McClellan (2001) on heart attack, depression and
cataract treatments. A policy implication of such results is that production growth in
health care is likely to be understated by the current accounting approach.

Moreover, the 'true' relative price of health care *vis-à-vis* other goods may decrease if new technologies increase the variety of products and if there is a demand
for product variety. Consider for example a model with a CES-type utility function:
$U = \Sigma_i x_i^{(\sigma-1)/\sigma}$, where $\sigma > 1$ is the elasticity of substitution among n products. Assuming price symmetry $(p_i = p, \forall i)$, the true composite price index is equal to
$P^* = n^{(1-\sigma)} \cdot p$. With two types of composite goods, say health (H) and all other
goods (O), the true relative price would be: $P_H^*/P_O^* = (n_H/n_O)^{(1-\sigma)} \cdot (p_H/p_O)$. Thus,
even if the usual price ratio (p_H / p_O) remains constant, the 'true' relative price P_H^*/P_O^*
would decrease when the pace of product creation in the health sector is faster than
in the rest of the economy.

2.3.2 *Impact of Insurance Systems and Regulatory Factors on Technological Progress*

The incentives to produce innovation in the health sector are dominated
by insurance systems and public provision. Weisbrod (1991) suggested that
expanding insurance has provided an increased incentive for the R&D
sector to develop new technologies. New products tend always to be vali-
dated *ex post* by the insurance system. The orientation of technological
progress is also not neutral, as certain types of innovations will be favoured,
depending on the design of health insurance and on the payment systems
implemented by the payers.

The cross-national comparisons performed by the TECH network, referred to above, have shown that there are big differences in patterns of
technological change across countries (McClellan and Kessler, 2002). The

absolute differences in innovative procedure growth rates between high-growth countries (Australia, the US, France, Israel) and slow-growth countries (Canada-Ontario, Finland) amount to a factor of two or more over a five-year period.

Countries in which the health-care system is characterized by a monopsonic third-party payer can control the implementation of new technologies through effective budget ceilings. In countries with several third-party payers, competition among them will tend to drive up technology adoption. Different providers' payment systems also matter: fee-for-services and per-case remuneration schemes are more likely to encourage a higher adoption of new technologies than fixed remuneration schemes (capitation, global budget). In some countries, hospitals have to apply separately for funds for large scale investments. In others, large investments are financed through the general remuneration of the hospitals. Direct control by a single payer through regulation of separate grants for large investments is likely to have a negative influence on the adoption rate of new technologies.

Bech *et al.* (2006) show that differences in technology use across countries and in their rates of adoption can be explained by these institutional factors. The main factors, which lead to lower utilization rates, appear to be the monopsonic payer and the funding of investments by specific grants. Baker and Brown (1999) suggest that managed care has slowed the rate of diffusion of new medical technologies. Dormont and Milcent (2006) show how a severe budget shortage induced by a global budget system makes it difficult for French public hospitals to finance the diffusion of angioplasty.

Improving efficiency and eliminating waste are important goals for regulation. However, it is critical to keep in mind that some policies may hinder technological progress. If the benefit induced by the new technologies is larger than their additional costs, such policies are not optimal.

2.3.3 *The Impact of Health Care on Longevity and Health*

The most common indicator of health-care outcomes is life expectancy at birth. As noted above, it has increased steadily over the 20th century, by about 30 years in the US and in comparable countries. In recent years, the EU-15 has performed better than the US in this respect (Figure 2.8), the latter displaying a persistent gap of around 1.5 years by 2004.

Has life in good health (or the health status) also increased over time? Life expectancy indicators fail to take into account morbidity differences. To address this issue, an increasingly used measure is the health-adjusted

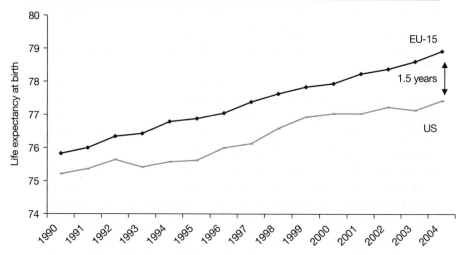

Figure 2.8. Life expectancy at birth in the EU-15 and the US, 1990–2004
Source: World Bank (2006).

life expectancy (HALE). The World Health Organization (WHO) has computed gender-specific HALEs for all countries of the world: the results show a large variability of HALEs between countries, also to the advantage of the EU-15 *vis-à-vis* the US by at least two years for each gender. However, no data have been produced by the WHO to make it possible to compare HALE over time, and to see how the evolution of HALE compares to that of life expectancy.

A European project, the European Health Expectancy Monitoring Unit (EHEMU), aimed at constructing comparable indicators on disability-free life expectancy (DFLE)[5] for European countries (Michel and Robine 2004). The results provide mixed evidence: while some countries have experienced an increase in lifetimes lived free of disability, others have shown hardly any change over the period examined. By age groups, mild and severe disability appears to have declined in several European countries, as well as in Japan. In some countries, the gains in DFLE are actually higher

---

[5] The difference between DFLE and HALE is that the former employs a dichotomous disability measure, while the latter uses a disability measure with different levels combined into a single value using utility weights specific for each level of disability. One advantage of the HALE method, as applied by WHO, is that it has been designed for use in a variety of countries with very different levels of data availability. However, the method relies on expert opinion for the development of the weights used for each condition.

than the gains in life expectancy at birth (e.g. France, Germany, Japan).[6] In the US and the UK, DFLE has increased but at a slower pace.

A study carried out by Fogel (2003) on a large sample of 45,000 US veterans does not support the idea that an increase in life expectancy translates into more years plagued by chronic illnesses. The average age of onset of various common chronic conditions (such as heart disease, arthritis, respiratory disease, etc.) increased by 10 years over an 80-year period, while life expectancy increased by 6.6 years. These results are in line with Freedman *et al.* (2002), who showed that elderly people, as they are living longer, are getting healthier in the US.

Has health care played a role in this reduced mortality and morbidity? Most studies point out several identification problems: many factors other than health care have influenced mortality, including behavioural changes, declines in pollution with the delivery of clean water and the removal of waste, increased education with advice about personal health practice, urbanization, etc. Nevertheless, evidence suggests that better health care has improved health status.

Cutler, Deaton, and Lleras-Muner (2006) show that, since the 1930s, mortality reductions have been driven by health care, first by vaccination and antibiotics, then by intensive care procedures. Murphy and Topel (2006) show that the gain in life expectancy is equal to about 9 years for men and women in the US between 1950 and 2000. They state that this gain in longevity is mainly due to the reduced mortality from heart disease and stroke (respectively, + 3.7 years and + 1 year for men, with comparable figures for women).

Hunink *et al.* (1997) showed that 43% of the decline in coronary heart disease (CHD) observed between 1980 and 1990 resulted from improvements in acute treatment and that 29% resulted from improvements in secondary prevention, that is, medications to reduce blood pressure and cholesterol level. Cutler, Landrum, and Stewart (2006) conclude that improved medical care for CHD explains up to 70% of mortality reduction in the US over the period 1984 to 1999. For England and Wales, 42% of the decrease in CHD mortality between 1981 and 2000 was found to be attributable to medical and surgical treatment (Unal *et al.*, 2005). Similar results were found for Scotland and the Netherlands (Capewell *et al.*, 1999; Bots and Grobbee, 1996).

---

[6] See Oliveira Martins *et al.* (2005), table 2.4.

Some results are also available concerning the impact of health care on reduced disability. Cutler, Landrum, and Stewart (2006) show that improved medical care explains up to 50% of the reduction in disability caused by cardiovascular disease in the US over the period 1984 to 1999. The increase in quality-adjusted life expectancy for these patients is around 3.7 years. Intensive procedures, such as hip replacement and other surgeries, rose particularly for people with muscular-skeletal problems between 1989 and 1999 in the US. Cutler (2004) shows that they led to a large decline in disability associated with those conditions during the same period.

The above evidence suggests that investment in and spending on health care have had a positive impact on health status, supporting the 'healthy ageing' regime experienced in the US, Europe, and Japan. But what is the likelihood of such a regime being maintained in the future? Actually, three scenarios have been considered in the literature, illustrated in Figure 2.9. Scenario I corresponds to the 'compression of morbidity' hypothesis, an optimistic theory suggested by Fries (1980). In that case, there would be a reduction in morbidity and disability in the last stages of life. Life expectancy would be close to disease-free and disability-free life expectancy. At the other extreme, scenario II corresponds to a pessimistic 'expansion of morbidity' (Grunenberg, 1977; Kramer, 1980), where all gains in longevity translate into years of poor health. An intermediate hypothesis can be considered (Manton, 1982), such as scenario III, where the gains in

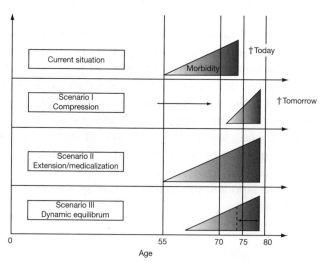

Figure 2.9. Three possible scenarios for future changes in morbidity at a given age

longevity gains translate one-to-one into years in good health (or 'healthy ageing').

To sum up, a fair amount of empirical evidence supports the view that health care (and/or expenditures) does matter for health outcomes. The evidence is far more solid when looking at the effects of specific interventions or treatments, such as CVD or depression treatments, compared to studies that examine aggregate relationships.[7]

Michel and Robine (2004) suggest that different patterns may evolve over time within the same country. In their model, the ageing population is based on a cyclical movement where, first, sicker people survive into old age and disability rises, then the number of years lived with disability decreases as new cohorts of healthier people enter old age, but, finally, the number of years lived with disability rises again, when the average age of death rises so much that many people spend their last years at an advanced age burdened by multiple chronic illnesses and frailty. If this is the case, then achieving healthy ageing seems possible but is not assured, and if achieved, it may not be permanent.

Looking ahead, a particular concern about the ability to maintain a healthy ageing regime arises from the extrapolation of recent trends in obesity, a challenge that is afflicting the US above all, yet many European countries are showing very similar, if delayed trends. Several studies in the US have documented a surprising increase in functional limitations among the middle-aged, caused by obesity, with obviously detrimental effects on late life functioning (Lakdawalla *et al.*, 2001; Freedman *et al.*, 2002). This research suggests that, at least in the US (where the compression of morbidity thesis has so far received rather widespread empirical support, e.g. Fries, 2005), there is reason to expect a reversal of the hard-fought gains of functional decline. Comparable findings do not exist for Europe, but this is a reflection of lack of suitable data rather than of the absence of the problem. If the US results are any guide to what might happen in Europe, they reinforce the importance of an active lifestyle and low-risk health habits, such as avoiding obesity, for maintaining the functional independence of elderly people. Jagger *et al.* (2008) investigated the link between life expectancies and Healthy Life Years (HLYs) in the European Union and found no conclusive evidence as to whether extra life years are spent in good health. If anything, substantial inequalities exist in the EU. Their findings suggest that, without major improvements in population health,

---

[7] For a survey on this area see Buck, Eastwood and Smith (1999).

the target of increasing participation by older people in the labour force may be difficult to achieve.

2.4 Efficiency in Health Expenditures

The fact that health expenditures have induced gains in longevity and health does not mean that they are necessarily efficient from a welfare point of view. Efficiency refers to efficiency in care delivery, but also to the fact that expenditures, as well as technology adoption and diffusion, should meet collective preferences.

2.4.1 *The Importance of Valuing Longevity Gains*

An important piece of evidence on the importance of properly evaluating longevity gains is provided by the *Future Elderly Model*. It is a micro-simulation model set up by RAND authors to construct simulated health histories for US Medicare enrollees (Goldman *et al.*, 2005). Transition probabilities are estimated on a sample of about 100,000 Medicare beneficiaries observed between 1992 and 1999. Within this framework, individual yearly probabilities of dying, or of having a particular health condition or disability state can be estimated. These probabilities can be used to simulate the impact of health improvements resulting from new technologies. Ten selected technologies were selected and their impact on Medicare costs by 2030 is projected.

Table 2.2 summarizes the results for three of these technologies: an intraventricular cardiovascular defibrillator, prevention of Alzheimer's disease, and a (hypothetical) chemical compound that extends life span. The three are cost-efficient in the sense that the cost of one year saved is lower or equals $100,000 (low bound for one year of life; see below). Prevention of Alzheimer's and the compound extending life span have about the same annual cost, but the compound is more efficient in terms of health outcomes, implying that is more costly in the long run: +13.8% (and 70.4% in the case of morbidity expansion) instead of +8% for the Prevention of Alzheimer's disease. Based on these results, Lubitz (2005) draws somewhat pessimistic conclusions on the role of technological progress: all technological advances may save costs from improved health in the short run, but over the long run the cumulated net costs increase. Given that a cost-saving criterion is not sufficient, a proper assessment requires an evaluation of the effects of a better health status on welfare.

Table 2.2. Micro-simulation results for three technologies by the Future Elderly Model

	Intraventricular cardio defibrillator	Prevention of Alzheimer's	Compound that extends life span (mythical)
Annual cost	US$37,500	US$720	US$365
Population concerned	50% AMI patients	100% Medicare recipients	100% Medicare recipients
Potential effect	Decrease in mortality rate: 10%	Delay of 3 years in incidence → decrease in prevalence of 1/3	Increase in life expectancy: +10 years
Cost of one year of life saved	US$100,000	US$80,300	US$8,800
Increase in total Spending for Medicare in 2030	+ 3.71%	+ 8.0%	+ 13.8% if healthy + 70.4% if unhealthy

Source: Goldman *et al.* (2005).

2.4.2 *The value of a statistical life*

One way to assess the value of health is to measure the extent to which one is willing to trade off health for specific market activities for which a price exists. This is the principle of so-called willingness-to-pay studies. Namely, the 'value of a statistical life' (hereafter, VSL) can be inferred from risk premiums in the job market: jobs that entail health risks, such as mining, pay more in the form of a risk premium. VSL can also be estimated by analysing market prices for products that reduce the likelihood of fatal injury. The VSL literature leads to estimates ranging from about $2 million to $9 million (Viscusi and Aldy, 2003; Ashenfelter and Greenstone, 2004; Murphy and Topel, 2006). Reviewing the literature, Cutler (2004) considers that a low bound of $100,000 per year of life saved could be adopted.

2.4.3 *Using the Value of a Statistical Life to Evaluate the Return on New Technologies in Health Care*

Assuming a VSL of $100,000 per year, Cutler and McClellan (2001) examine whether new treatments are worth the additional costs. For heart attack, the gain in life expectancy is about one year, which corresponds, once the cost of living is deducted, to a present value of the benefit from technological change of about $70,000, while the increase in the cost of treatment is around $10,000 per year. They conclude that the return to technological change in heart attack treatments is high—1:7. For depression, the time spent in ill health is reduced by eight weeks with new treatments. This amounts to a benefit of about $6,000, around six times greater than the cost of treatment ($1,000). For cataract, the result is even more impressive: the present value of benefit is equal to $95,000, to compare with a cost for the operation equal to about $3,000. These assessments are rather conservative, because they do not take into account the social gains arising from the fact that a cured person is able to work and produce more. This remark may apply less for those heart attacks and cataracts which occur at a great age, but is more relevant for depression, which increases the probability of early retirement (Conti *et al.*, 2006).

Cutler, Rosen, and Vijan (2006) find that increased spending on health care at birth resulted in an average cost of $19,900 per year of life gained (for the period 1960–2000). Assuming that 50% of improvements in longevity resulted from medical care (Bunker *et al.*, 1994; Bunker, 2001), Cutler, Rosen, and Vijan (2006) conclude that health care led to gains in welfare. A comparable study is proposed by Luce *et al* (2006). Using life-year values of $99,000 to $173,000, and conservatively considering only the health care-related improvements in survival over the past two decades, they find that one dollar of health-care spending in the US could generate from $1.55 to $1.94 in overall health gains.

Murphy and Topel (2006) provided what was undoubtedly the most striking result in this respect. Using individuals' willingness to pay, they found that gains in life expectancy from 1970 to 2000 had added a gain of around 50% of annual GDP to US wealth! Rising medical expenditures (reaching around 14% of GDP in 2000) would have absorbed only 36% of the value of increased longevity. The authors distinguish between length and quality of life: life extension is valued because utility from goods and leisure is enjoyed longer, and improvements in health status raise utility from given amounts of good and leisure. They show that the social value of improvements in health is an increasing function of the size of the population, the lifetime income, the existing level of health, and of the proximity of the ages of the population to the age of most disease onset. These factors make it possible to predict that the valuation of health improvements will continue to rise in the future, as the population and incomes grow, especially as the baby-boom generation approaches the age of disease-related death. Finally, they show that improvements in life expectancy raise willingness to pay for further improvements in health by increasing the value of remaining life.

2.4.4 *Efficiency in Health-Care Use and Adoption of Innovation*

Bech *et al.* (2006) have provided empirical evidence that the organization of health insurance systems has an influence on the pace of adoption of technological innovations (see Section 2.3.2). Obviously, the design of health insurance, as well as of payment systems, influences efficiency in health-care use. The lack of efficiency may correspond to underuse or overuse of health care and technology, in the sense that the level of consumption is below or above the level that would match preferences.[8] Prospective payment systems, such as a global budget for hospitals, may hinder the use of costly innovations, while fee-for-services payments encourage more numerous and invasive procedures (there are examples relative to Caesarian section for deliveries; other examples can be found in McKinsey, 1996). Even in the context of a prospective payment per diagnosis-related group (DRG), McClellan (1997) has shown that the definition of the DRG can be closely linked to the implementation of a procedure, and can thus create incentives for their excessive use. This is the case for angioplasty in the treatment of heart attack (Delattre *et al.*, 2002). Comparing the cost-effectiveness of revascularization (such as angioplasty) with more simple medical management in the population with a myocardial infarction, Rosen *et al.* (2007) show that the cost of revascularization is $55,100 per life-year gained, which is much higher than the cost per life-year gained thanks to medical management, that is, $15,900. These results suggest that revascularization is overprovided: there is room for improvement in efficiency.

To sum up this section, three main insights emerge on the links between health expenditures, health status, and welfare:

1. Technological progress, rather than ageing, is the main driver of health expenditure growth. Two mechanisms are involved: *substitution*, where old technologies are replaced by better ones, and *extension*, where more goods and services are available and consumed. The growth in health expenditures is likely to be mostly explained by the latter effect.
2. The diffusion of technologies leads to additional costs over the long run but also generates value in terms of longevity and better health, so that it contributes to welfare. These welfare gains induced by better health and longevity could be large.

---

[8] Individual or collective preferences are at stake, depending on whether the basic insurance is public or private.

3. A healthy ageing regime seems therefore possible, but is by no means ensured. Proper individual incentives for an active lifestyle and low-risk health habits, such as avoiding obesity, seem essential to increase longevity without incapacity. Without significant improvements in population health, increased participation of older workers in the labour force may be difficult to achieve.

The next question is how far our societies are ready to invest in the health status of the population?

3

Preferences towards Health Care:
Is Health a Luxury Good?

Since Newhouse (1977), an extensive empirical literature has sought to assess whether health care is a luxury (income elasticity above one) or a necessity (elasticity below one). This is still an unsettled issue, which is unfortunate since most projections of future expenditures rely on assumptions regarding this elasticity. An income elasticity greater than one implies that consumers' preferences drive health expenditure above income growth and could explain the increase in the share of health care in GDP. In this context, Getzen (2000) argues that empirical studies often fail to distinguish between sources of variation between groups and within groups: an individual within an insured group may have little incentive to limit health expenditures, especially if the group is large and the individual's effect on the group is insignificant. Thus, an individual's health-care spending is insensitive to income. In contrast, the group's total expenditure on health care is limited by its aggregate income. Total group spending will be more responsive to income than individual spending, and wider groups (countries) will be even more responsive. This stylized fact points out the importance of heterogeneity across groups of agents.

Confirming this argument, it can be observed that the higher the level of aggregation, the higher the estimated income elasticity of health-care spending. Studies at the individual level show that variation in spending is mostly associated with individual differences in health status (50% to 90%), while income elasticities are small or even negative (Newhouse and Phelps, 1976; Manning *et al.*, 1987; Sunshine and Dicker, 1987; Wagstaff *et al.*, 1991; AHCPR, 1997). Nevertheless, analysis of pre-1960 data, where insurance is less prevalent and most payments are made out-of-pocket, shows much larger individual income elasticities (from 0.2 to 0.7).

Similarly, consumption of dentistry, plastic surgery, counselling, eyeglasses, and other types of care that are less reimbursed show income elasticities strongly positive and sometimes exceeding one (Parker and Wong, 1997). At the macro-level, estimates of national health expenditures consistently show income elasticities greater than one, with above 90% of cross-sectional and time-series variation explicable by difference in per capita income, and differences in health status having negligible effects (Abel-Smith, 1967; Kleiman, 1974; Newhouse, 1977, 1987; Maxwell, 1981; Leu, 1986; Culyer, 1988; Getzen, 1990; Gerdtham et al., 1992).

3.1 An Econometric Investigation of the Income Elasticities

Against this background, we propose new evidence on the elasticity of per capita public, private, and total health-care services. The model is essentially a reduced-form equation, with the choice of right-hand-side variables influenced by different possible determinants of health-care spending.[1] Our starting point builds on Newhouse (1977), assuming GDP per capita as the main determinant of health-care expenditures per capita:

$$HCE_{i,t} = \alpha_i + \beta.GDP_{i,t} + u_{i,t} \qquad (3.1)$$

where $HCE_{i,t}$ stands for per capita health-care expenditures, $GDP_{i,t}$ is per capita GDP, $u_{i,t}$ is an error term, $t = 1, \ldots, T$ (number of years), and $i = 1, \ldots, N$ (number of countries). But other right-hand-side variables should be considered, such as a trend to capture technology advances or health prices, as discussed in the previous chapter. The risk of omitted-variable bias may be high. Recent studies (Hall and Jones, 2007; Okunade and Murthy, 2002; Blomqvist and Carter, 1997) have stressed that the observed increasing health-care expenditure as a share of GDP is likely due to other factors, such as insurance coverage. Di Matteo and Di Matteo (1998) also argue that because health is labour intensive, its cost may increase as a function of average income, so that measured income elasticity is blurred by the price effect. Since the price elasticity is presumably negative, the income coefficient is likely to be biased downward. This conflicting evidence suggests

---

[1] To explain the results of the macro-elasticity of demand for (per capita) health-care services with respect to (per capita) income, a first strand of explanations focuses on data. In this respect, one can quote the comparability of OECD data on health-care expenditures, the definition of (per capita) GDP, the sampling period, and the transformation of variables (log-transformation, PPP-adjusted measure). See Blomquist and Carter (1997); Gerdtham et al. (1992).

testing the robustness of standard estimates using various explanatory variables.[2]

Three main econometric methods have been used in the literature: (i) cross-section analysis, (ii) time-series analysis, and (iii) panel analysis. Two key issues are the degree of heterogeneity and the finite sample bias of standard time-series estimates (especially when T is small). As panel data techniques are a standard method of dealing with heterogeneity issues, this option was followed here.

We conducted an econometric test with three different samples derived from the OECD Health Data Base (OECD, 2005a). The first sample (group 1) corresponds to an unbalanced panel, where not all years are available, for all 30 OECD countries. The second sample (group 2) corresponds to a nearly balanced panel of 19 OECD countries.[3] The third sample (group 3) comprises 17 OECD countries over the same time period.[4] All samples cover the period 1970–2002. For group 3, it was possible to gather some institutional variables characterizing health systems.

We conducted separate regressions for per capita public, private, and total health-care expenditures. For each independent variable, we consider a subset of the following explanatory variables: GDP per capita; a trend over the period 1970–2002 (common to all OECD countries), as a loose proxy for the role of long-term technological change; POPY, the share of young (0–14), POPP, middle-age (15–54), and POPO old-age people (55–74) over the total population; the share of very old people (75+) serving as the reference group; and three dummy variables, which control respectively for the existence of gate-keeping and for the type of health-care system (public or integrated).

Four different specifications are tested. First, the *pooled regression* model:

$$\log(HCE_{i,t}) = \alpha + \beta \cdot \log(GDP_{i,t}) + X_{i,t}^{T} \cdot \delta + u_{i,t} \qquad (3.2)$$

where *HCE* denotes health expenditures per capita; $X_{I,\,t}$ is a vector of the other regressors included in the specifications (the superscript T denoting its transpose).

---

[2] Despite the fact that empirical studies have mainly focused on omitted-variable bias, a reduced-form model relating health expenditures to income can also be affected by endogeneity bias.

[3] Group 2 includes Australia, Austria, Canada, Denmark, Finland, France, Germany, Iceland, Ireland, Japan, Luxembourg, the Netherlands, New Zealand, Norway, Portugal, Spain, Sweden, the United Kingdom, and the USA.

[4] Group 3 comprises the countries of group 2, excluding Luxembourg and the Netherlands.

Second, the *one-way fixed-effects* model (in the individual dimension), where α_i denotes the ith individual effect:

$$\log(HCE_{i,t}) = \alpha_i + \beta \cdot \log(GDP_{i,t}) + X_{i,t}^T \cdot \delta + u_{i,t} \qquad (3.3)$$

Third, the *two-way fixed-effects* models, where λ_t denotes the t_{th} temporal effect:

$$\log(HCE_{i,t}) = \alpha_i + {}_t + \beta \cdot \log(GDP_{i,t}) + X_{i,t}^T \cdot \delta + u_{i,t} \qquad (3.4)$$

Finally, the *one-way error component model* (in the individual dimension) where $\alpha_i \sim N(0, \sigma_\alpha^2)$:

$$\log(HCE_{i,t}) = \alpha + \beta \cdot \log(GDP_{i,t}) + X_{i,t}^T \cdot \delta + v_{i,t} v_{i,t} = \alpha_i + u_{i,t} \qquad (3.5)$$

Tables 3.1 to 3.3 report the results of the pooled OLS regressions. *P*-values are in brackets and standard errors have been determined using the White's correction or the Arellano's correction. Results are broadly robust across groups and across time periods.[5] Several points are worth noting. First, the income elasticity depends on the type of health-care spending. Income elasticity is in general below or close to one in the case of per capita private health expenditures, whereas it exceeds one when considering per capita public or total health expenditures. Second, the inclusion of a common trend or time dummies over sub-periods leads to a decrease in the income elasticities for public and total expenditures, though they remain above one for the most part. Third, the population variables are often statistically significant at conventional levels, but their sign depends on the specification. In most cases, they tend to be positive for public and total expenditures, while negative for private expenditures. This result could be due to the fact that public systems provide universal coverage to the elderly and thus are positively affected by the larger shares of the younger groups vis-à-vis those aged 75+ (the reference group). The pattern is opposite for private expenditures, as in most countries the spending of the eldest people are supported by the public sector.

These results are in line with earlier studies, at least for per capita total health expenditures, in the sense that cross-sectional model estimates of

---

[5] We also estimated cross-section regressions over the period 1980–2002. The estimates are quite close to the pooled estimates. The results are not reported here but are available upon request.

Table 3.1. Pooled OLS regressions: per capita public health expenditures

Variable	Group 1			Group 2			Group 3		
	[1]	[2]	[3]	[1]	[2]	[3]	[1]	[2]	[3]
Per capita GDP	1.661	1.649	1.428	1.48	1.342	1.314	1.557	1.441	1.406
	[0.000]	[0.000]	[0.000]	[0.000]	[0.000]	[0.000]	[0.000]	[0.000]	[0.000]
Time trend		0.002	0.011		0.007	0.001		0.005	0.002
		[0.168]	[0.000]		[0.000]	[0.289]		[0.000]	[0.161]
POPY			0.762			−1.561			−1.178
			[0.000]			[0.000]			[0.000]
POPP			0.278			−4.067			−3.337
			[0.417]			[0.417]			[0.000]
POPO			1.332			−1.231			−0.836
			[0.000]			[0.000]			[0.000]
Observations	773	773	773	614	614	614	557	557	557
Countries	30	30	30	19	19	19	17	17	17

Notes: P-values are in square brackets. Group 1 corresponds to an unbalanced panel of 30 OECD countries for the period 1970–2002; group 2 corresponds to a nearly balanced panel of 19 OECD countries; group 3 corresponds to group 2 excluding Luxembourg and Netherlands. POPY is the share of young (0–14), POPP is middle-age (15–54), and POPO is old-age people (55–74) over the total population.

Table 3.2. Pooled OLS regressions: per capita private health expenditures

Variable	Group 1 [1]	[2]	[3]	Group 2 [1]	[2]	[3]	Group 3 [1]	[2]	[3]	[4]
Per capita GDP	1.084	0.962	1.124	1.159	0.678	0.527	1.459	1.117	1.034	1.291
	[0.000]	[0.000]	[0.000]	[0.000]	[0.000]	[0.000]	[0.000]	[0.000]	[0.000]	[0.000]
Time trend		0.017	0.007		0.023	0.019		0.016	0.018	0.025
		[0.001]	[0.000]		[0.000]	[0.000]		[0.000]	[0.000]	[0.000]
POPY			-0.791			-0.343			1.646	1.305
			[0.014]			[0.000]			[0.000]	[0.000]
POPP			0.387			2.651			2.471	1.348
			[0.629]			[0.000]			[0.000]	[0.029]
POPO			-1.213			-1.333			0.967	-0.045
			[0.000]			[0.000]			[0.006]	[0.847]
Gate-keeping										-0.309
										[0.000]
Public System										-0.206
										[0.000]
Integrated System										-0.736
										[0.000]
Observations	773	773	773	614	614	614	557	557	557	557
Countries	30	30	30	19	19	19	17	17	17	17

Notes: P-values are in square brackets. Group 1 corresponds to an unbalanced panel of 30 OECD countries for the period 1970–2002; group 2 corresponds to a nearly balanced panel of 19 OECD countries; group 3 corresponds to group 2 excluding Luxembourg and Netherlands. POPY is the share of young (0–14), POPP is middle-age (15–54), and POPO is old-age people (55–74) over the total population.

Table 3.3. Pooled OLS regressions: per capita total health expenditures

Variable	Group 1 [1]	[2]	[3]	Group 2 [1]	[2]	[3]	[4]	Group 3 [1]	[2]	[3]	[4]
Per capita GDP	1.471 [0.000]	1.426 [0.000]	1.345 [0.000]	1.441 [0.000]	1.269 [0.000]	1.243 [0.000]	1.311 [0.000]	1.559 [0.000]	1.459 [0.000]	1.456 [0.000]	1.502 [0.000]
Time trend		0.007 [0.000]	0.008 [0.000]		0.008 [0.000]	0.005 [0.000]	0.005 [0.000]		0.004 [0.000]	0.004 [0.000]	0.006 [0.000]
POPY			0.087 [0.164]			-0.997 [0.000]	-0.909 [0.000]			-0.093 [0.438]	-0.091 [0.512]
POPP			-0.14 [0.271]			-2.215 [0.000]	-2.652 [0.000]			-0.268 [0.343]	-1.062 [0.002]
POPO			0.318 [0.000]			-1.104 [0.000]	-1.111 [0.000]			-0.032 [0.810]	-0.179 [0.000]
Gate-keeping							-0.119 [0.000]				-0.102 [0.000]
Public system							-0.171 [0.000]				-0.104 [0.000]
Integrated system							-0.101 [0.000]				-0.109 [0.000]
Observations	773	773	773	614	614	614	614	557	557	557	557
Countries	30	30	30	19	19	19	19	17	17	17	17

Notes: P-values are in square brackets. Group 1 corresponds to an unbalanced panel of 30 OECD countries for the period 1970–2002; group 2 corresponds to a nearly balanced panel of 19 OECD countries; group 3 corresponds to group 2 excluding Luxembourg and Netherlands. POPY is the share of young (0–14), POPP is middle-age (15–54), and POPO is old-age people (55–74) over the total population.

the GDP elasticity of HCE are typically above unity.[6] However, cross-sectional models are fragile in small data sets and use an implicit assumption
of homogeneity across countries. This leads to unrealistic assumptions,
such as the homogeneity of tastes and preferences across countries, as
well as the homogeneity of health systems, which could severely bias the
estimates (Pesaran *et al.*, 1996).

In addressing these drawbacks, panel estimates offer a number of advantages over cross-sectional or time-series studies (see Baltagi, 2008). In particular, having multiple years of data for each country enables the inclusion
of (time) country-specific fixed (or random) effects, thereby controlling for
a wide range of time-invariant country characteristics, which may bias
the estimate of income elasticity in cross-section (or time-series analysis).
Tables 3.4 to 3.6 reports estimates of the one-way fixed-effects model in the
individual dimension. Since the dummy variables (gate-keeping, public
system and integrated system) are not time-varying, they could not be
estimated in the fixed-effect model.[7]

When controlling for individual fixed effects, the inclusion of a common
time trend significantly reduces the income elasticity to below one. If this
common trend captures technological progress, it confirms the fact that
neglecting the role of technology change tends to bias long-term income
elasticity upward (see Dreger and Reimers, 2005).[8] A second result is that
the income elasticity further decreases when introducing the population
variables. These variables have the expected sign in the case of per capita
public and total health-care expenditures. These results are relatively robust
across the three different country samples. When testing the pooled model
against the one-way fixed-effects model, the test statistic strongly supports
the latter. When compared with the pooled regressions, it can be seen that
the results for the income elasticities are less volatile across the three
different samples of countries. This also suggests that the one-way fixed-
effect estimates are more robust.

To assess the role of the time dimension, we ran two-way fixed-effects
regressions (Table 3.7). Except for a few estimates of the per capita private
health-care expenditures regressions, we consistently find the income elas-

---

[6] A non-exhaustive list includes Cullis and West (1979), Leu (1986), Culyer (1990),
Gerdtham *et al.* (1992), Hitiris and Posnett (1992).

[7] Using the method suggested by Canova (2007), we also regressed the individual effects on
these variables. Results are generally not statistically significant.

[8] Note we assume here that cross-section effects are independent. This assumption may lead
to the spurious interpretation of this common trend as technology progress in the sense that
other factors may explain this term when accounting for cross-sectional dependence. For
instance, this trend may also reflect the effect of relative prices.

Table 3.4. One-way fixed-effects regressions in the individual dimension: per capita public health expenditures

Variable	Group 1			Group 2			Group 3		
	[1]	[2]	[3]	[1]	[2]	[3]	[1]	[2]	[3]
Per capita GDP	1.591	0.936	0.698	1.551	0.933	0.884	1.597	1.017	0.931
	[0.000]	[0.000]	[0.000]	[0.000]	[0.000]	[0.000]	[0.000]	[0.000]	[0.000]
Time trend		0.017	0.021		0.015	0.013		0.014	0.014
		[0.000]	[0.000]		[0.000]	[0.116]		[0.000]	[0.000]
POPY			1.074			0.175			0.241
			[0.000]			[0.111]			[0.000]
POPP			3.704			1.357			1.347
			[0.000]			[0.000]			[0.000]
POPO			1.668			0.814			0.858
			[0.000]			[0.000]			[0.000]
Observations	773	773	773	614	614	614	557	557	557
Countries	30	30	30	19	19	19	17	17	17

Notes: P-values are in square brackets. Group 1 corresponds to an unbalanced panel of 30 OECD countries for the period 1970–2002; group 2 corresponds to a nearly balanced panel of 19 OECD countries; group 3 corresponds to group 2 excluding Luxembourg and Netherlands. POPY is the share of young (0–14), POPP is middle-age (15–54), and POPO is old-age people (55–74) over the total population.

Table 3.5. One-way fixed-effects regressions in the individual dimension: per capita private health expenditures

Variable	Group 1 [1]	[2]	[3]	Group 2 [1]	[2]	[3]	Group 3 [1]	[2]	[3]
Per capita GDP	1.612 [0.000]	0.903 [0.000]	1.053 [0.000]	1.681 [0.000]	0.926 [0.000]	0.935 [0.000]	1.745 [0.000]	0.982 [0.000]	1.026 [0.000]
Time trend		0.018 [0.001]	0.015 [0.000]		0.019 [0.000]	0.019 [0.000]		0.018 [0.000]	0.019 [0.000]
POPY			-0.905 [0.000]			-0.612 [0.001]			-0.406 [0.022]
POPP			-2.224 [0.000]			-1.69 [0.000]			-1.351 [0.009]
POPO			-1.619 [0.000]			-1.506 [0.000]			-1.351 [0.000]
Observations	773	773	773	614	614	614	557	557	557
Countries	30	30	30	19	19	19	17	17	17

Notes: P-values are in square brackets. Group 1 corresponds to an unbalanced panel of 30 OECD countries for the period 1970–2002; group 2 corresponds to a nearly balanced panel of 19 OECD countries; group 3 corresponds to group 2 excluding Luxembourg and Netherlands. POPY is the share of young (0–14), POPP is middle-age (15–54), and POPO is old-age people (55–74) over the total population.

Table 3.6. One-way fixed-effects regressions in the individual dimension: per capita total health expenditures

Variable	Group 1			Group 2			Group 3		
	[1]	[2]	[3]	[1]	[2]	[3]	[1]	[2]	[3]
Per capita GDP	1.554	0.863	0.779	1.541	0.919	0.877	1.579	0.971	0.905
	[0.000]	[0.000]	[0.000]	[0.000]	[0.000]	[0.000]	[0.000]	[0.000]	[0.000]
Time trend		0.018	0.017		0.015	0.014		0.015	0.014
		[0.000]	[0.000]		[0.000]	[0.000]		[0.000]	[0.000]
POPY			0.039			0.098			0.194
			[0.686]			[0.275]			[0.049]
POPP			0.887			0.981			1.048
			[0.008]			[0.000]			[0.000]
POPO			0.361			0.477			0.581
			[0.002]			[0.000]			[0.000]
Observations	773	773	773	614	614	614	557	557	557
Countries	30	30	30	19	19	19	17	17	17

Notes: P-values are in square brackets. Group 1 corresponds to an unbalanced panel of 30 OECD countries for the period 1970–2002; group 2 corresponds to a nearly balanced panel of 19 OECD countries; group 3 corresponds to group 2 excluding Luxembourg and Netherlands. POPY is the share of young (0–14), POPP is middle-age (15–54), and POPO is old-age people (55–74) over the total population.

Table 3.7. Two-way fixed-effects regressions

Variable	Group 1 Per capita public health expenditures		Group 2		Group 3		Group 1 Per capita private health expenditures		Group 2		Group 3		Group 1 Per capita total health expenditures		Group 2		Group 3	
	[1]	[3]	[1]	[3]	[1]	[3]	[1]	[3]	[1]	[3]	[1]	[3]	[1]	[3]	[1]	[3]	[1]	[3]
Per capita GDP	0.952 [0.000]	0.719 [0.000]	0.927 [0.000]	0.935 [0.000]	0.972 [0.000]	0.967 [0.000]	0.921 [0.000]	1.047 [0.000]	0.976 [0.000]	0.969 [0.000]	1.089 [0.000]	1.131 [0.000]	0.876 [0.000]	0.814 [0.000]	0.917 [0.000]	0.923 [0.000]	0.949 [0.000]	0.944 [0.000]
POPY		1.097 [0.000]		-0.068 [0.471]		-0.01 [0.918]		-0.973 [0.000]		-0.506 [0.003]		-0.255 [0.127]		0.081 [0.384]		-0.067 [0.414]		0.026 [0.759]
POPP		3.308 [0.000]		-0.013 [0.954]		0.03 [0.899]		-1.857 [0.005]		-1.175 [0.009]		-0.958 [0.040]		0.531 [0.184]		-0.038 [0.837]		0.114 [0.565]
POPO		1.716 [0.000]		0.504 [0.000]		0.544 [0.000]		-1.685 [0.000]		-1.388 [0.000]		-1.224 [0.000]		0.421 [0.000]		0.264 [0.000]		0.362 [0.000]
Observations	773	773	614	614	557	557	773	773	614	614	557	557	773	773	614	614	557	557
Countries	30	30	19	19	17	17	30	30	19	19	17	17	30	30	19	19	17	17

Notes: P-values are in square brackets. Group 1 corresponds to an unbalanced panel of 30 OECD countries for the period 1970–2002; group 2 corresponds to a nearly balanced panel of 19 OECD countries; group 3 corresponds to group 2 excluding Luxembourg and Netherlands. POPY is the share of young (0–14), POPP is middle-age (15–54), POPO is old-age people (55–74) over the total population.

ticity to be below one. Specification [3] is preferred by standard specification tests. However, there is no clear-cut evidence between the one-way and two-way fixed-effects models.[9]

Finally, we also tested a one-way error component model in the individual variables for each type of per capita health-care expenditure (Tables 3.8 to 3.10). The variance-covariance parameters are estimated using the Swamy-Arora method.[10] Results are fairly close to those of the one-way fixed-effects model.[11] Overall, results confirm that the inclusion of a common trend significantly lowers the income elasticity (below one).[12] The additional variables capturing the institutional features of health systems, available for country groups 2 and 3, do not yield sufficiently significant results.

Some caveats and qualifications are in order. First, variables can be integrated and a co-integration relationship may exist. Second, we assume that there is cross-sectional independence. Third, income elasticity is obtained from a reduced-form equation in which potentially important determinants are not taken into consideration due to missing or unreliable data. Moreover, we disregard the endogeneity problem of per capita GDP by choosing not to use instruments in the previous regressions (although the determination of non-redundant and reliable instruments is a difficult task in the present setting; see below). Fourth, we suppose that heterogeneity is modelled through individual or time effects, and random effects. Finally, the specifications retained here are static, which may bias the results. To address some to these caveats, additional tests for the existence of a co-integration relationship, cross-sectional dependence and convergence were also carried out. To save space, they are not reported here.[13] Importantly, they do not qualitatively change the results concerning the value of the income elasticity.

Acemoglu *et al.* (2009) addressed several of these caveats and provide a thorough econometric investigation on the income elasticity of health

---

[9] Results are not reported here but are available upon request.

[10] Results are robust to other methods.

[11] The Hausman and Augmented-Hausman tests tend to favour the latter specification. Note that the use of a one-way or two-way error component model might be questionable since OECD countries represent a closed population, i.e. the sample population is the same as the total population.

[12] We also ran a one-way error component model in the time dimension, as well as a two-way error component model; the previous results are quite robust. Results are not reported here but are available upon request.

[13] These results are available upon request. As a robustness check, we assume that the slope coefficients can be different across groups of countries. Empirical evidence still tends to support the assumption of an income elasticity equal to or below one.

Table 3.8. One-way error component model in the individual dimension: per capita public health expenditures

Variable	Group 1			Group 2				Group 3			
	[1]	[2]	[3]	[1]	[2]	[3]	[4]	[1]	[2]	[3]	[4]
Per capita GDP	1.591	1.121	0.913	1.547	0.981	0.971	0.992	1.596	1.074	1.045	1.053
	[0.000]	[0.000]	[0.000]	[0.000]	[0.000]	[0.000]	[0.000]	[0.000]	[0.000]	[0.000]	[0.000]
Time trend		0.013	0.016		0.014	0.011	0.01		0.013	0.011	0.011
		[0.000]	[0.000]		[0.000]	[0.000]	[0.000]		[0.000]	[0.000]	[0.000]
POPY			0.969			0.041	0.027			0.138	0.129
			[0.000]			[0.812]	[0.874]			[0.453]	[0.484]
POPP			3.247			0.896	0.943			0.902	0.958
			[0.000]			[0.046]	[0.035]			[0.053]	[0.040]
POPO			1.636			0.661	0.658			0.724	0.725
			[0.000]			[0.000]	[0.000]			[0.000]	[0.000]
Gate-keeping							0.015				0.009
							[0.857]				[0.922]
Public System							0.011				0.011
							[0.919]				[0.929]
Integrated System							0.184				0.181
							[0.003]				[0.008]
Observations	773	773	773	614	614	614	614	557	557	557	557
Countries	30	30	30	19	19	19	19	17	17	17	17

Note: The variance-covariance parameters are estimated by using the Swamy-Arora method. P-values are in square brackets. Group 1 corresponds to an unbalanced panel of 30 OECD countries for the period 1970–2002; group 2 corresponds to a nearly balanced panel of 19 OECD countries; group 3 corresponds to Group 2 excluding Luxembourg and Netherlands. POPY is the share of young (0–14), POPP is middle-age (15–54), and POPO is old-age people (55–74) over the total population.

Table 3.9. One-way error component model in the individual dimension: per capita private health expenditures

Variable	Group 1 [1]	[2]	[3]	Group 2 [1]	[2]	[3]	[4]	Group 3 [1]	[2]	[3]	[4]
Per capita GDP	1.599 [0.000]	0.938 [0.000]	1.102 [0.000]	1.675 [0.000]	0.913 [0.000]	0.918 [0.000]	0.922 [0.000]	1.745 [0.000]	0.987 [0.000]	1.023 [0.000]	1.035 [0.000]
Time trend		0.018 [0.000]	0.014 [0.000]		0.019 [0.000]	0.02 [0.000]	0.019 [0.000]		0.018 [0.000]	0.019 [0.000]	0.019 [0.000]
POPY			−0.933 [0.000]			−0.589 [0.063]	−0.596 [0.060]			−0.376 [0.262]	−0.369 [0.270]
POPP			−2.292 [0.000]			−1.585 [0.054]	−1.677 [0.042]			−1.216 [0.153]	−1.299 [0.126]
POPO			−1.618 [0.000]			−1.489 [0.000]	−1.517 [0.000]			−1.319 [0.000]	−1.334 [0.000]
Gate-keeping							−0.239 [0.518]				−0.245 [0.379]
Public System							−0.361 [0.435]				−0.059 [0.871]
Integrated System							−0.672 [0.010]				−0.662 [0.002]
Observations	773	773	773	614	614	614	614	557	557	557	557
Countries	30	30	30	19	19	19	19	17	17	17	17

Note: The variance-covariance parameters are estimated by using the Swamy-Arora method. P-values are in square brackets. Group 1 corresponds to an unbalanced panel of 30 OECD countries for the period 1970–2002; Group 2 corresponds to a nearly balanced panel of 19 OECD countries; group 3 corresponds to group 2 excluding Luxembourg and Netherlands. POPY is the share of young (0–14), POPP is middle-age (15–54), and POPO is old-age people (55–74) over the total population.

Table 3.10. One-way error component model in the individual dimension: per capita total health expenditures

Variable	Group 1 [1]	[2]	[3]	Group 2 [1]	[2]	[3]	[4]	Group 3 [1]	[2]	[3]	[4]
Per capita GDP	1.543 [0.000]	1.039 [0.000]	0.947 [0.000]	1.537 [0.000]	0.955 [0.000]	0.919 [0.000]	0.913 [0.000]	1.578 [0.000]	1.058 [0.000]	0.994 [0.000]	1.003 [0.000]
Time trend		0.014 [0.000]	0.013 [0.000]		0.015 [0.000]	0.013 [0.000]	0.013 [0.000]		0.013 [0.000]	0.013 [0.000]	0.013 [0.000]
POPY			-0.038 [0.697]			0.058 [0.696]	0.03 [0.685]			0.169 [0.273]	0.152 [0.324]
POPP			0.591 [0.015]			0.837 [0.030]	0.846 [0.029]			0.879 [0.025]	0.814 [0.037]
POPO			0.343 [0.000]			0.417 [0.006]	0.421 [0.005]			0.879 [0.001]	0.503 [0.001]
Gate-keeping							-0.031 [0.803]				-0.033 [0.707]
Public System							0.014 [0.924]				0.087 [0.453]
Integrated System							0.017 [0.841]				0.016 [0.805]
Observations	773	773	773	614	614	614	614	557	557	557	557
Countries	30	30	30	19	19	19	19	17	17	17	17

Note: The variance-covariance parameters are estimated by using the Swamy-Arora method. P-values are in square brackets. Group 1 corresponds to an unbalanced panel of 30 OECD countries for the period 1970–2002; group 2 corresponds to a nearly balanced panel of 19 OECD countries; group 3 corresponds to Group 2 excluding Luxembourg and Netherlands. POPY is the share of young (0–14), POPP is middle-age (15–54), and POPO is old-age people (55–74) over the total population.

expenditures using US regional data. Their strategy is to identify truly exogenous income shocks not correlated with health and thus not affected by an endogeneity bias. Their instrument is the changes in the price of oil weighted by oil reserves. Their central estimate for the income elasticity is 0.7, with a maximum bound of 1.1 at the 95% confidence interval. Overall, the elasticity tends to be below one. This result is robust to alternative specifications.

While our econometric estimates and other empirical evidence favour an assumption of income elasticity around, if not below, one, it should be stressed this value is not low in absolute terms. It implies that, *ceteris paribus*, health expenditures will grow at least in line with GDP per capita. Public health-care budgets cannot rely on economic growth to smooth or reduce expenditure pressures over the coming decades.

3.2 Can an Optimal Share of Health-Care Spending in GDP be Estimated?

Given preferences towards health goods, could an optimal level of health expenditures be estimated? Hall and Jones (2007) proposed a model where the key parameter is the curvature of the marginal utility of consumption (a simple static version of their model is spelled out in Box 3.1). When the marginal utility of consumption of non-health goods declines quickly with income, the optimal health spending share rises rapidly. This growth reflects a value of life that grows faster than income.

To see how technology interacts with preferences, Hall and Jones (2007) consider a health production function, $f(h)$ (equation (3.9) in Box 3.1), of the following specific form:

$$x = (zh)^\theta \tag{3.6}$$

where technological progress is denoted by z. Hall and Jones (2007) set up a full dynamic model that allows for age-specific mortality, age-specific elasticities of the health production function (θ_a, for a given age a), as well as growth in total resources and productivity growth in the health sector. The health production function identifies three different causes in the decline in age-specific mortality: technological progress in health care, resource allocation (i.e. the share of income devoted to health spending), and other causes (pollution, education, trends in risky behaviours such as

Box 3.1 THE MODEL OF HALL AND JONES (2007)

Denote by x the individual's health status, which is assumed to be equal to its life expectancy. The mortality rate of the individual is thus equal to $1/x$. y is the individual's income; c consumption, which is supposed to be stationary over the life cycle, and h health expenditures. Expected lifetime utility for the representative individual is then defined by:

$$U(c,x) = \int_0^\infty e^{-(1/x)t} u(c) dt = x.u(c) \qquad (3.7)$$

The income can be spent on either consumption or health:

$$c + h = y \qquad (3.8)$$

A health production function defines the value of health for a given level of expenditures h:

$$x = f(h) \qquad (3.9)$$

The optimal allocation of resources maximizes the expected lifetime utility (3.7) subject to the budget constraint (3.8) and the health production function (3.9). The problem of the individual becomes:

$$\underset{c,h}{Max}\ f(h)u(c) \text{ s.t. } c + h = y$$

The first-order conditions for this problem imply that the marginal benefit of saving a life equals the marginal cost of saving a life. Let $L(c, x) = U(c, x)/u'(x)$ denote the value of life in units of output. The optimal allocation of resources verifies:

$$L(c,x) = \frac{x^2}{f'(h)} \qquad (3.10)$$

The share of income devoted to health expenditures is denoted by $s = h/y$. The elasticity of the health production function with respect to health expenditures is denoted by η_h and the elasticity of the utility function with respect to consumption by η_c. From condition (3.10), one can derive that the optimal share of income devoted to health care (i.e. the share that maximizes social welfare) verifies condition (3.11):

$$s = \eta_h = \frac{L(c,x)/x}{y} \qquad (3.11)$$

The production elasticity is likely to fall as spending rises. Therefore, from condition (3.11) it can be seen that the optimal share of income devoted to health care s increases if the value of one year of life $L(c, x) / x$ rises faster than income. This condition can also be expressed as follows:

$$\frac{s}{1-s} = \frac{\eta_h}{\eta_c}$$

(3.12)

This shows that a rising share of income devoted to health care is optimal if η_c is decreasing more rapidly than η_h. The thrust of the argument behind this result is that satiation occurs more rapidly with non-health rather than with health consumption.

Does the rising share of health expenditures observed in all developed countries fit collective preferences? In other words, are preferences likely to meet condition (3.12)? Hall and Jones assume the following utility function:

$$u(c) = b + \frac{c^{1-\gamma}}{1-\gamma}$$

(3.13)

When γ is high, the marginal utility of consumption of non-health goods declines quickly and the optimal share of health spending rises rapidly. Empirical literature suggests $\gamma = 2$, or at least $\gamma > 1$. These values imply that the marginal utility of consumption declines quickly, which is a condition for the value of life to grow rapidly. From (3.13), one can derive the expression of the value of one year of life:

$$\frac{L(c, x)}{x} = bc^{\gamma} - \frac{c}{\gamma - 1}$$

(3.14)

With, $\gamma > 1$, the value of one year of life will grow faster than consumption and income, implying that the optimal health share in GDP (s) should rise continuously over time.

smoking, etc.). Depending on assumptions relative to the pace of techno-logical progress, Hall and Jones find that technological progress and increased health spending each account for around one-third of the decline in age-specific mortality.

The marginal cost of saving a life can be derived from the health produc-tion function. Hall and Jones obtain a baseline value of about $1.9 million for an individual aged 40–44. The literature leads to estimates of the value of a statistical life (VSL) which range from about $2 million to $9 million (Viscusi and Aldy, 2003). If VSL is equal to the bottom of the range provided by the literature, that is, US$2 million, health expenditure is roughly at its efficient level for this age group. With a higher VSL, current health spend-ing would be too low.

The optimal share of health spending depends on various assumptions regarding preferences and the value of life. Hall and Jones (2007) use a benchmark of $\gamma=2$ (cf. equation (3.13) in Box 3.1), but simulations are also performed for $\gamma = 2.5$, 1.5, and 1.01. Income per person is assumed to grow at an average (historical) rate of 2.3% per year. Their simulations suggest that a rising share of the spending devoted to health care is a robust feature of the optimum, as long as γ is not too small, which is equivalent to saying that health is a superior good. Only in the extreme case where $\gamma = 1.01$, does the marginal utility of consumption fall more slowly than the diminishing returns in the production of health, implying that the optimal health share declines over time (cf. equation (3.12) in Box 3.1).

Hall and Jones (2007) also analysed how the optimal share of health spending in GDP depends on assumptions regarding the value of life and the pace of technological progress. The assumption relative to VSL influences positively the optimal level of health share. Conversely, the higher the productivity gains in the health production function, the lower the optimal level of the health share in GDP. Overall, the optimal health spending is invariably high—ranging from 23% in the case where $\gamma = 1.01$ to 45%! Although somewhat unrealistic, these results suggest that historical and future increases in the health spending share could be desirable from a welfare-enhancing point of view.

Nevertheless, these calculations are fragile. The crux of Hall and Jones' argument for a rising share of health consumption in GDP is the fact that the marginal utility of consumption of non-health goods falls relative to that of health as income rises. In other words, as satiation occurs more rapidly in non-health consumption than in health consumption, the latter can be viewed as a luxury good (or its income elasticity is greater than one). Thus we are back to the empirical evidence presented in Section 3.1, which contradicts somewhat the assumption used by Hall and Jones (2007), as well as in other studies, to derive expenditure projections. We also show, in Appendix I, that their implicit income elasticity also depends critically on the specific form of the utility function, namely the presence of a constant term (coefficient b in Box 3.1, equation (3.13)). While the share of health expenditures in GDP is set to rise in the future, determining their optimal level remains therefore an open question.

4

Integrating the Different Drivers: Projections of Total Health Expenditures, 2025–2050

The above estimates of the income elasticity of health expenditures are a key element in assessing the amount of resources that could be devoted to future health-care spending and investment, but have to be combined with other *demographic* and other *non-demographic* drivers (see Chapter 2) to provide a complete picture. This chapter proposes an integrated framework for these different drivers and derives different scenarios for total health spending with a horizon of 2050.

4.1 Demographic Drivers of Expenditure

Assessing demographic drivers requires the breakdown of health expenditures by age groups. These data are relatively scarce. For public expenditures only, an average profile by age is available for the year 1999 (Figure 4.1).[1] As discussed above, the shape of these expenditure curves reflects the interaction between health-care costs incurred near to death and mortality rates. While mortality rates increase with age, the costs of health care near death (or 'costs of death') tend to be higher at young and prime ages than for elderly people (Aprile, 2004). This explains why expenditures first increase with age, then peak, and after that, decline at very old ages. The little spike in health expenditures at the beginning of the curve just reflects the fact that early infant mortality is higher than young and prime-age mortality.

[1] For European countries, the data are based on the EU-AGIR Project; see Westerhout and Pellikaan (2005).

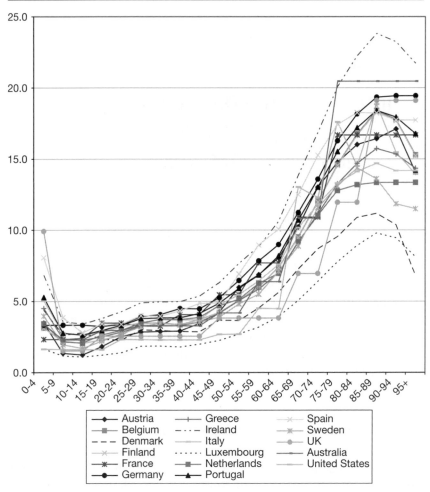

Figure 4.1. Public health-care expenditures by age groups,[1] 1999 (in % of GDP per capita)

Note: [1] Expenditure per capita in each age group divided by GDP per capita, 1999.

Source: ENPRI-AGIR (cf. Westerhout and Pellikaan, 2005), national authorities and authors' calculations.

For European countries, where health provision is dominated by the public sector, these public expenditure profiles can capture well the profile of total expenditures. For the United States, private expenditures play a much more important role. Nonetheless, the available breakdown of public and private expenditures for the US still shows a sharp increase in health expenditures at older ages only for public expenditures (Figure 4.2). Private expenditures tend to decline after 60 years of age. We conclude that, even

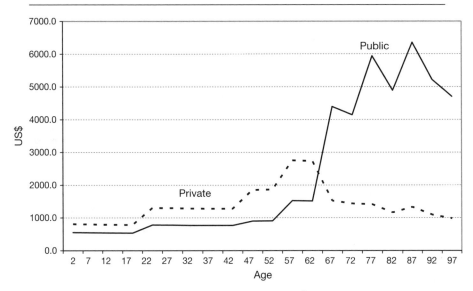

Figure 4.2. Public and private health expenditure per capita[1] (in US$ PPPs), United States

Note: [1]Excluding long-term care.

Source: US Centers for Medicare and Medicaid Services, Office of Actuary, National Health Statistics Group.

in the case of the US, the profile of public expenditures captures most of the increase in health spending with age.

On the basis of the public expenditure profiles and population estimates, expenditures on the segment of the population aged over 65 is around four times higher than for those of younger cohorts. The ratio rises to between six to nine times higher for the older groups (Productivity Commission, 2005a, 2005b; OECD, 2005a). As discussed in Chapter 2, this fact is not a reason for expecting demographic pressures to be a major driver of the growth in health expenditures.[2] One should take into account a dynamic and positive link between health status and longevity gains, possibly reflecting a 'healthy ageing' regime. This is likely to lower the average cost per individual in older age groups, all the more so as major health costs tend to come at the end of life.

---

[2] The effect of ageing on health expenditures per capita has also been weak in the past; see Culyer (1990), Gerdtham *et al.*, (1992), Hitiris and Posnett (1992), Zweifel *et al.* (1999), Richardson and Robertson (1999), Moise and Jacobzone (2003), and Jönsson and Eckerlund (2003).

For the purpose of projecting health expenditures we need then to disentangle the expenditures on survivors and non-survivors. The expenditures for the *non-survivors* can be estimated by multiplying the health costs near to death by the number of deaths per age group. Here the proxy for the 'costs of death' is the health expenditure per capita for the group 95+, assuming that after this age all health costs are death-related. In our estimates, this amount was multiplied by a factor, equal to 4 for an individual between 0 to 59 years old[3] and declining linearly to 1 afterwards, to reflect the decline of the 'costs of death' with age.

Two different effects are at play concerning expenditures for *non-survivors*. On the one hand, the number of deaths is set to rise due to the *transitory* effect of the post-war baby-boom. On the other hand, if mortality falls over time, due to a *permanent* increase in longevity, fewer will be at the very end of life in each given year, mitigating the health-care costs.[4] The total effect on public health-care expenditures will depend on the relative size of these effects.

The expenditure curve for *survivors* is simply derived by subtracting the death-related costs, as described above, from the total expenditure curves. Given that data were available only for 18 OECD countries and the uncertainties surrounding these calculations, it seemed preferable to estimate an average expenditure curve for survivors and then calibrate this curve to reflect the level of expenditures in each country. In this way, projections are less sensitive to initial conditions and country-specific idiosyncrasies.

An average expenditure curve for *survivors* was estimated econometrically in a panel of 18 OECD countries by 20 age groups, using a spline function, as follows (all the estimated coefficients are significant):

$$\frac{\text{Health Exp}}{\text{Population}}\bigg|_{agegroup} = -137.8 \cdot age + 9.94 \cdot age^2 - 0.29 \cdot age^3$$
$$+0.004 \cdot age^4 - 0.00002 \cdot age^5 + 1222.6$$

where *age* is the central point in each age bracket (e.g. 2, 7, 12, ..., 97).

Under the hypothesis that health costs are mostly death-related, the projected increase in life expectancy must be accompanied by an equivalent gain in the numbers of years spent in good health. Otherwise, an increasing share of the population living in 'bad health' would emerge

---

[3] This proportion is based on Aprile (2004) and some evidence gathered by the EC-Ageing Working group (EC-EPC, 2005). The results are not very sensitive to the alternative assumptions, because mortality rates are rather low for young and prime-age people.

[4] See e.g. Fuchs (1984), Zweifel *et al.* (1999), Jacobzone (2003), and Gray (2004).

and health-care costs would then cease to be mainly driven by the costs of death, as initially assumed. In such a scenario, the expenditure curve for *survivors* is allowed to shift rightwards in line with longevity gains, progressively postponing the age-related increases in expenditure.[5] This development tends to reduce costs compared with a situation in which life expectancy does not increase. The baseline projections presented in this chapter follow this 'healthy ageing' scenario. The sensitivity of the results to alternative assumptions is tested below.

4.2 Non-demographic Drivers of Expenditure

Evidence provided in Chapter 3 suggests that a reasonable approach would be to assume unit income elasticity in the baseline projections. This has the effect of increasing health spending in line with GDP (though we will test the sensitivity of the projections to this assumption).[6] Assuming unit income elasticity and accounting for the effect of demographic developments, Oliveira Martins and Maisonneuve (2006) derived an average residual growth for OECD countries of around 1% per year for the 1990s. In principle, this residual expenditure growth captures the effect of technological progress and other drivers (e.g. prices and policies). Our baseline projection assumes that such an average 1% per year residual growth will remain constant in the future.

These assumptions will be applied to all countries and there are two main reasons for following this approach. First, in countries where cost-containment policies have resulted in a low or negative residual (e.g. Austria, Denmark, Ireland, Italy, and Sweden), there could be a trend reversal, notably because new staff have to be attracted to the health sector or run-down facilities renewed. Second, in countries where the residual growth was very high (e.g. Portugal, the United States), it is likely that cost-containment policies will be implemented in the future. These effects would lead to a certain cross-country convergence of the expenditure residual over time.

---

[5] In contrast, in 'pure demographic' projections (see Dang *et al.*, 2001), the expenditure curves would not shift rightwards with longevity, reflecting the implicit assumption of unchanged health status at any given age. When the cost curves stay put in the presence of longevity gains, the share of life lived in 'bad health' increases when life expectancy increases. This corresponds to the 'expansion of morbidity' scenario referred to in Chapter 2.

[6] It should be noted that unit income elasticity also makes the projections less sensitive to alternative GDP per capita projections. This seems to be a desirable feature given the considerable uncertainty concerning long-run growth scenarios.

4.3 A Projection Model for Health-Care Expenditures

Defining *HE*, *Y*, and *N* as real health-care expenditures, real income, and population, respectively; ε as the income elasticity of health expenditures, and *NDF* as the other non-demographic factors, the growth of health expenditures can be decomposed as follows:

$$\Delta\log\left(\frac{HE}{N}\right) = \Delta\log(Adjusted\ age\ factor) + \varepsilon\cdot\Delta\log\left(\frac{Y}{N}\right) \\ +\Delta log(NDF) \tag{4.1}$$

or expressed as the share of expenditure in GDP:

$$\Delta\log\left(\frac{HE}{Y}\right) = \Delta\log(Adjusted\ age\ factor) + (\varepsilon - 1)\cdot\Delta\log\left(\frac{Y}{N}\right) \\ +\Delta log(NDF) \tag{4.2}$$

Intuitively, the mechanical effect of population ageing on expenditures can be seen as moving along the expenditure curve, assuming that the age profile of expenditures remains constant over time. This demographic effect is adjusted for 'healthy ageing' by shifting the expenditure curve rightwards, implying that old people still cost more than young people, but at progressively older ages. The cost curve also shifts upwards due to the non-demographic drivers (i.e. income and other non-demographic effects).

In order to make the projections less sensitive to the starting year and allow for some convergence of expenditures to GDP across countries,[7] the

---

[7] Without this specification, spending patterns of countries with equivalent expenditure drivers would diverge in terms of share of expenditure to GDP merely due to different initial expenditure to GDP ratios. Such a divergent scenario is not very appealing in the context of long-term projections. This issue has been explored in a few empirical papers. Hitiris (1997) examines total health expenditures convergence for a group of ten European countries and finds no evidence of convergence. Narayan (2007) examines the catch-up hypothesis, especially whether or not per capita total health expenditures for Canada, Japan, Switzerland, Spain, and the United Kingdom converge on those of the US over the period 1960–2000. He uses univariate and panel Lagrange Multiplier (LM) unit root tests that potentially allow for structural breaks and provides evidence of relative convergence when incorporating one or two structural breaks (see also Barros, 1998; Okunade and Karakus, 2001). However, the unit root approach to convergence has been criticized on the ground that non-stationary processes can meet the definition of convergence (Nahar and Inder, 2002; Bentzen, 2005). We investigated the convergence hypothesis for per capita public, private, and total health-care expenditures using the recent approaches developed by Nahar and Inder (2002) and Phillips and Sul (2007). The results, available upon request, support the hypothesis of convergence of GDP and total health expenditures per capita. Health expenditures as a share of GDP also converge across countries.

Box 4.1 EXOGENOUS VARIABLES AND ASSUMPTIONS UNDERLYING THE PROJECTIONS

The projections require a set of exogenous data, as follows:

(1) Population projections (N). The population projections were gathered by the OECD Directorate on Employment, Labour and Social Affairs, directly from national sources.
(2) Labour force projections (L/N) rely on Burniaux *et al.* (2003). These projections are constructed on the basis of a so-called cohort approach. They correspond to a baseline scenario, that is, the impact of current policies is assumed to influence labour participation over the coming decades, but no additional assumptions are made concerning future policy changes.
(3) Labour productivity (Y/L) growth is assumed to converge linearly from the initial rate (1995–2003) to 1.75% per year by 2030 in all countries, except former transition countries and Mexico, where it converges only by 2050.

The projected GDP per capita is directly derived from the above exogenous variables $(Y/N = Y/L \times L/N)$. This simple framework is not supposed to capture in the best possible way productivity differentials across countries, but to isolate, as far as possible, the effect of ageing and other demographic factors on the projections. Further details can be found in Oliveira Martins and Maisonneuve (2006).

total logarithmic growth rates derived from equation (4.2) for each country are applied to the OECD cross-country average expenditure share to GDP in 2005 (a sort of 'representative' country). The changes in expenditure shares calculated from this common base are then added to the country-specific shares in 2005 to obtain the projected ratios of expenditure to GDP (see Appendix II).

Additional exogenous assumptions underlying the projections are listed in Box 4.1 (more details are also provided in Appendix II).

4.4 Expenditure Projections for the US, EU-15, and Japan

The framework described above was used to project expenditures at the horizon of 2050. The demographic effects can be decomposed into health-care spending for survivors, an adjustment for 'healthy ageing', and death-related costs (Figure 4.3(a)). Pure age effects vary substantially across countries, mapping differences in evolving old-age dependency ratios (Figure 4.3(b)). They can be quite large for some countries, but, as longevity increases, they tend to be compensated by better health status. Death-

(a)

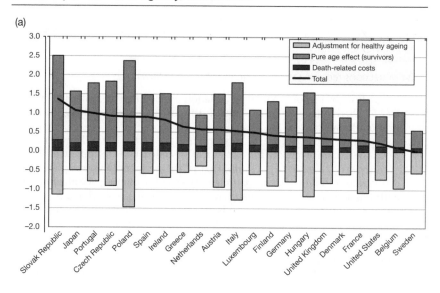

(b)

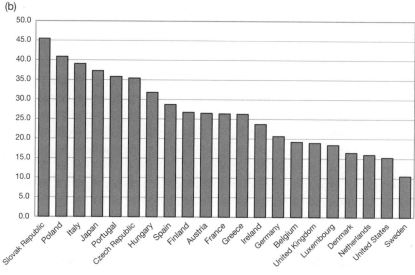

Figure 4.3. Demographic effects on health-care expenditure (a) **Public health-care expenditure** (increase in % points of GDP 2005–2050) (b) **Increase in the old-age dependency ratio between 2005 and 2050**[1] (in percentage points of working-age population)

Note: Ratio of population aged 65 and over to population aged 15–64.

Source: Oliveira Martins and de la Maisonneuve (2006).

related costs account for only a small fraction of the increase in expenditures (around 7% of total health-care spending in the OECD by 2050).[8] Overall, the net effect of demographics on health-care expenditures ranges from virtually zero in Sweden to nearly 1.5 percentage points of GDP for Slovakia. Admittedly, the 'healthy ageing' assumption can be viewed as relatively optimistic, albeit in line with observed patterns of morbidity regimes in the US and European countries.

We carried out several simulations. Scenario I is our baseline. It assumes, on top of the demographic effects adjusted for 'health ageing', an expenditure residual growth of 1% per year over the projection period and an income elasticity equal to 1. In scenario II, we keep the same assumptions of scenario I but the income elasticity is set at 1.5. This reflects strong preferences towards health goods, as some studies have argued. In scenario III, we keep the same assumptions as in scenario I but the residual is set at 2% growth per year. This scenario is purely illustrative, as the high growth of the expenditure residual just compounds over time without limit. Finally, a voluntarily 'cost-containment' scenario (IV) was simulated, where the residual expenditure growth is assumed to start at 1% per year, but to converge on zero by 2050. The income elasticity is kept unitary, but to be consistent with a lower residual growth over the projection period, it is assumed that lower technology improvements lead to an 'expansion of morbidity'. This implies that expenditure curves do not shift rightwards over time in line with longevity gains. The results from these simulations are as follows.

In scenario I, the US expenditure share reaches 19% of GDP by 2050, or around a 5 percentage-point increase compared with 2005. A similar increase is obtained for the EU-15 and there is a 6 percentage-point increase for Japan (Table 4.1). In most countries, health-care expenditures would exceed 10% of GDP by 2050. This looks like a relatively mild scenario.

In scenario II, average expenditures more than double, with a projected increase of above 9 percentage points of GDP (Table 4.2). Driven by the income effect, which accounts for almost 4 percentage points of GDP in the US and EU-15, expenditure shares would reach nearly 23% in the US, and around 16% of GDP in Europe and Japan by 2050.

Scenario III illustrates the type of assumptions about the role of technology that are required to generate very high shares of health care to GDP, as put forward in some studies (Hall and Jones, 2007). On average, expenditures increase above 12 percentage points of GDP (Table 4.3). The US

---

[8] See Oliveira Martins and Maisonneuve (2006).

Table 4.1. Projections of total health-care expenditures, scenario I (residual at 1% per year (with no transversality condition) and income elasticity 1)

Health expenditure as % of GDP	2000	2005	Increase in % points of GDP, 2005–2025						Increase in % points of GDP, 2005–2025						Health expenditure as % of GDP 2050
			Death-related costs	Pure age effect (survivors)	Adjustment for healthy ageing	Income effect	Non-ageing residual effect	Total	Death-related costs	Pure age effect (survivors)	Adjustment for healthy ageing	Income effect	Non-ageing residual effect	Total	
United States	12.0	14.3	0.1	0.8	−0.5	0.0	1.7	2.1	0.1	1.1	−1.0	0.0	4.4	4.7	19.0
Europe															
Austria	8.1	8.3	0.1	0.8	−0.6	0.0	1.7	2.1	0.2	1.9	−1.3	0.0	4.4	5.2	13.4
Belgium	7.2	9.4	0.1	0.7	−0.7	0.0	1.7	1.7	0.1	1.3	−1.3	0.0	4.4	4.5	13.9
Czech Republic	6.4	7.1	0.1	1.0	−0.6	0.0	1.7	2.3	0.2	2.3	−1.3	0.0	4.4	5.6	12.7
Denmark	5.8	6.3	0.1	0.7	−0.6	0.0	1.7	2.0	0.1	1.1	−0.8	0.0	4.4	4.8	11.1
Finland	4.2	4.8	0.1	1.2	−0.6	0.0	1.7	2.4	0.2	1.6	−1.3	0.0	4.4	4.9	9.8
France	7.9	9.3	0.1	0.9	−0.7	0.0	1.7	2.0	0.2	1.7	−1.5	0.0	4.4	4.8	14.0
Germany	9.0	9.3	0.1	0.8	−0.6	0.0	1.7	2.0	0.2	1.4	−1.1	0.0	4.4	4.9	14.2
Greece	9.3	6.4	0.1	0.7	−0.4	0.0	1.7	2.1	0.2	1.4	−0.8	0.0	4.4	5.3	14.7
Hungary	6.8	7.9	0.1	1.0	−0.8	0.0	1.7	2.1	0.2	1.9	−1.6	0.0	4.4	4.9	12.8
Ireland	5.7	6.6	0.1	0.7	−0.3	0.0	1.7	2.2	0.2	1.8	−1.0	0.0	4.4	5.5	12.1
Italy	7.1	7.7	0.1	1.0	−0.7	0.0	1.7	2.1	0.2	2.2	−1.8	0.0	4.4	5.1	12.8
Luxembourg	4.4	6.5	0.1	0.5	−0.5	0.0	1.7	1.8	0.2	1.3	−0.8	0.0	4.4	5.1	11.6
Netherlands	6.5	7.8	0.1	0.9	−0.4	0.0	1.7	2.3	0.1	1.1	−0.5	0.0	4.4	5.2	13.0
Poland	5.3	6.3	0.1	1.5	−0.8	0.0	1.7	2.5	0.2	3.0	−2.1	0.0	4.4	5.6	11.9
Portugal	8.8	9.6	0.1	0.9	−0.6	0.0	1.7	2.1	0.2	2.2	−1.1	0.0	4.4	5.7	15.3
Slovak Republic	5.2	5.8	0.1	1.4	−0.8	0.0	1.7	2.5	0.3	3.1	−1.6	0.0	4.4	6.2	12.0
Spain	6.6	7.6	0.1	0.7	−0.4	0.0	1.7	2.2	0.2	1.8	−0.8	0.0	4.4	5.6	13.2
Sweden	5.5	6.1	0.1	0.5	−0.4	0.0	1.7	1.9	0.1	0.6	−0.8	0.0	4.4	4.4	10.5
United Kingdom	5.9	6.8	0.1	0.8	−0.7	0.0	1.7	1.9	0.2	1.4	−1.2	0.0	4.4	4.8	11.7
EU-15 average	*6.8*	*7.7*	*0.1*	*0.8*	*−0.5*	*0.0*	*1.7*	*2.1*	*0.2*	*1.5*	*−1.1*	*0.0*	*4.4*	*5.1*	*12.8*
Japan	6.8	7.4	0.1	1.2	−0.4	0.0	1.7	2.6	0.2	1.9	−0.7	0.0	4.4	5.8	13.2

Notes: Assumptions used in this scenario: health ageing: dynamic equilibrium (1 year gain in life expectancy = 1 year in good health); income elasticity =1; residuals =1 with no transversality condition.

Source: Oliveira Martins and de la Maisonneuve (2006) and author's calculations.

Table 4.2. Projections of total health-care expenditures, scenario II (residual at 1% per year (with no transversality condition) and income elasticity 1.5)

Health expenditure as a % of GDP	2000	2005	Increase in % points of GDP, 2005–2025						Increase in % points of GDP, 2005–2050						Health expenditure as a % of GDP 2050
			Death-related costs	Pure effect age (survivors)	Adjustment for healthy ageing	Income effect	Non-ageing residual effect	Total	Death-related costs	Pure age effect (survivors)	Adjustment for healthy ageing	Income effect	Non-ageing residual effect	Total	
United States	12.0	14.3	0.1	0.8	−0.5	1.6	1.7	3.7	0.1	1.1	−1.0	3.8	4.4	8.5	22.8
Europe															
Austria	8.1	8.3	0.1	0.8	−0.6	1.4	1.7	3.5	0.2	1.9	−1.3	3.1	4.4	8.3	16.6
Belgium	7.2	9.4	0.1	0.7	−0.7	1.4	1.7	3.2	0.1	1.3	−1.3	3.4	4.4	7.9	17.2
Czech Republic	6.4	7.1	0.1	1.0	−0.6	0.9	1.7	3.2	0.2	2.3	−1.3	1.9	4.4	7.6	14.6
Denmark	5.8	6.3	0.1	0.7	−0.6	1.4	1.7	3.4	0.1	1.1	−0.8	3.5	4.4	8.3	14.6
Finland	4.2	4.8	0.1	1.2	−0.6	2.0	1.7	4.4	0.2	1.6	−1.3	4.3	4.4	9.3	14.1
France	7.9	9.3	0.1	0.9	−0.7	1.1	1.7	3.0	0.2	1.7	−1.5	2.8	4.4	7.6	16.9
Germany	9.0	9.3	0.1	0.8	−0.6	1.0	1.7	3.0	0.2	1.4	−1.1	2.8	4.4	7.7	17.0
Greece	9.3	9.4	0.1	0.7	−0.4	2.1	1.7	4.2	0.2	1.4	−0.8	3.8	4.4	9.0	18.4
Hungary	6.8	7.9	0.1	1.0	−0.8	2.2	1.7	4.3	0.2	1.9	−1.6	4.4	4.4	9.3	17.2
Ireland	5.7	6.6	0.1	0.7	−0.3	4.2	1.7	6.4	0.2	1.8	−1.0	6.9	4.4	12.4	19.0
Italy	7.1	7.7	0.1	1.0	−0.7	1.1	1.7	3.2	0.2	2.2	−1.8	2.5	4.4	7.6	15.3
Luxembourg	4.4	6.5	0.1	0.5	−0.5	3.3	1.7	5.1	0.2	1.3	−0.8	5.7	4.4	10.7	17.2
Netherlands	6.5	7.8	0.1	0.9	−0.4	1.3	1.7	3.7	0.1	1.1	−0.5	3.5	4.4	8.7	16.5
Poland	5.3	6.3	0.1	1.5	−0.8	3.4	1.7	5.9	0.2	3.0	−2.1	6.4	4.4	12.0	18.2
Portugal	8.8	9.6	0.1	0.9	−0.6	2.0	1.7	4.1	0.2	2.2	−1.1	3.7	4.4	9.4	19.0
Slovak Republic	5.2	5.8	0.1	1.4	−0.8	1.6	1.7	4.1	0.3	3.1	−1.6	2.8	4.4	9.0	14.8
Spain	6.6	7.6	0.1	0.7	−0.4	1.1	1.7	3.3	0.2	1.8	−0.8	2.7	4.4	8.3	15.9
Sweden	5.5	6.1	0.1	0.5	−0.4	1.6	1.7	3.6	0.1	0.6	−0.8	4.0	4.4	8.4	14.5
United Kingdom	5.9	6.8	0.1	0.8	−0.7	1.6	1.7	3.6	0.2	1.4	−1.2	3.8	4.4	8.6	15.4
EU-15 average	*6.8*	*7.7*	*0.1*	*0.8*	*−0.5*	*1.8*	*1.7*	*3.8*	*0.2*	*1.5*	*−1.1*	*3.8*	*4.4*	*8.8*	*16.5*
Japan	6.8	7.4	0.1	1.2	−0.4	0.8	1.7	3.5	0.2	1.9	−0.7	2.5	4.4	8.3	15.7

Notes: Assumptions used in this scenario: healthy ageing: dynamic equilibrium (1 year gain in life expectancy = 1 year in good health); income elasticity = 1.5, residuals = 1 with no transversality condition.

Source: Oliveira Martins and de la Maisonneuve (2006) and author's calculations.

expenditure share would reach 26% of GDP by 2050, while the share would be around 20% in both the EU-15 and Japan.

Scenario IV implicitly embodies a policy reaction to growing expenditures. This could be justified on the grounds that health-care expenditures relative to GDP could not continue to grow without limit.[9] A continuing increase in the share of income going to health-care spending could reflect individual preferences, but the health-care market is not perfect and governments are footing most of the bill. Thus, rapid growth of the share of health-care spending in income would have to be compensated by reductions in other public spending items, which may be difficult to achieve, and/or increased health-care charges for individuals. This implicitly means that policies would have to progressively rein in the expenditure residual, for example, by ensuring that future technology improvements are mainly used in a cost-saving way. This may imply some trade-offs. Reining in the impact of technological progress on health-care demand without foregoing the benefits it provides to patients could be a difficult task.

Despite the cost-containment assumptions, total health-care expenditures would still increase on average by nearly 4 percentage points between 2005 and 2050, from 7–8% to above 11% of GDP in the EU and Japan (cf. Table 4.4). Moreover, larger increases by 2050 are to be found in countries in Central and Eastern Europe, which are experiencing rapid demographic change. In the US, the share of expenditure to GDP would stabilize at around 18%.

These different scenarios illustrate how uncertainties concerning projections' parameters may drive very different levels of health expenditures by 2050. Despite these uncertainties, even in the more conservative scenarios, the amount of resources channelled to the health sector is substantial.

---

[9] Similar transversality conditions have also been imposed in other projection exercises. For example, Englert (2004) assumes that income elasticity ultimately converges to one.

Table 4.3. Projections of total health-care expenditures, scenario III (residual at 2% per year (with no transversality condition) and income elasticity 1)

| Health expenditure as a % of GDP | 2000 | 2005 | Increase in % points of GDP, 2005–2025 | | | | | | Increase in % points of GDP, 2005–2050 | | | | | | Total Health expenditure as a % of GDP 2050 |
			Death-related costs	Pure age effect (survivors)	Adjustment for healthy ageing	Income effect	Non ageing residual effect	Total	Death-related costs	Pure age effect (survivors)	Adjustment for healthy ageing	Income effect	Non-ageing residual effect	Total	2050
United States	12.0	14.3	0.1	0.8	-0.5	0.0	3.8	4.2	0.1	1.1	-1.0	0.0	11.4	11.6	25.9
Europe															
Austria	8.1	8.3	0.1	0.8	-0.6	0.0	3.8	4.2	0.2	1.9	-1.3	0.0	11.4	12.1	20.4
Belgium	7.2	9.4	0.1	0.7	-0.7	0.0	3.8	3.9	0.1	1.3	-1.3	0.0	11.4	11.5	20.8
Czech Republic	6.4	7.1	0.1	1.0	-0.6	0.0	3.8	4.4	0.2	2.3	-1.3	0.0	11.4	12.6	19.7
Denmark	5.8	6.3	0.1	0.7	-0.6	0.0	3.8	4.1	0.1	1.1	-0.8	0.0	11.4	11.8	18.1
Finland	4.2	4.8	0.1	1.2	-0.6	0.0	3.8	4.5	0.2	1.6	-1.3	0.0	11.4	11.9	16.7
France	7.9	9.3	0.1	0.9	-0.7	0.0	3.8	4.1	0.2	1.7	-1.5	0.0	11.4	11.7	21.0
Germany	9.0	9.3	0.1	0.8	-0.6	0.0	3.8	4.1	0.2	1.4	-1.1	0.0	11.4	11.9	21.1
Greece	9.3	9.4	0.1	0.7	-0.4	0.0	3.8	4.3	0.2	1.4	-0.8	0.0	11.4	12.2	21.6
Hungary	6.8	7.9	0.1	1.0	-0.8	0.0	3.8	4.2	0.2	1.9	-1.6	0.0	11.4	11.8	19.7
Ireland	5.7	6.6	0.1	0.7	-0.3	0.0	3.8	4.3	0.2	1.8	-1.0	0.0	11.4	12.4	19.0
Italy	7.1	7.7	0.1	1.0	-0.7	0.0	3.8	4.2	0.2	2.2	-1.8	0.0	11.4	12.0	19.8
Luxembourg	4.4	6.5	0.1	0.5	-0.5	0.0	3.8	3.9	0.2	1.3	-0.8	0.0	11.4	12.0	18.5
Netherlands	6.5	7.8	0.1	0.9	-0.4	0.0	3.8	4.4	0.1	1.1	-0.5	0.0	11.4	12.1	19.9
Poland	5.3	6.3	0.1	1.5	-0.8	0.0	3.8	4.6	0.2	3.0	-2.1	0.0	11.4	12.5	18.8
Portugal	8.8	9.6	0.1	0.9	-0.6	0.0	3.8	4.2	0.2	2.2	-1.1	0.0	11.4	12.7	22.3
Slovak Republic	5.2	5.8	0.1	1.4	-0.8	0.0	3.8	4.6	0.3	3.1	-1.6	0.0	11.4	13.2	19.0
Spain	6.5	7.6	0.1	0.7	-0.4	0.0	3.8	4.3	0.2	1.8	-0.8	0.0	11.4	12.5	20.2
Sweden	5.5	6.1	0.1	0.5	-0.4	0.0	3.8	4.0	0.1	0.8	-0.8	0.0	11.4	11.3	17.4
United Kingdom	5.9	6.8	0.1	0.8	-0.7	0.0	3.8	4.0	0.2	1.4	-1.2	0.0	11.4	11.8	18.6
EU-15 average	6.8	7.7	0.1	0.8	-0.5	0.0	3.8	4.2	0.2	1.5	-1.1	0.0	11.4	12.0	19.7
Japan	6.8	7.4	0.1	1.2	-0.4	0.0	3.8	4.7	0.2	1.9	-0.7	0.0	11.4	12.8	20.2

Notes: Assumptions used in this scenario: healthy ageing: dynamic equilibrium (1 year gain in life expectancy = 1 year in good health); income elasticity = 1; residuals = 2 with no transversality condition.

Source: Oliveira Martins and de la Maisonneuve (2006) and author's calculations.

Table 4.4. Projections of total health-care expenditures, scenario IV (residual at 1% per year (with no transversality condition) and income elasticity 1 and expansion of morbidity)

Health expenditure as a % of GDP	2000	2005	Death-related costs	Pure age effect (survivors)	Adjustment for healthy ageing	Income effect	Non-ageing residual effect	Total	Death-related costs	Pure age effect (survivors)	Adjustment for healthy ageing	Income effect	Non-ageing residual effect	Total	Health expenditure as a % of GDP 2050
			Increase in % points of GDP, 2005–2025						Increase in % points of GDP, 2005–2050						
United States	12.0	14.3	0.1	0.8	0.0	0.0	1.3	2.2	0.1	1.1	0.0	0.0	1.9	3.2	17.5
Europe															
Austria	8.1	8.3	0.1	0.8	0.0	0.0	1.3	2.2	0.2	1.9	0.0	0.0	1.9	4.0	12.2
Belgium	7.2	9.4	0.1	0.7	0.0	0.0	1.3	2.0	0.1	1.3	0.0	0.0	1.9	3.3	12.7
Czech Republic	6.4	7.1	0.1	1.0	0.0	0.0	1.3	2.4	0.2	2.3	0.0	0.0	1.9	4.4	11.5
Denmark	5.8	6.3	0.1	0.7	0.0	0.0	1.3	2.1	0.1	1.1	0.0	0.0	1.9	3.1	9.4
Finland	4.2	4.8	0.1	1.2	0.0	0.0	1.3	2.6	0.2	1.6	0.0	0.0	1.9	3.7	8.5
France	7.9	9.3	0.1	0.9	0.0	0.0	1.3	2.2	0.2	1.7	0.0	0.0	1.9	3.8	13.0
Germany	9.0	9.3	0.1	0.8	0.0	0.0	1.3	2.2	0.2	1.4	0.0	0.0	1.9	3.5	12.8
Greece	9.3	9.4	0.1	0.7	0.0	0.0	1.3	2.1	0.2	1.4	0.0	0.0	1.9	3.5	12.9
Hungary	6.8	7.9	0.1	1.0	0.0	0.0	1.3	2.4	0.2	1.9	0.0	0.0	1.9	4.0	11.9
Ireland	5.7	6.6	0.1	0.7	0.0	0.0	1.3	2.1	0.2	1.8	0.0	0.0	1.9	3.9	10.5
Italy	7.1	7.7	0.1	1.0	0.0	0.0	1.3	2.4	0.2	2.2	0.0	0.0	1.9	4.4	12.1
Luxembourg	4.4	6.5	0.1	0.5	0.0	0.0	1.3	1.9	0.2	1.3	0.0	0.0	1.9	3.4	9.9
Netherlands	6.5	7.8	0.1	0.9	0.0	0.0	1.3	2.3	0.1	1.1	0.0	0.0	1.9	3.2	11.0
Poland	5.3	6.3	0.1	1.5	0.0	0.0	1.3	2.9	0.2	3.0	0.0	0.0	1.9	5.1	11.4
Portugal	8.8	9.6	0.1	0.9	0.0	0.0	1.3	2.3	0.2	2.2	0.0	0.0	1.9	4.3	13.9
Slovak Republic	5.2	5.8	0.1	1.4	0.0	0.0	1.3	2.9	0.3	3.1	0.0	0.0	1.9	5.3	11.1
Spain	6.6	7.6	0.1	0.7	0.0	0.0	1.3	2.1	0.2	1.8	0.0	0.0	1.9	3.9	11.5
Sweden	5.5	6.1	0.1	0.5	0.0	0.0	1.3	1.9	0.1	0.6	0.0	0.0	1.9	2.7	8.8
United Kingdom	5.9	6.8	0.1	0.8	0.0	0.0	1.3	2.2	0.2	1.4	0.0	0.0	1.9	3.5	10.3
EU-15 average	6.8	7.7	0.1	0.8	0.0	0.0	1.3	2.2	0.2	1.5	0.0	0.0	1.9	3.6	11.3
Japan	6.8	7.4	0.1	1.2	0.0	0.0	1.3	2.6	0.2	1.9	0.0	0.0	1.9	4.0	11.4

Notes: Assumptions used in this scenario. expansion of morbidity: gains in life expectancy do not translate into years in good health; income elasticity = 1; residuals = 1 with a transversality condition.
Source: Oliveira Martins and de la Maisonneuve (2006) and author's calculations.

5

The Impact of Health on Productivity and Growth

After having analysed the impact of income growth on health spending, this chapter closes the loop by investigating the likely impacts of better health and longevity on economic growth. There are reasons to believe that health matters for growth, through both labour participation and productivity. First, health impacts labour supply. A good health status increases the time available for both work and leisure. Moreover, health also influences the decision to supply labour through its impact on wages, preferences, and expected life horizon—the net effect depending on substitution and income effect. Second, healthier individuals could reasonably be assumed to produce more per hour worked, thus increasing productivity. Third, according to human capital theory, better health contributes to more educated people and thus to more productive people. An increasing life expectancy will also encourage people to acquire more education. Fourth, the state of health of an individual (or the total population) is likely to impact upon not only the level of income but also the distribution of this income between savings and consumption and hence the willingness to undertake investment, which in turn promotes growth. Fifth, R&D in health, which represents a substantial share of total R&D, may contribute as an engine of innovation and growth.

5.1 Health, Human Capital, and Growth: General Results

Since the seminal work of Becker (1964),[1] there is a sound theoretical and empirical basis to the argument that human capital matters for economic

[1] In the original formulation of his theory, Becker (1964) pointed to health as one component of the stock of human capital, but then focused in his early empirical work exclusively on education.

growth, but until recently, human capital has been mostly narrowly defined as education. At the same time, the idea of health representing—next to education—an important component of human capital was introduced most prominently by Grossman (1972), but has been acknowledged more widely. Grossman (1972) distinguishes between health as a consumption good and health as a capital good. As a consumption good, health enters directly into the utility function of the individual, since one enjoys being healthy. As a capital good, health reduces the number of days spent ill, and therefore increases the number of days available for both market and non-market activities. Health is not only demanded, but also produced, by individuals. They inherit an initial stock of health that depreciates with time, but they can invest to maintain and increase this stock. The production of health also requires the use by individuals of time away from market and non-market activities. These two ideas have been introduced in growth models where the growth rate of total factor productivity can be endogenized.

Van Zon and Muysken (2001) analyse the trade-off between health and human capital accumulation in the endogenous growth framework of Lucas (1988). Health influences inter-temporal decision-making in three different ways. First, health generates positive utility of its own, through the average health level in the economy. The average effect also affects longevity.[2] Second, the provision of health-care services directly competes with the provision of labour services allocated to the production and human capital sector. In other words, more health services lead to less human capital accumulation. Finally, health serves as a prerequisite to the provision of human capital services. In this respect, health enters both the utility and the production function. In particular, the generation of health services is defined by decreasing returns (Forster, 1989; Ehrlich and Chuma, 1990; Grossman, 1998), whereas human capital accumulation is modelled using constant returns to scale (the well-known knife-edge condition on the human capital accumulation dynamics). In this context, the social planner chooses the fractions that are respectively spent on human capital accumulation and health services production. This choice impacts on the average health level, and thus on the human capital accumulation, the production of the final good, and the utility function. Two polar cases can be distinguished from this model. If the impact of the average health level on longevity is an externality, health becomes a pure complement to

---

[2] Longevity being proportional to the average health level of the population.

growth, that is, any reallocation of labour from the health sector towards the human capital sector leads to a decline in growth. In contrast, if the impact of the average health level on longevity is internalized (as in their model), then increases in the demand for health services, as for instance caused by an ageing population, will adversely affect growth.

Other elements relating longevity, human capital, and growth have been considered in the theoretical literature. Indeed, the expansion of life expectancy allows for higher returns to be obtained over a longer period of time and thus creates incentives to invest more in education (Kalemli-Ozcan *et al.*, 2000; De la Croix and Licandro, 1999). In contrast, a reduction in life expectancy leads to higher competition for resources between the consumption and health needs of the elderly and the investment in education of the young population (Zhang *et al.*, 2003). In particular, Zhang *et al.* (2001) show that the effect of a life expectancy extension on long-run economic growth will depend on the utility parameters and the social security system. For instance, with a pay-as-you-go social security system, an increase in longevity will increase the value to parents of the welfare of their children and not of the number of their children.

5.2 Does Health Contribute to Growth in Rich Countries?

Confirming the above theoretical arguments, on a worldwide level, better health, typically measured by life expectancy, appears among the few robust predictors of a country's subsequent economic growth, in some cases contributing even more than education (see Levine and Renelt, 1992; Sala-i-Martin *et al.*, 2004, Hongbin *et al.*, 2007; López-Casanovas *et al.*, 2005).[3] But the effect of health and longevity on growth is not so clear-cut for developed countries. The economic literature has tried to investigate this puzzle.

If non-active people are getting older and older through an increase in life expectancy, this will not expand the labour force or the returns on investment in education or training. However, longevity also affects agents' willingness to substitute consumption over the life cycle. Individuals with a higher life expectancy tend to be more patient and thus have higher levels

---

[3] It could be noted that disentangling the role of health in the context of standard growth regressions faces several general econometric challenges that have been highlighted in the literature (Pritchett, 2006; Rodrick, 2005; Sala-i-Martin *et al.*, 2004), notably a possible reverse causality. In this context, recent papers have developed alternative approaches, for instance a macroeconomic production function model of growth (Bloom and Canning, 2005).

of savings. *Ceteris paribus*, this should yield higher growth (Reinhart, 1999). To sum up, life expectancy could affect growth via three different links: (i) the savings decision; (ii) labour market participation; and (iii) competition for resources between different activities. Therefore, there is no consensus about whether an increase in longevity has a positive or a negative effect on growth, or simply does not affect it at all.

It should be stressed that empirical studies often rely on poor proxies of the health status of the population. The contribution of health is typically measured by life expectancy, total health-care expenditures, child mortality, or the mortality of some specific diseases. These explanatory variables do not capture all the plausible effects through which health may enhance growth by its effects on labour market participation, worker productivity, investment in R&D and human capital, savings, and population age structure (Bloom and Canning, 2000; Bloom *et al.*, 2003; Easterlin, 1999).

In addition, the fact that the relation between health (or its proxies) and growth is weaker for developed countries could be due to a non-linear relationship, positive at low levels of development and insignificant or negative at higher levels. Bhargava *et al.* (2001) use adult survival rates (i.e. the inverse of adult mortality rates) between ages 15 and 60 as a health proxy in order to assess the effect of health on economic growth in a worldwide panel data set for the period 1965 to 1990. Using an interaction term between the health proxy and per capita income, they detected a threshold income level beyond which adult survival rates have negligible or even negative effects on growth rates.

Using data from more than 50 developing and developed countries, Jamison *et al.* (2004) find that increases in physical capital stock dominate (accounting for 67% of total growth), but both educational improvements (14%) and health improvements (11%) have an important role, too. Most importantly, investment in health presents diminishing returns, consistent with the results reported by Bhargava (2001). These results require some qualifications. First, given lack of morbidity or disability data, only mortality rates are used as a proxy for overall health conditions. However, it is plausible that changes in morbidity may also be significant for income growth, while they are only partially correlated with mortality decline and might lag mortality decline. Second, health improvements above the age of 60 (the threshold used in Bhargava *et al.*, 2001) may have an impact on the retirement decision and may further improve even if adult survival rates have already reached high levels.

Focusing on high-income countries, Knowles and Owen (1995) incorporated a proxy for health in Mankiw, Romer, and Weil's (MRW) empirical growth model. They examine a cross-section of 84 countries for the period 1960 to 1985, using Ordinary Least Squares (OLS) estimates.[4] Their results suggest a stronger, more robust, relationship between per capita income and life expectancy than between income and educational human capital. For a sub-sample of 22 high-income countries, no statistically significant impact of life expectancy was found.

Rivera and Currais (1999a, 1999b) examine the impact of health in a cross-section of 24 high-income countries using an augmented Mankiw-Romer-Weil model. In contrast to Knowles and Owen (1995), they use health expenditures as a proxy for health status, arguing that mortality rates represent a very limited indicator of the output of health-care systems. Indeed, medical care is not exclusively or primarily aimed at influencing directly the probability of dying. In the absence of reliable time-series data capturing both mortality and morbidity, the choice of health expenditures cannot be entirely dismissed. Both OLS and Two-Stage Least Squares (2SLS) estimates are carried out (using several instruments, such as alcohol consumption, rate of population over 65 years old, in-patient beds per 1,000 population, etc). Results suggest a fairly robust positive impact of health (expenditures) on income. Following a similar approach, Gyimah-Brempong and Wilson (2004) and Beraldo *et al.* (2005) also found a fairly robust, statistically significant positive contribution of health expenditures to growth. The endogeneity of health expenditures to GDP per capita could nevertheless be a serious drawback in this type of studies.

Along these lines, recent contributions have focused more narrowly on the links between government health spending and growth. Agenor (2005) concentrates on the potential trade-off between health and other public services, such as education, security, and infrastructure services. The optimal allocation of government spending is determined in an endogenous growth model where public expenditure is an input in the production of final goods as well as health services. In his model, health is treated as labour-augmenting and not as a separate factor of production. In particular, the amount of effective labour services provided by a worker is assumed to be proportional to his average health level. At the same time, health services enter into the household's utility function and thus affect welfare directly. The specification of Agenor (2005) is close to the model proposed

---

[4] The authors argue that (non-reported) 2SLS estimates gave qualitatively similar results. The 2SLS estimates use lagged values of potentially endogenous regressors—a strategy they acknowledge to be the natural choice in time-series regressions but not in cross-country regressions.

by Barro (1990), and thus does not display any transitional dynamics when the flow of health services is considered. An increase of public spending on infrastructure increases growth through an increase in infrastructure services to both production and to health services. But it also reduces the resources allocated to health and hence leads to lower productivity and growth. The net effect is ambiguous and depends on the calibration of the parameters of the economy. When both the production and utility function depend on the stock of public capital in health, no general results can be derived.

In contrast, Aisa and Pueyo (2004, 2006) analyze the impact of government spending in a model of endogenous longevity. Aisa and Pueyo (2004) endogenize life expectancy by allowing the probability of survival to depend on health-care public expenditures. Moreover, the accumulation of the health status depends on public health-care expenditures as a percentage of income.[5] Their model also follows Barro (1990). The production of final goods is obtained by combining private capital, labour, and productive public services. Public expenditures, which represent a constant fraction of GDP, are financed through taxes. Therefore, there is a trade-off between the amount of productive public services allocated to the production of final goods and the amount of health expenditures, which leads to a higher health status and thus increases the survival probability. Their theoretical results show that a higher life expectancy leads to a higher savings rate and to an expansion of the labour force (the labour participation effect). Depending on the parameters, these effects may enhance growth. But Aisa and Pueyo (2004) acknowledge that this effect is likely to be less clear-cut in OECD countries, where efforts to increase life expectancy may have a negative effect on long-run growth. By modelling a non-monotonic effect of government spending on economic growth, Aisa and Pueyo (2006) obtain similar results. Public expenditures have two opposite effects. On the one hand, they reduce the impatience of consumers by lengthening life, which promotes saving and growth. On the other hand, resources devoted to health are at the expense of other factors, especially the accumulation of physical capital, which reduces growth. All in all, the effect of public health expenditures is mixed.

Surrounding this analysis, an important question is whether health-care expenditures contribute to health outcomes. Echoing some of the results obtained at the micro or individual level presented in Chapter 2, results

---

[5] They also assume a constant depreciation rate as in standard accumulation equations.

appear particularly mixed when examining the relationship at the aggregate level. Earlier commentators have argued that the role of health care was rather small and may even have been detrimental (Illich, 1976; McKeown, 1979). In fact, the impact of 'curative medical measures' may reasonably be assumed to have had little effect on mortality decline prior to the mid-20th century (Colgrove, 2002). Since then, however, the scope and quality of health care have changed almost beyond recognition, but the debate about the relative role of health care continues.

Explaining the mixed results obtained so far, Suhrcke and Urban (2006) argued that there is very little variation in life expectancy among rich countries (in sharp contrast to the wide variation among poor countries). They also share the view that the link between health expenditures and health outcomes is far too poorly understood for the former to serve as a proxy for the latter. For this reason, they use a health proxy that at least displays significantly greater variation among rich countries and is particularly characteristic of the health challenges that these countries are facing: cardiovascular disease (CVD) mortality among the working-age population. Starting from a worldwide sample of countries (acknowledging data problems on CVD data for low- and middle-income countries), they find that the effect of working-age CVD mortality rates on growth was dependent on the level of initial per-person GDP. They therefore split the sample into (broadly defined) low- and middle-income countries, on the one hand, and high-income countries, on the other hand. Results are remarkably robust across different specifications and methods. In their preferred estimate, a 1% increase in the CVD mortality rate was found to decrease the growth rate of per-person income in the subsequent five years by about 0.1% in the high-income country sample.[6] While 0.1% is a small amount in growth terms, it is sizeable in absolute money terms when accumulated over many years. As an aside, the authors did not find a significant influence of CVD mortality on growth in the low- and middle-income country sample.

Weil (2007) uses three microeconomic indicators of health: average height of adult men, the adult survival rate for men, and age of menarche for women. His preferred estimate leads to the conclusion that eliminating health differences among countries would reduce the variance of (log) per capita GDP by 9.9%. But this effect tends to be smaller than what is derived

---

[6] The result is based on a panel of five-year intervals between 1960 and 2000, and includes a set of standard controls (including initial income, openness, secondary schooling, etc.). The authors used a dynamic panel growth regression framework, taking into account potential endogeneity problems from reverse causality or omitted variables, which might determine both CVD mortality and growth simultaneously.

from cross-country regressions. Bloom and Canning (2005) compared the size of the microeconomic estimates of effect of health on wages with the macroeconomic estimates of the effect of health on worker productivity using a calibrated macroeconomic production function model. However, their database, derived from the Penn World Tables, also includes non-OECD countries, thus making a comparison difficult.

A reason why the impact of health on growth may not appear as strong as might be expected is related to *level* versus *growth* effects. Indeed, health could be a labour-augmenting factor increasing the level of individual productivity, but it would only generate a growth-enhancing mechanism if it increases steadily every year. Aghion *et al.* (2010) combine the approach of Acemoglu and Johnson (2007), which regresses income growth on the increase in life expectancy, with that of Lorentzen *et al.* (2008), which regresses GDP per capita growth on average child and mortality rates. The former had found that an increase in life expectancy had little effect on GDP per capita growth, in particular because it increases the rate of population growth. The latter, on the contrary, found that mortality reductions have a strong effect on income growth. The model of Aghion *et al.* includes both a level effect, using the initial life expectancy, and a growth effect, through increases in life expectancy. Their explanation is based on the fact that life expectancy has converged across countries, with developed countries having had lower increases in longevity, and only mortality rates below 40 years old have an impact on growth. Both could explain why the relationship between health and growth has weakened over time for OECD countries.

All these results are consistent with the fact that a positive impact of improved health on economic growth could have been hindered in many countries by a fixed and too low retirement age. Once institutional incentives for early retirement are lifted and the effective retirement age increases, health status could have a more important role on economic activity through labour market participation of the elderly. The next simulations illustrate this potential increased labour participation induced by longevity.

5.3 Potential Labour Resources Associated with Longevity Gains

Due to the baby-boom, the labour force in the OECD has increased steadily since the early 1970s, but this situation will radically change over the next decades. Following Burniaux *et al.* (2003), with unchanged labour market and immigration conditions, the labour force could decline in the EU-15 by around 25 million workers by 2050 (or −14%) compared to the peak to be reached by 2010 (Figure 5.1). In Japan, the labour force has already started this decline and is projected to fall by 22 million workers (−36%) by 2050 compared with 1995. Only in the United States is the labour force projected to continue increasing, by around 37 million workers (+26%) between 2005 and 2050.

The decline in the European labour force is mainly due to the marked reduction in the number of young (age 15–29) and prime-age (age 30–49) workers, while the number of older workers (50–64) in Europe will increase by around 5% (Figure 5.1). In Japan, all age groups are declining markedly. The sustained decline in total labour force could induce a substantial drag on potential growth, which could reach 1% in Japan and 0.8% per year in Germany (cf. Oliveira Martins *et al.*, 2005). With unchanged conditions, it is unlikely that increased capital deepening and/or total factor productivity could fully compensate for this shock.

To investigate the contribution of longevity to counteract these worrying trends, we carried out two 'thought experiments'. First, we shifted the observed participation ratios[7] by age group over time in line with the average increase in life expectancy. In a second experiment, we shifted the old-age threshold (usually 65+) that usually defines the working-age population (15–64 years) in line with longevity gains. It can be seen that some compensation can be found for the declining numbers of young and prime-age workers in the labour force. The gains are limited in Europe due to low participation in the labour force by older workers, which is assumed to remain constant throughout the simulation period.

However, when the same simulations are carried out for the working-age population (i.e. assuming that all potential workers participate in the labour market; Figure 5.2), the gains are substantially larger, leading to a near stabilization of the European labour force over the period 2005–50. This has both a level and a growth effect compared with the baseline scenario, as the additional labour resources increase steadily over time.

Using these counterfactual scenarios for labour force and working-age population, we also simulated alternative old-age dependency ratios (i.e. old-age people over working-age population), with the old-age threshold increasing in line with longevity. This 'longevity indexation' appears to be

---

[7] Note that the baseline projections of Burniaux *et al.* (2003) assumed unchanged policies and thus the participation ratios of older workers were also assumed to remain constant over time.

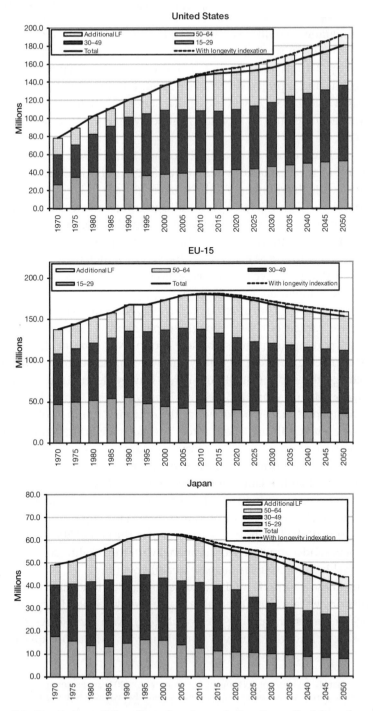

Figure 5.1. Simulations of the effect of ageing an longevity on the labour force[1]

Note: [1]The labour force (LF) projections are derived from the baseline scenario of Burniaux *et al*. (2003). The longevity indexation method is described in Oliveira Martins *et al*. (2005).

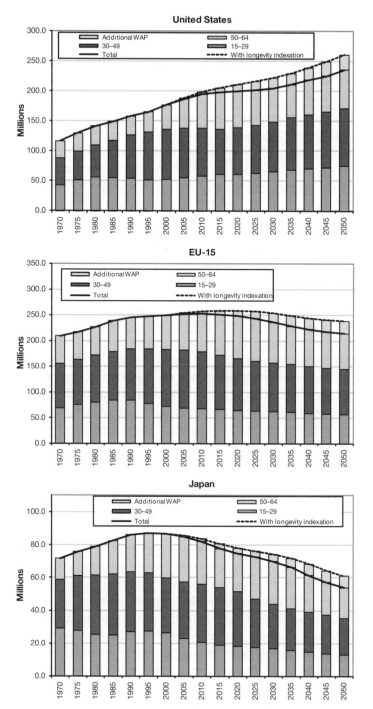

Figure 5.2. Simulations of the effect of ageing and longevity on the working-age population (WAP)[1]

Note: [1]The labour force projections are derived from the baseline scenario of Burniaux *et al.* (2003). The longevity indexation method is described in Oliveira Martins *et al.* (2005).

sufficient to stabilize, or even reverse, the upward trends in dependency ratios defined over the working-age population. The effect is stronger in the United States and EU-15 than in Japan, where the ageing process is particularly strong. In contrast, when considering the ratios over labour force projections, the effect of the longevity indexation is powerful in the United States and in Japan, but becomes much weaker for the EU-15 (Figure 5.3). This is due to the much lower labour market participation ratios of older workers in Europe, as noted above. The effect of indexation is therefore conditioned by the functioning of labour markets, indicating a strong complementarity between the two types of policies. Along the same lines, a recent paper by Lievre *et al.* (2007) computed an indicator of healthy working life expectancy and concluded that there is an untapped reservoir of healthy years that could be used to extend the length of the working life in Europe.

These simple back-of-the-envelope calculations suggest that 'healthy ageing', combined with appropriate management of longevity gains, could be used to compensate for the ageing of populations in labour markets, as well as for the increase of old-age dependency ratios, a key parameter for the sustainability of pension systems. The potential could be even larger if past longevity trends are maintained, contrary to what is assumed in the national population projections used in this study (see Chapter 1 note 1). Of course, increased participation needs to be combined with appropriate labour reforms, highlighting the need for complementarity of policies dealing with ageing.

5.4 Would an Ageing Labour Force have a Negative Impact on Aggregate Productivity?

If individual productivity declines with age, there may be concerns that a massive increase in the participation rate of older workers will hinder aggregate productivity. A rather pessimistic assumption would be a (quadratic) inverted U-shaped age profile (e.g. Miles, 1999). However, progress in health care could counteract this decline in individual productivity. One could therefore envisage a more optimistic ('healthy ageing') scenario, where productivity peaks after 40 years old and then stabilizes up to retirement (see Aubert and Crépon, 2003). These two different scenarios are depicted in Figure 5.4.

What difference might these individual profiles make to aggregate labour productivity? To answer this question, each hypothetical individual age-

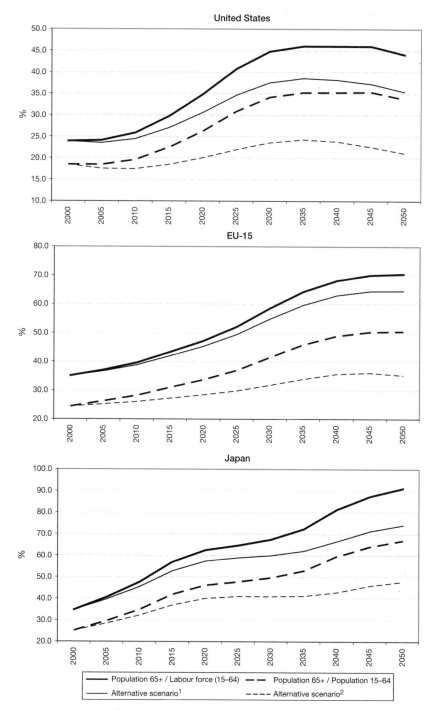

Figure 5.3. Simulations of longevity indexation on dependency ratios

Note: [1] Population in retirement/labour force, indexed on longevity. [2] Population in retirement/working-age population, indexed on longevity.

Source: Oliveira Martins *et al.* (2005) and authors' calculations.

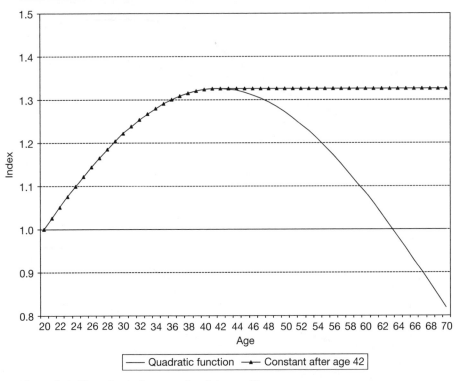

Figure 5.4. Hypothetical age-productivity profiles

productivity profile was applied to the population projections for 2005–50 used in this chapter. The results of this calculation for the US, Japan, Germany, and France are displayed in Figure 5.5. Comparing the most optimistic scenario, assuming a flat productivity profile for old-age workers, with the more pessimistic one, where productivity declines steadily, a positive level difference emerges; however, the order of magnitude of the change is small (+/−2.5%) and this *level* effect stabilizes around 2020. Thus, even under rather pessimistic scenarios, the effect of employing older workers would not induce a significant negative impact on aggregate productivity.

5.5 The Health Sector as an Engine of Innovation: Europe vs. the US

An important channel through which the health sector could influence growth is R&D activities. Sanso and Aisa (2006) propose a model in which a

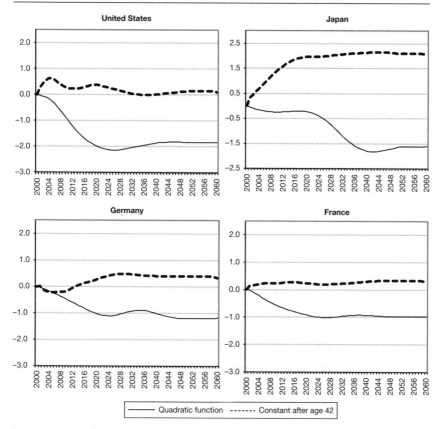

Figure 5.5. Mechanical impact of ageing on aggregate labour productivity levels (% changes relative to 2000 levels)

Note: Impact of multiplying the projected change in the structure of the labour force by productivity-age profiles of Figure 5.4.

Source: Oliveira Martins *et al*. (2005).

biological deterioration rate—'the rate at which the effectiveness of health goods in maintaining a given level of health decreases as individuals grow older'—is a key parameter in determining the steady-state growth rate. They develop a dynamic general equilibrium model integrating accumulation of human capital, innovation in medical technology, health, and longevity. In this framework, where agents decide on their 'quantity' of life, the need to offset the biological deterioration rate encourages medical research, and thus growth, which in turn permits medical research and health care expenditures to be financed.

From the perspective of health-related innovation, the situation in the US contrasts with that in Europe. In the pharmaceutical sector,[8] the US is increasingly outperforming Europe (and Japan) as the main player in medical innovation by standard measures of R&D inputs (e.g. R&D expenditures) and outputs (e.g. number of patents registered and patent citations). The comparatively stronger emphasis in Europe on cost-containment through health-care price and reimbursement regulations goes a long way to explaining these differences. In the US, with very limited incentives for agents to consider the costs of treatment, there has accordingly been very limited incentive to invest in cost-reducing R&D. The EU health sector has therefore been in the position to take advantage of the development of new technologies produced elsewhere—chiefly the US—as it has been able to introduce them slowly, after the expensive early stages of implementation. While this has certainly contributed to lower average costs (at the expense of delay in implementation), it is hard to say what the effect on overall health sector productivity in the EU has been. In evaluating the comparative performance of the different systems, it is also important to take into account the trade-offs involved in terms of the effect on access to health care, which has become much skewed in the US.

The basic characteristics of the pharmaceutical market differ between the EU, the US, and Japan. The US market is the largest and has grown faster than European markets (measured by sales at ex-factory prices; Table 5.1). By 2003, the US market was currently twice as large as the EU-15 aggregate, and accounted for approximately 50% of the world market for pharmaceuticals (up from 31.2% in 1995). Europe held a 30% share of the global pharmaceutical market in 2003, while Japan's share in 2003 was nearly 12%. It is noteworthy that China, Brazil, and India—not shown here—are growing fast, gaining shares in the international market (EC, 2006).

Table 5.1. The size of pharmaceutical markets (million)

	1999	2000	2001	2002	2003
EU-15	72,094	29,962	90,100	96,825	103,142
US	124,261	163,439	197,351	208,970	194,061
Japan	50,246	62,606	59,744	55,736	52,092

Source: EC (2006).

[8] For a description and analysis of the medical devices sector, see Pammolli et al. (2005).

5.4.1 A Comparison of Pharmaceutical Innovation Input and Output

Research and Development (R&D) is particularly important in the pharmaceutical industry. Despite data limitations and methodological problems, there have been some attempts to measure pharmaceutical R&D expenditures (Figure 5.6). The data show an increase in R&D expenditures, at least in Europe and the US, with the US overtaking Europe in recent years.

Although R&D expenditures have increased globally, innovative output, measured by the number of new chemical entities, has declined over the past few decades (Figure 5.7). The European pharmaceutical industry had for many years been the world's leading inventor of new medicines, but was overtaken after the 1990s by the United States. Europe is also underrepresented in some crucial research fields such as R&D biotechnology. Between 1960 and 1965, European companies invented 65% of new chemical entities (NCEs) placed on the world market. Forty years later this share had fallen to 34%. According to data for the period 2001–5, the United States has become the leading inventor of new molecules in the world.

Other widely used indicators in the empirical literature for the measurement of innovation are patents and patent citations. Patents are a unique source of information about innovative activities, particularly in the pharmaceutical industry, where they play a prominent role in protecting returns from R&D. Table 5.2 covers all pharmaceutical and biotechnological patents granted from 1974 to 2003 by the United States Patent and Trademark Office (USPTO) to inventors and institutions located in the US, Japan, and the EU.[9]

The table shows that the majority of patents in biotechnology and pharmaceuticals are held by inventors located in the US. The number of pharmaceutical patents held by US-based inventors increased by 7 percentage points between 1984–93 and 1994–2003. The increase is even more striking if each patent is weighted by the number of citations it receives (Table 5.3).

Interestingly, the share of EU inventors is higher than the share of EU institutional assignees. The opposite is true for the US, even if the imbalance is gradually disappearing. In other words, there are more European inventors involved in research assigned to US organizations and

[9] Note that there could be a 'registration effect' in the US market, probably in favour of 'Other countries'. It would be useful to compare these figures with the data from the European Patent Office. Unfortunately, comparable data were not available.

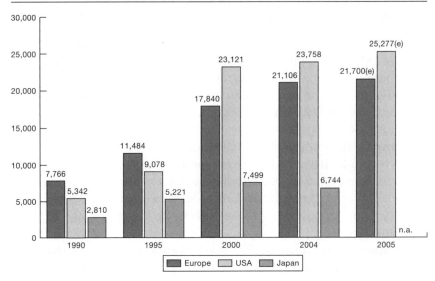

Figure 5.6. Pharmaceutical R&D expenditure in Europe, the US, and Japan (million euros, current exchange rates)

Source: EFPIA (2006).

Note: (e) stands for estimates.

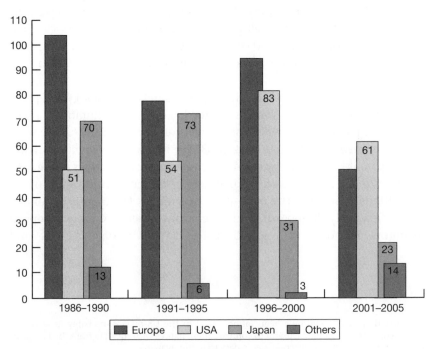

Figure 5.7. Production of new chemical or biological entities

Source: EFPIA (2006).

Table 5.2. Shares of USPTO-granted pharmaceutical patents by countries based on the nationality of the assignee (A) and location of the inventor (I)

	1974–1983			1984–1993			1994–2003		
	Assignee	Inventor	I-A	Assignee	Inventor	I-A	Assignee	Inventor	I-A
EU	28.3%	30.9%	2.6%	27.3%	29.2%	1.9%	23.1%	24.8%	1.7%
USA	59.0%	52.3%	−6.7%	55.2%	50.8%	−4.4%	60.1%	57.3%	−2.8%
Japan	9.3%	9.4%	0.2%	13.4%	13.6%	0.1%	9.2%	9.3%	0.2%

Source: EC (2006).

Table 5.3. Shares of patent citations of USPTO-granted pharmaceutical patents by countries based on the nationality of the assignee (A) and location of the inventor (I)

	1974–1983			1984–1993			1994–2003		
	Assignee	Inventor	I-A	Assignee	Inventor	I-A	Assignee	Inventor	I-A
EU	23.57%	25.50%	1.92%	19.43%	21.33%	1.90%	17.47%	19.06%	1.59%
USA	63.71%	59.33%	−4.38%	67.12%	63.52%	−3.60%	70.39%	68.13%	−2.26%
Japan	9.26%	8.99%	−0.27%	9.55%	9.64%	0.09%	6.00%	6.07%	0.07%

Source: EC (2006).

performing their research in the US than vice versa, although the globalization of R&D activities is gradually eroding this disparity.[10]

US dominance appears even stronger when we consider patent citations data. In fact, Table 5.4 suggests that on average patents assigned to US institutions have a much greater impact on future innovative activity. US biopharmaceutical patents received 5.6 citations on average between 1994 and 2003, far more than European (2.9) and Japanese (2.1) ones. Furthermore, the largest share (almost half) of European and Japanese citations go to US patents, although this finding must be interpreted with caution, since we are considering data on patents granted by the USPTO. Nevertheless, trends

Table 5.4. Biopharmaceutical Patent citations

Country	1974–1983	1984–1993	1994–2003
USA			
Patent count	8,943	14,860	36,271
Number of citations	6,680	40,332	201,510
Mean number of citations	0.75	2.71	5.56
of which:			
US→US	74.70%	73.00%	74.70%
US→EU	18.29%	18.51%	18.82%
US→Japan	5.09%	7.06%	6.77%
EU-25			
Patent count	5,238	8,525	1,5904
Number of citations	3,153	15,004	46,396
Mean number of citations	0.60	1.76	2.92
of which:			
EU→EU	55.25%	51.18%	43.64%
EU→US	36.12%	38.83%	49.11%
EU→Japan	5.49%	7.96%	7.49%
Japan			
Patent count	1,582	3,845	5,678
Number of citations	959	5,833	11,746
Mean number of citations	0.61	1.52	2.07
of which:			
Japan→Japan	40.88%	36.57%	35.96%
Japan→US	33.99%	37.68%	42.23%
Japan→EU	23.46%	23.90%	22.26%

Source: EC (2006).

[10] It is important to note that, in recent years, the number of patents in pharmaceuticals and biotechnology granted by the Chinese patent office has increased. The same applies to US patents granted to Chinese inventors. These increases indicate a process of accumulation of scientific and technological capabilities. India's recent performance in biopharmaceutical innovation, as reflected in patents granted, is similar to that of China. If these trends persist, China and India will strengthen their positions, becoming attractive and competitive destinations for foreign direct outward investment by multinational corporations (EC, 2006).

in the pattern of EU and Japanese citations of the US reveal the increasing importance of US research for inventors located in Europe and Japan.

5.4.2 Market structure characteristics explain differences in innovative performance

Market structure characteristics may account for the observed differences between Europe and the US. Concerning pharmaceutical prices, the differences between the US and EU-15 are mostly due to branded drugs. Indeed, prices of US generic drugs are largely aligned with those of the EU-15. In a few countries, such as Germany, generic prices are even higher than in the US. The entry price for branded drugs is 43.4% higher in the US than the average market price. The corresponding price gap in the EU-15 is only 28.2%, and in Japan just 3.9%. US generic products, by contrast, are priced at 60.3% of the average prices in the market.

These price differentials between the US and Europe reflect radical differences in market regulation. Countries with free or semi-regulated prices for branded drugs—such as the US and, to a lesser extent, UK and Germany—have higher prices than in Italy or France. However, the relatively unregulated markets tend to experience fierce price competition after patent expiration, since the higher prices of branded drugs represent a strong incentive for generic entry and price competition à la Bertrand (Pammolli *et al.*, 2002; Magazzini *et al.*, 2004). The net effect is that generic penetration in terms of volume is much higher in the US market (33.7% in 2004) and the UK (31%) than in the EU-15 average (13.8%) and Japan (2.6%). The opportunity to command substantially higher market prices for new and branded drugs can act as a powerful incentive for R&D and capital investments that can explain, to a certain extent at least, the different trends characterizing the EU and US pharmaceutical industries.

Overall, the US market is more concentrated than the most important EU markets (Germany, France, Italy, and Spain, but not the UK), as well as Japan, China, and India. On average, the three leading products in each of 100 different therapeutic categories account for 85.6% of total market share in the US, as compared with a total market share of 76.5% in the EU-25. In other words, European markets are more fragmented. To a large extent, the high concentration of the US market is due to the 'premium price' that best-in-class products can command. The relative price of the market leader in the US is 44% higher than the average market price—more than in Europe (22%) and Japan (15%).

The higher concentration in the US market does not imply less competition, however. On the contrary, firm turnover in the US is almost double that of the EU-15 and EU-25. The lower turnover of EU markets translates into a higher persistency and a lower contestability of the leading products. The US average persistency of the leading product is slightly less than 6 years, while in the EU it is almost 10 years and in Japan more than 15 years.

The US market has also the highest product turnover. The US rate is 59.5% higher than the EU-15's, and 38.8% higher than Japan's. The most striking difference is found in product exit rate, which is on average 77.2% higher in the US than in the EU-15, and 40.7% higher than in Japan. Product entry rates are 51.3% higher in the US than in the EU-15, and 38.8% higher than in Japan. As a result, the process of creative destruction is much more intense in the US market than in European or Japanese markets. US market behaviour is therefore more consistent with Schumpeterian competition, where innovators can gain temporary quasi-monopoly profits, which in turn spur innovation efforts by competitors that quickly lead to more innovative products and a high turnover of market shares. Dynamic competition is less evident in the EU as a whole, and especially in certain continental European countries. As documented extensively in Gambardella *et al.* (2000), there is too little market-based competition in some of the European countries, resulting in a less efficient industry, as reflected in productivity indicators and market performance.

6

Summary and Policy Discussion

Since human capital is the main driver of productivity and growth in knowledge-based economies, health should also matter for economic outcomes. In the context of rapid population ageing, the contribution of health to human capital and hence to growth potential could become even more important. This part has tackled these issues by offering an integrated view of the relationships between health spending, medical innovation, health status, growth, and welfare.

We started with the observation that longevity has increased steadily in developed countries. This is good for welfare and for the economy providing that a virtuous cycle exists between longevity and health status (so-called 'healthy ageing'). Despite the uncertainties over whether healthy ageing can continue in the future, improved health status can be (and has been) achieved to a significant extent through improved health care. The evidence reviewed here suggests that the value attributed to the resulting reduction in mortality and/or morbidity, at least for specific interventions or treatments, most often exceed the costs and thus has been a worthwhile investment.

But health care is costly and developed societies are spending an increasing share of their income on health services and products, with already strained public budgets paying most of the bill. This rising expenditure trend has little relation to demography, but rather is driven by consumers' preferences for longer lives and the diffusion of technological progress. We have provided empirical evidence that health expenditures tend to grow in line with incomes (unitary income elasticity); on the top of this income effect, it is the change in medical practices that explains most of the drift of health expenditures per capita.

The structure of health insurance, as well as the regulation of health care supply, might also encourage some costly innovations with a small benefit in terms of social welfare. Prevention policies should also be considered in this regard. This part has focused on curative treatments, adopting a somewhat narrow perspective of 'health investment'. The potential for (especially primary) prevention—through the health-care system or beyond—to improve health and thereby perhaps even to alleviate the future health expenditures burden is still a matter of some debate (Fries *et al.*, 1998; Harvey, 1998). While more work to clarify the potential health and fiscal benefits of prevention is clearly warranted, the value of non-clinical prevention may become even more important in the future, given the already significant and growing challenge of obesity, essentially affecting all (but not only) rich countries.

Policies have to define the boundary between the package of health-care services which are covered through a mandatory health insurance (public or private and regulated through a managed competition scheme), and the other services which will be covered by private voluntary insurance. In each country, fine tuning should allow social preferences to be taken into account relative to the pace of technological progress, equity in access to innovations, and the tax burden.

Given the various determinants of health expenditures, we carried out several projection exercises leading to the conclusion that the expected increase in resources directed to health care by 2050 is substantial (ranging from 4 percentage points in the most conservative scenario to above 12 percentage points of GDP). The question then arose as to what might be the likely impact of these developments on economic growth, and what might be the impact if longevity was 'better managed'. In particular, would there be a role for investing in health to act as a driver for Europe to catch up with the US in terms of GDP per capita?

Despite convincing theoretical arguments, the empirical evidence reviewed in this chapter on the impact of health and health spending on economic growth in rich countries is rather mixed. Probably, the positive impact of improved health on the economy has been hindered by a fixed and too low retirement age. Once institutional incentives for early retirement are lifted and the effective retirement age increases, through labour market participation of the elderly, health status could have a more important role in growth. It may seem a bit paradoxical that Europe is doing better than the US in terms of life expectancy, but is failing to capitalize on these additional human resources by having early retirement and long inactive lives. Providing labour market and pension reforms offer the right environment, we showed that longevity gains could be used to smooth the negative effects of baby-boom bust on the labour force, notably in Europe.

Given the role of preferences and the demographic transition, the global market for health services and products is huge. Satisfying this demand offers the potential for growth, but the EU is lagging behind the US in terms of health-related R&D and innovation. This is partly due to differences in regulation and market structure, which would require appropriate product market reforms. In this context, countries with ageing populations could take advantage of longevity and develop goods and services targeted at the older segments of the population. This would build new dynamic comparative advantages, reinforced by fast technical progress in biotech sectors. Overall, health policies are often complementary with other areas (e.g. public budgets, labour market, pensions, etc.), so reforms need to be designed in a coherent and broad-based manner. (Ch. 5)

APPENDIX I: SPECIFICATION OF THE UTILITY FUNCTION AND THE INCOME ELASTICITY

In this appendix, we show the relation between the specification of the utility function used in Hall and Jones (2007) and the value of the income elasticity. Assume that a social planner chooses consumption and health spending to maximize the utility of the individual, for example, solving the following program:

$$max_{c,h} f(h)u(c) \text{ s.t. } c + h = y$$

where:

$$u(c) = b + \frac{c^{1-\gamma}}{1-\gamma}$$

$$f(h) = A_a h^{\theta_a}.$$

This program is similar to the Hall and Jones' model (see Box 3.1 in the main text). Under standard regularity conditions, the first-order conditions are given by:

$$f(h)u'(c) - \lambda = 0 \qquad (A.1)$$

$$f'(h)u(c) - \lambda = 0 \qquad (A.2)$$

$$c + h = y. \qquad (A.3)$$

Using (A.1) and (A.2), we have:

$$\frac{f(h)}{f'(h)} = \frac{u(c)}{u'(c)}$$

or

$$\frac{h}{c} = \frac{\eta_h}{\eta_c}$$

where $\eta_h = h \frac{f'(h)}{f(h)}$ and $\eta_c = c \frac{u'(c)}{u(c)}$.

Solving the first-order conditions, we obtain:

$$h = \theta_a \left(\frac{b + \frac{c^{1-\gamma}}{1-\gamma}}{c^{-\gamma}} \right)$$

which implies from equation (A.3):

$$c + \theta_a \left(\frac{b + \frac{c^{1-\gamma}}{1-\gamma}}{c^{-\gamma}} \right) = y.$$

It is straightforward to see that:

$$\frac{dc}{dy} = \frac{1}{(1-\gamma)\left(1 + \frac{\theta_a}{1-\gamma}\right) + \gamma \frac{y}{c}}$$

$$\eta^*_{y/c} = \frac{1}{(1-\gamma)\left(1 + \frac{\theta_a}{1-\gamma}\right)(1 - s^*) + \gamma}$$

where $s^*=h/y$ is the optimal share of health spending in GDP. Some algebraic manipulations yield the income elasticity of the demand for health:

$$\eta^*_{y/h} = \frac{\theta_a \left(b\gamma(c^*)^{1-\gamma} + \frac{1}{1-\gamma} \right) \left(\frac{1-s^*}{s^*} \right)}{(1-\gamma)\left(1 + \frac{\theta_a}{1-\gamma}\right)(1 - s^*) + \gamma}.$$

The income elasticity depends on b, γ, and θ_a (since s^* depends on η_h and η_c, which in turn depend on the parameters of u and f). In particular, it could be larger or less than one, depending on the values of the parameters and the optimal consumption allocation. However, in the particular case where $b=0$, we have $s^* = h/y = 1/(1 + \eta_c/\eta_h) = 1/(1 + (1 - \gamma)/\theta_a)$ and the income elasticity is equal to one. In other words, the fact that the optimal share of health spending is rising with GDP depends critically on a strictly positive b parameter. Hall and Jones acknowledge the critical importance of this condition for their results, without establishing the formal relationship between the form of the utility function and the income elasticity.

APPENDIX II: DATA SOURCES AND METHODS OF HEALTH EXPENDITURE PROJECTIONS[1]

Estimating Death-Related Costs

The primary data for 18 OECD countries are drawn from the Ageing, Health and Retirement in Europe (AGIR data set) (Westerhout and Pellikaan, 2005, based on EC-EPC, 2001) for the EU-15 countries and from national sources for Australia, Canada, and United States.

The cost of death for the oldest group (95+) is assumed to be the lowest and was proxied by their observed health expenditure per person when available. For France, Germany, Italy, United Kingdom, Spain, Netherlands, and Australia, for which the expenditure data for the oldest group were not available, the cost for people aged 75–9 was taken as a proxy. In fact, when available, expenditure at age 95+ is roughly equal to the level of expenditure at age 75–9. For countries where no cost expenditures were available, the cost of death for the oldest group was estimated as three times the average health expenditure per capita.

The costs of death for other age groups are then derived by multiplying this estimate by an adjustment factor equal to four between ages 0–4 to 55–9, gradually decreasing to one afterwards. Multiplying these costs of death by the estimated number of deaths by age group (using mortality data) gives the death-related cost (DRC) curve.

Calibration of the Expenditure Curves on the OECD Health Database

The cost curves derived for the year 2000 were first calibrated in order to fit with levels for 2005, the starting point for the projections. The total health and long-term care expenditures for 2005 being not yet available in the OECD (2005a), an estimate was made by applying the observed growth rate in expenditures 2000–3 (or 2002, depending on the countries) for the whole period 2000–5. A second step was to split total spending into health and long-term care. The details of this split are provided below and involved an estimate of the shares of long-term care expenditures based on OECD (2005b).

---

[1] This appendix draws on Oliveira Martins and Maisonneuve (2006).

The costs of death by age group for 2005 were derived by applying the same growth rate as for total health expenditures between 2000 and 2005. The total death-related costs in 2005 were computed as the product of the cost of death by the projected number of deaths by age group in that year. The total survivor expenditures were then derived by subtracting total death-related costs from total health spending. Using this information, the survivor cost curve was calibrated proportionally for each age group.

Projecting Demographic Effects under a 'Healthy Ageing' Scenario

Shifting the survivor cost curve according to longevity gains involves two steps:

(1) The survivor expenditure curve by five-year age groups is interpolated in order to derive a profile by individual age. In this way, the cost curve can be shifted smoothly over time in line with life expectancy gains.
(2) An 'effective age' is calculated by subtracting the increase in life expectancy at birth according to national projections from current age. For example, a 70-year-old person in Germany is projected to have an effective age of 67 by 2025 and 64 by 2050.

The Starting Point of the Projections

The projected changes in spending expressed as a percentage of GDP were calculated from a common base applied to all OECD countries. This base was taken as the OECD average expenditure in 2005. These changes were added to the initial level of expenditures in each country. This approach makes the projected changes (expressed as a percentage of GDP) less dependent on the base year levels and also allows for a certain catch-up of expenditure ratios across countries. More precisely, the variation of the share of expenditure to GDP in country j between, say, 2005 and 2050, is calculated as:

$$\Delta\left(\frac{Expenditure}{GDP}\Big|_{2050-2005}^{country\,j}\right) = \exp\left[\Delta\log(Drivers)\Big|_{2050-2005}^{country\,j}\right.$$
$$+ \log\left(\frac{Expenditure}{GDP}\Big|_{year=2005}^{averageOECD}\right)\right] - \left(\frac{Expenditure}{GDP}\Big|_{year=2005}^{OECDaverage}\right)$$

References

Abel-Smith, B. (1967), 'An International Study of Health Expenditure', Public Health Papers No. 32, WHO, Geneva.

Acemoglu, D., A. Finkelstein, and M. Notowidigdo (2009), 'Income and Health Spending: Evidence from Oil Shocks', CEPR Discussion Papers No. 7255.

——and S. Johnson (2007), 'Disease and Development: The Effect of Life Expectancy on Economic Growth', *Journal of Political Economy*, 115(6), 925–85.

Agenor, P. R. (2005), 'Health and Infrastructure in Models of Endogenous Growth', *Center for Growth and Business Cycle Research Discussion Paper Series*.

Aghion, P., and P. Howitt (1992), 'A Model of Growth through Creative Destruction', *Econometrica*, 51, 323–51.

——P. Howitt and F. Murtin (2010), 'The Relationship between Health and Growth: When Lucas Meets Nelson-Phelps', NBER Working Paper No. 15813.

AHCPR (1997), *Trends in Personal Health Care Expenditures, Health Insurance and Payment Sources, Community Based Population, 1987–1995*, Agency for Health Care Policy and Research, Center for Cost and Financing Studies, National Medical Survey Data, Mar. 1997, Table 8.

Aisa, R., and F. Pueyo (2004), 'Endogenous Longevity, Health and Economic Growth: A Slow Growth for a Longer Life', *Economics Bulletin*, 9(3), 1–10.

————(2006), 'Government Health Spending and Growth in a Model of Endogenous Longevity', *Economics Letters*, 90, 249–53.

Aprile, R. (2004), 'How to Take Account of Death-related Costs in Projecting Health Care Expenditure—Updated Version', mimeo, Ragioneria Generale Dello Stato.

Ashenfelter, O., and M. Greenstone (2004), 'Using Mandated Speed Limits to Measure the Value of a Statistical Life', *Journal of Political Economy*, Feb., 112(1), S226–67, Part 2.

Aubert, P., and B. Crépon (2003), 'La productivité des salaries âgés: une tentative d'estimation', *Economie et Statistique*, No. 368, 95–119.

Auerbach, A., and L. Kotlikoff (1987), *Dynamic Fiscal Policy*, Cambridge: Cambridge University Press.

Baker, L., and M. Brown (1999), 'Managed Care, Consolidation among Health Care Providers, and Health Care: Evidence from Mammography', *Rand Journal of Economics*, 30(Summer), 351–74.

Baltagi, B. H. (2008), *Econometric Analysis of Panel Data*, 4th edition, Chichester: John Wiley & Sons.

Barbi, E. (2003), 'Assessing the Rate of Ageing of the Human Population', Max Planck Institute for Demographic Research Working Paper WP 003–008.

Barro, R. J. (1990), 'Government Spending in a Simple Model of Endogenous Growth Model', *Journal of Political Economy*, 98, S103–25.

Barros, P. P. (1998), 'The Black Box of Health Care Expenditure Growth Determinants', *Health Economics*, 7, 538–44.

Baumol, W. J. (1967), 'Macroeconomics of Unbalanced Growth: The Anatomy of Urban Crisis', *American Economic Review*, 57, 415–26.

——(1993), 'Health Care, Education and the Cost of Disease: A Looming Crisis for Public Choice,' *Public Choice*, 77, 17–28.

Bech, M. *et al.* (2006), 'How do Economic Incentives and Regulatory Factors Influence Adoption of New Medical Technologies? Result from the TECH Project'.

Becker, G. (1964), *Human Capital: A Theoretical Analysis with Special Reference to Education*, New York: Columbia University Press for NBER.

Bentzen, J. (2005), 'Testing for Catching-up Periods in Time Series Convergence', *Economic Letters*, 88, 323–8.

Beraldo, S., D. Montolio, and G. Turati (2005), 'Healthy, Educated and Wealthy: Is the Welfare State Really Harmful for Growth?', Espai de Recerca en Economia Universitat de Barcelona Working Papers in Economics No. 127.

Berndt, E. *et al.* (2000), 'The Medical Treatment of Depression, 1991–1996: Productive Inefficiency, Expected Outcome Variations, and Price Indexes', NBER Working Paper No. 7816.

Bhargava, A., D. T. Jamison, L. J. Lau, and C. J. L. Murray (2001), 'Modeling the Effects of Health on Economic Growth.' *Journal of Health Economics*, 20, 423–40.

Blomqvist, A. G., and R. A. L. Carter (1997), 'Is Health Care Really a Luxury?', *Journal of Health Economics*, 16(2), 207–30.

Bloom, D., and D. Canning (2000), 'The Health and Wealth of Nations', *Science*, 287 (5456), 1207–9.

————(2005), 'Health and Economic Growth: Reconciling the Micro and Macro Evidence', mimeo.

————and J. Sevilla (2003), 'Longevity and Life Cycle Savings', *Scandinavian Journal of Economics*, 105: 319–38.

Börsch-Supan, A., A. Ludwig, and J. Winter (2002), 'Ageing, Pension Reform and Capital Flows', in A. Auerbach and H. Hermann (eds.), *Ageing, Financial Markets and Monetary Policy*, Heidelberg: Springer, 55–83.

Börsch-Supan, A. *et al.* (2005), *Health, Ageing and Retirement in Europe: First Results from the Survey of Health, Ageing and Retirement in Europe*, Manheim Research Institute for the Economics of Ageing, Manheim.

Börsch-Supan A., A. Brugiavini, H. Jurges, J. Machenback, J. Siegrist, and G. Weber (2005), 'First Results from the Survey of Health, Ageing and Retirement in Europe', MEA, available at www.share-project.org.

——A. Ludwig, and J. Winter (2006), 'Ageing, Pension Reform and Capital Flows: A Multi-country Simulation Model', *Economica*, 73, 625–58

Bots, M. L., and D. E. Grobbee (1996), 'Decline of Coronary Heart Disease Mortality in The Netherlands from 1978 to 1985: Contribution of Medical Care and Changes over Time in Presence of Major Cardiovascular Risk Factors', *Journal of Cardiovascular Risk*, 3(3), 271–6.

Buck, D., A. Eastwood, and P. Smith (1999), 'Can We Measure the Social Importance of Health Care?', *International Journal of Technology Assessment in Health Care*, 15(1), 89–107.

Bunker, J. P. (2001), 'The Role of Medical Care in Contributing to Health Improvements within Societies', *International Journal of Epidemiology*, 30(6), 1260–3.

——H. S. Frazier, and F. Mosteller (1994), 'Improving Health: Measuring Effects of Medical Care', *Milbank Memorial Fund Quarterly*, 72, 225–58.

Burniaux, J.-M., R. Duval, and F. Jaumotte (2003), 'Coping with Ageing: A Dynamic Approach to Quantify the Impact of Alternative Policy Options on Future Labour Supply in OECD Countries', OECD Economics Department Working Papers No. 371.

Canova, F. (2007), *Applied Macroeconomic Research*, Princeton: Princeton University Press.

Capewell, S., C. E. Morrison, and J. J. McMurray (1999), 'Contribution of Modern Cardiovascular Treatment and Risk Factor Changes to the Decline in Coronary Heart Disease Mortality in Scotland between 1975 and 1994', *Heart*, 81, 380–6.

Cheung, S. L., and J. M. Robine (2007), 'Increase in Longevity and the Compression of Mortality: The Case of Japan', *Population Studies*, 61(1), 85–97.

Colgrove, J. (2002), 'The McKeown Thesis: A Historical Controversy and its Enduring Influence', *American Journal of Public Health*, 92(5), 725–9.

Conti, R., E. Berndt, and R. Frank (2006), 'Early Retirement and Public Disability Insurance Applications: Exploring the Impact of Depression', NBER Working Paper 12237.

Cullis, J. G., and P. A. West (1979), *The Economics of Health, an Introduction*, London: Martin Robertson.

Culyer, A. J. (1988), 'Health Care Expenditures in Canada: Myth and Reality; Past and Future', Canadian Tax Paper No. 82, Canadian Tax Foundation, Toronto.

——(1990), 'Cost Containment in Europe', *Health Care Systems in Transition*, Paris: OECD.

Cutler, D. (2004), 'Your Money or your Life: Strong Medicine for America's Health Care System', New York: Oxford University Press.

——A. S. Deaton, and A. Lleras-Muner (2006), 'The Determinants of Mortality', *Journal of Economic Perspectives*, 20, 97–120.

——M. Landrum, and K. Stewart (2006), 'Intensive Medical Care and Cardiovascular Disease Disability Reductions', NBER Working Paper No. 12184.

——and M. McClellan (1996), 'The Determinants of Technological Change in Heart Attack Treatment', NBER Working Paper No. 5751.

————(2001), 'Is Technological Change in Medicine Worth It?', *Health Affairs*, 20, 11–29.

———J. P. Newhouse, and D. Remler (1998), 'Are Medical Prices Falling?' *Quarterly Journal of Economics*, 113(4), 991–1024.

———A. B. Rosen, and S. Vijan (2006), 'The Value of Medical Spending in the United States, 1960–2000', *New England Journal of Medicine*, 355, 920–7.

Dang, T. T., P. Antolin, and H. Oxley (2001), 'Fiscal Implications Ageing: Projections of Age-related Spending', OECD Economics Department Working Papers No. 305, Paris.

De la Croix, D., and O. Licandro (1999), 'Life Expectancy and Endogenous Growth', *Economic Letters*, 65, 255–63.

Delattre, E., B. Dormont, M. McClellan, and C. Milcent (2002), 'Systèmes de tarification et évolutions de la variabilité des coûts hospitaliers en France et aux Etats-Unis', in *De la tarification à la pathologie: les leçons de l'expérience étrangère*, Dossiers Solidarité et Santé, La Documentation française, Paris.

Di Matteo, L., and R. Di Matteo (1998), 'Evidence on the Determinants of Canadian Provincial Government Health Expenditures: 1965–1991', *Journal of Health Economics*, 17(2), 211–28.

Docteur, E., and H. Oxley (2003), 'Health-Care Systems: Lessons from the Reform Experience', OECD Economics Department Working Papers No. 374.

Dormont, B., M. Grignon, and H. Huber (2006), 'Health Expenditure Growth: Reassessing the Threat of Ageing', *Health Economics*, 15(9), 947–63.

———and C. Milcent (2006), 'Innovation Diffusion under Budget Constraints. Microeconometric Evidence on Heart Attack in France', Annals of Economics and Statistics No. 79/80.

Dreger, C., and H.-E. Reimers (2005), 'Health Care Expenditures in OECD Countries: A Panel Unit Root and Cointegration Analysis', IZA Discussion Paper 1469, Bonn.

Duval, R. (2003), 'The Retirement Effects Of Old-Age Pension and Early Retirement Schemes in OECD countries', OECD Economics Department Working Papers No. 370.

Easterlin, R. (1999), 'How Beneficent is the Market? A Look at the Modern History of Mortality,' *European Review of Economic History*, 3(3), 257–94.

EC-Economic Policy Committee (2001), *Budgetary Challenges Posed by Ageing Populations: The Impact on Public Spending on Pensions, Health and Long-Term Care for the Elderly and Possible Indicators of the Long-Term Sustainability of Public Finances*, EPC/ECFIN/655/01-EN final, Oct.

EC-Economic Policy Committee (2005), 'The 2005 EPC Projection of Age-Related Expenditure: Agreed Underlying Assumptions and Projection Methodologies', *European Economy*, Occasional Papers No. 19.

EC (European Commission) (2006), *European Competitiveness Report 2006*, Brussels.

EFPIA (2006), *The Pharmaceutical Industry in Figures*, The European Federation of Pharmaceutical Industries and Associations, Brussels.

Ehrlich, I., and H. Chuma (1990), 'A Model of the Demand for Longevity and the Value of Life Extension', *Journal of Political Economy*, 98, 760–82.

Englert, M. (2004), 'Assessing the Budgetary Cost of Ageing and Projecting Health Care (+ Care for Elderly) Expenditure: The Belgian Experience', Federal Planning Bureau, Brussels.

Fisher, F. M., and K. Shell (1972), *The Economic Theory of Price Indices*, New York: Academic Press.

Fogel, R. (2003), 'Changes in the Process of Aging during the Twentieth Century: Findings and Procedures of the Early Indicators Project', NBER Working Paper 9941.

Forster, B. A. (1989), 'Optimal Health Investment Strategies', *Bulletin of Economic Research*, 41, 45–57.

Freedman, V., L. Martin, and R. Schoeni (2002), 'Recent Trends in Disability and Functioning among Older Americans: A Systematic Review', *Journal of the American Medical Association*, 288(24), 3137–46.

Fries, J. F. (1980), 'Ageing, Natural Death, and the Compression of Morbidity', *New England Journal of Medicine*, 303, 130–5.

——C. E. Koop, J. Sokolov, C. E. Beadle, and D. Wright (1998), 'Beyond Health Promotion: Reducing Need and Demand for Medical Care', *Health Affairs*, 17(2), 70–84.

Fuchs, V. (1984), 'Though Much is Taken: Reflections on Ageing, Health and Medical Care', NBER Working Paper No. 1269.

Galasso, V. (2006), *The Political Future of Social Security in Aging Societies*, Cambridge, Mass.: MIT Press.

Gambardella A., L. Orsenigo, and F. Pammolli (2000), 'Global Competitiveness in Pharmaceuticals: A European Perspective', European Commission, November.

Gelijns, A., and N. Rosenberg (1994), 'The Dynamics of Technological Change in Medicine', *Health Affairs*, Summer, 29–46.

Gerdtham, U., B. Jonsson, M. MacFarlan, and H. Oxley (1998), 'The Determinants of Health Expenditure in the OECD Countries: A Pooled Data Analysis', *Health, the Medical Profession and Regulation*, Dordrecht: Kluwer Academic Publisher, 113–34.

——J. Sogaard., F. Anderson, and B. Jonsson (1992), 'An Econometric Analysis of Health Care Expenditure: A Cross-Section Study of the OECD Countries', *Journal of Health Economics*, 11(1), 63–84.

Getzen, T. (1990), 'Macro Forecasting of National Health Expenditures', in L. Rossiter and R. Scheffler (eds.), *Advances in Health Economics*, 11, 27–48.

——(1992), 'Population Ageing and the Growth of Health Care Expenditures', *Journal of Gerontology*, 47, S98–104.

——(2000), 'Health Care is an Individual Necessity and a National Luxury: Applying Multilevel Decision Models to the Analysis of Health Care Expenditure', *Journal of Health Economics*, 19, 259–70.

Goldman *et al.* (2005), 'Consequences of Health Trends and Medical Innovation for the Future Elderly', *Health Affairs*, W5-R5.

Gray, A. (2004), 'Estimating the Impact of Ageing Populations on Future Health Expenditures', Public lecture to the National Institute of Economics and Business and the National Institute of Health and Human Science, 4 Nov., Canberra.

Griliches, Z. (1971), *Price Indexes and Quality Change*, Cambridge, Mass.: Harvard University Press.

Grossman, M. (1972), 'On the Concept of Health Capital and the Demand for Health', *Journal of Political Economy*, 80: 223–55.

——(1998), 'On Optimal Length of Life', *Journal of Health Economics*, 17(4), 499–509.

Grunenberg, E. M. (1977), 'The Failure of Success', *Milbank Memorial Fund Quarterly/Health and Society*, 55, 3–24.

Gyimah-Brempong, K., and M. Wilson (2004), 'Health Human Capital and Economic Growth in Sub-Saharan African and OECD Countries', *The Quarterly Review of Economics and Finance*, 44(2), 296–320.

Hall, R., and C. Jones (2007), 'The Value of Life and the Rise in Health Spending', *The Quarterly Journal of Economics*, Feb., 39–72.

Harvey, K. (1998), 'Health Promotion is a Waste of Time and Money', *British Medical Journal*, 317(7162): 887.

Hitiris, T. (1997), 'Health Care Expenditure and Integration in the Countries of the European Union', *Applied Economics*, 29, 1–6.

——and J. Posnett (1992), 'The Determinants and Effects of Health Expenditure in Developed Countries', *Journal of Health Economics* 11(2), 173–81.

Hongbin, L., J. Zhang, and J. Zhang (2007), 'Effects of Longevity and Dependency Rates on Saving and Growth: Evidence from a Panel of Cross Countries', *Journal of Development Economics*, 84, 138–54.

Hunink, M. G., L. Goldman, A. N. Tosteson, *et al.* (1997), 'The Recent Decline in Mortality from Coronary Heart Disease, 1980–1990: The Effect of Secular Trends in Risk Factors and Treatment', *Journal of the American Medical Association*, 277, 535–42.

Illich, I. (1976), *Limits to Medicine: Medical Nemesis—The Expropriation of Health*, Harmondsworth: Penguin.

Ingenue (2001), 'Macroeconomic Consequences of Pension Reforms in Europe: An Investigation with the INGENUE World Model', CEPII Working Papers No. 17.

Jacobzone, S. (2003), 'Ageing and the Challenges of New Technologies: Can OECD Social and Health Care Systems Provide for the Future?', *The Geneva Papers on Risk and Insurance*, 28(2), 254–74.

Jagger, C. *et al.* (2008), 'Inequalities in Healthy Life in the 25 Countries of the European Union in 2005: a Cross-National Meta-regression Analysis', *The Lancet*, 17 Nov.

Jamison, D., Lawrence J. Lau, and Jia Wang (2004), 'Health's Contribution to Economic Growth in an Environment of Partially Endogenous Technological Progress', Disease Control Priorities Project Working Paper No. 10.

Jones, C. I. (2004), 'Why Have Health Expenditures as a Share of GDP Risen So Much?', U.C. Berkeley Working Paper.

Jönsson, B., and I. Eckerlund (2003), 'Why do Different Countries Spend Different Amounts on Health Care?', *A Disease-Based Comparison of Health Systems*, Paris: OECD.

Kalemli-Ozcan, S., H. E. Ryder, and D. N. Weil (2000), 'Mortality Decline, Human Capital Investment and Economic Growth', *Journal of Development Economics*, 62, 1–23.

Kleiman, E. (1974), 'The Determinants of National Outlay on Health', in M. Perlman (ed.), *The Economics of Health and Medical Care*, London: Macmillan.

Knowles, S., and P. Owen (1995), 'Health Capital in Cross-Country Variation in Income per Capita in the Mankin-Romer-Weil Model', *Economic Letters*, 48, 99–106.

Kramer, M. (1980), 'The Rising Pandemic of Mental Disorders and Associated Chronic Diseases and Disabilities', *Acta Psychiatrica Scandinavica*, 62(suppl. 285), 282–97.

Lakdawalla, D., J. Bhattacharya, and D. Goldman (2004), 'Are the Young Becoming more Disabled?' *Health Affairs*, 23(1), 168–76.

Leu, R. E. (1986), 'The Public-Private Mix and International Health Care Costs', *Public and Private Health Services: Complementarities and Conflicts*, Oxford: Blackwell Scientific Publications, 41–63.

Levine R. and D. Renelt (1992), 'A Sensitivity Analysis of Cross-Country Growth Regressions', *American Economic Review*, 80, 942–63.

Lichtenberg, F. R. (2003), 'The Impact of New Drug Launches on Longevity: Evidence from Longitudinal, Disease-Level Data from 52 Countries, 1982–2001', NBER Working Paper Series No. 9754.

Lievre, A., F. Jusot, T. Barnaby, C. Serment, N. Brouard, J. M. Robine, M. A. Brieu, and F. Forette (2007), 'Healthy Working Life Expectancies at Age 50 in Europe: A New Indicator', *The Journal of Nutrition, Health and Aging*, 11(6), 508–14.

López-Casanovas, G., B. Rivera. and L. Currais (2005), *Health and Economic Growth*, Cambridge, Mass.: MIT Press.

Lorentzen, P., J. McMillan, and R. Wacziarg (2008), 'Death and Development', *Journal of Economic Growth*, 13(2), 81–124.

Lubitz, J. B. (2005), 'Health, Technology, and Medical Care Spending', *Health Affairs*, W5-R81.

Lubitz, J. B., and G. F. Riley (1993), 'Trends in Medicare Payments in the Last Year of Life', *New England Journal of Medicine*, 328, 1092–96.

Lucas, R. E. (1988), 'On the Mechanisms of Economic Development', *Journal of Monetary Economics*, 22, 3–42.

Luce, B. R., J. Mauskopf, F. Sloan, J. Ostermann, and L. Paramore (2006), 'The Return on Investment in Health Care: From 1980 to 2000', *Value Health*, 9(3), 146–56.

McClellan, M. (1997), 'Hospital Reimbursement Incentives: An Empirical Analysis', *Journal of Economics and Management Strategy*, 6(1), 91–128.

——and D. B. Kessler (2002), *Technological Change in Health Care: A Global Analysis of Heart Attack*, Ann Arbor: The University of Michigan Press.

McKeown, T. (1979), *The Role of Medicine: Dream, Mirage, or Nemesis?* Princeton: Princeton University Press.

McKinsey (1996), *Health Care Productivity*, Report, Advisory Committee: K. Arrow, M. N. Baily, A. Börsch-Supan, and A. M. Garber.

Magazzini, L., F. Pammolli, and M. Riccaboni (2004), 'Dynamic Competition in Pharmaceuticals: On Patent Expiry, Generic Penetration and Industry Structure', *European Journal of Health Economics*, 5, 175–82.

Manning, W. *et al.* (1987), 'Health Insurance and the Demand for Medical Care: Evidence from a Randomized Experiment', *American Economic Review*, 77, 251–77.

Manton, K. G. (1982), 'Changing Concepts of Morbidity and Mortality in the Elderly Population', *Milbank Memorial Fund Quarterly, Health and Society*, 60, 183–244.

Maxwell, R. (1981), *Health and Wealth: An International Study of Health Care Spending,*, Lexington, Mass.: Lexington Books, MA.

Michel, J.-P., and J.-M. Robine (2004), 'A "New" General Theory of Population Ageing', *The Geneva Papers on Risk and Insurance*, 29(4), 667–78.

Miles, D. (1999), 'Modelling the Impact of Demographic Change upon the Economy', *Economic Journal*, 109(452), 1–36.

Moise, P., and S. Jacobzone (2003), 'Population Ageing, Health Expenditure and Treatment: An ARD Perspective', *A Disease-Based Comparison of Health Systems*, Paris: OECD.

Murphy, K., and R. H. Topel (2006), 'The Value of Life and Longevity', *Journal of Political Economy*, 114(5), 871–904.

Nahar, S., and B. Inder (2002), 'Testing Convergence in Economic Growth for OECD Countries', *Applied Economics*, 34, 2011–22.

Narayan, P. K. (2007), 'Do Health Expenditures "Catch-up"? Evidence from OECD Countries', *Health Economics*, 16(10), 993–1008.

Newhouse, J. P. (1977), 'Medical Care Expenditure: A Cross-National Survey', *Journal of Human Resources*, 12, 115–25.

——(1987), 'Cross-National Differences in Health Spending: What do they Mean?', *Journal of Health Economics*, 6, 159–62.

——(1992), 'Medical Care Costs: How Much Welfare Loss?', *Journal of Economic Perspectives*, 6(3), 3–21.

——and C. E. Phelps (1976), 'New Estimates of Price and Income Elasticities of Medical Care Services', in R. N. Rosett (ed.), *The Role of Health Insurance in the Health Services Sector*, New York: NBER.

Norton, E. (2000), 'Long-Term Care', in A. J. Culyer and J. P. Newhouse (eds.), *Handbook of Health Economics*, Vol. 1B, Amsterdam: Elsevier.

O'Connell, J. (1996), 'The Relationship between Health Expenditures and the Age Structure of the Population in OECD Countries', *Health Economics*, 5, 573–78.

OECD (1987), 'Financing and Delivering Health Care: A Comparative Analysis of OECD Countries', *OECD Social Policy Studies* No. 4.

——(2005a), *Health Database*, Paris: OECD.

——(2005b), *Long-Term Care for Older People*, Paris: OECD.

Oeppen, J., and J. Vaupel (2002), 'Broken Limits to Life Expectancy', *Science*, 296 (5570), 1029–31.

Okunade, A. A., and V. N. R. Murthy (2002), 'Technology as a Major Driver of Health Costs: A Cointegration Analysis of the Newhouse Conjecture', *Journal of Health Economics*, 21, 147–59.

Okunade, A. A., and V. N. R. Murthy (2001), 'Unit Root and Cointegration Tests: Time Series versus Panel Estimates for International Health Expenditures', *Applied Economics*, 33, 1131–7.

Oliveira Martins, J., and C. de la Maisonneuve (2006), 'The Drivers of Public Expenditure on Health and Long-Term Care: An Integrated Approach', *OECD Economic Studies*, 43/2.

——F. Gonand, P. Antolin, C. de la Maisonneuve, and K. Yoo (2005), 'The Impact of Ageing in Demand, Factor Markets and Growth', OECD Economics Department Working Papers No. 420.

Olshansky, J. *et al.* (2005), 'A Potential Decline in Life Expectancy in the United States in the 21st Century', *The New England Journal of Medicine*, 352(11), 1138–45.

Pammolli, F. *et al.* (2005), 'Medical devices: competitiveness and impact on public health expenditures', study prepared for the European Commission-Directorate Enterprise and Industry.

——L. Magazzini, and L. Orsenigo (2002), 'The Intensity of Competition after Patent Expiry in Pharmaceuticals: A Cross-Country Analysis', *Revue d'Economie Industrielle*, 99, 107–32.

Parker, S., and R. Wong (1997), 'Household Income and Health Care Expenditures in Mexico', *Health Policy*, 40, 237–55.

Pesaran, H., R. P. Smith, and K. S. Im (1996), 'Dynamic Linear Models for Heterogenous Panels', in L. Mátyás and P. Sevestre (eds.), *The Econometrics of Panel Data*, Dordrecht, the Netherlands: Kluwer Academic Publishers, 145–95.

Phillips, P. C. B., and D. Sul (2007), 'Transition Modeling and Econometric Convergence Tests', Cowles Foundation Discussion Paper No. 1595.

Pritchett, L. (2006), 'The Quest Continues', *Finance and Development*, Mar., 18–22.

Productivity Commission (2005a), *Economic Implications of an Ageing Australia*, Research Report, Canberra.

——(2005b), *Impacts of Medical Technology in Australia*, Progress Report, Melbourne, Apr.

Reinhart, V. R. (1999), 'Death and Taxes: Their Implications for Endogenous Growth', *Economic Letters*, 92, 339–45.

Richardson, J., and I. Robertson (1999), 'Ageing and the Cost of Health Services', in *Policy Implications of the Ageing of Australia's Population*, Productivity Commission and Melbourne Institute, Canberra.

Rivera, B., and L. Currais (1999a), 'Economic Growth and Health: Direct Impact or Reverse Causation?' *Applied Economics Letters*, 6(11), 761–4.

————(1999b), 'Income Variation and Health Expenditure: Evidence for OECD Countries', *Review of Development Economics*, 3(3), 258–67.

Rodrik, D. (2005), 'Why We Learn Nothing from Regressing Economic Growth on Policies', Harvard University, mimeo.

Rosen, A. B., D. M. Cutler, D. M. Norton, H. M. Hu, and S. Vijan (2007), 'The Value Of Coronary Heart Disease Care for The Elderly: 1987–2002', *Health Affairs*, 23(1), 111–23.

Sala-i-Martin, X., G. Doppelhofer, and R. Miller (2004), 'Determinants of Long-Term Growth: A Bayesian Averaging of Classical Estimates (BACE) Approach', *The American Economic Review*, 94, 813–35.

Sanso, M., and R. Aisa (2006), 'Endogenous Longevity, Biological Deterioration, and Economic Growth', *Journal of Health Economics*, 25, 555–78.

Seshamani, M. and A. M. Gray (2004a), 'A Longitudinal Study of the Effects of Age and Time to Death on Hospital Costs', *Journal of Health Economics*, 23(2), 217–35.

————(2004b), 'Aging and Health-Care Expenditure: The Red Herring Argument Revisited', *Health Economics*, 13, 303–14.

Shapiro, I., M. D. Shapiro, and D. Wilcox (2001), 'Measuring the Value of Cataract Surgery', in D. Cutler and E. Berndt (eds.), *Medical Care Output and Productivity*, NBER Studies in Income and Wealth No. 62, NBER.

Stearns, S. C., and E. C. Norton (2004), 'Time to Include Time to Death? The Future of Health Care Expenditure Predictions', *Health Economics*, 13, 315–27.

Suhrcke, M., and D. Urban (2006), 'Are Cardiovascular Diseases Bad for Economic Growth?', CESifo Working Paper No. 1845.

Sunshine, J. H., and M. Dicker (1987), 'Total Family Expenditures for Health Care, United States, 1980', *National Medical Care Utilization and Expenditure Survey, Series B*, Report No. 15, DHHS pub. No. 87-20215, National Center for Health Statistics, Public Health Service, Washington: US Government Printing Office.

TECH (The Technological Change in Health Care Research) Network (2001), 'Technological Change around the World: Evidence from Heart Attack Care', *Health Affairs*, 20(3), 25–42.

Triplett, J. E., and B. P. Bosworth (2000), 'Productivity in the Services Sector', Brookings Institution, mimeo.

Unal, B., J. A. Critchley, and S. Capewell (2005), 'Modelling the decline in coronary heart disease deaths in England and Wales, 1981–2000: Comparing Contributions from Primary Prevention and Secondary Prevention', *British Medical Journal*, 331, 614.

Van Zon, A., and J. Muysken (2001), 'Health and Endogenous Growth', *Journal of Health Economics*, 20, 169–85.

Vaupel, J. W. (2002), 'Post-Darwinian Longevity', Max Planck Institute for Demographic Research Working Papers No. 2002-043.

Viscusi, W., and J. Aldy (2003), 'The Value of a Statistical Life: A Critical Review of Market Estimates throughout the World', *Journal of Risk and Uncertainty*, 27, 5–76.

Wagstaff, A., E. van Doorslaer, and P. Paci (1991), 'Equity in the Finance and Delivery of Health Care: Some Tentative Cross-Country Comparisons', in A. McGuire, P. Fenn, and K. Mayhew (eds.), *Providing Health Care*, Oxford: Oxford University Press.

Weil, D. (2007), 'Accounting for the Effect of Health on Economic Growth', *Quarterly Journal of Economics*, 122(3), 1265–306.

Weisbrod, B. A. (1991), 'The Health Care Quadrilemma: An Essay on Technological Change, Insurance, Quality of Care, and Cost Containment', *Journal of Economic Literature*, 29, 523–55.

Werblow, A., S. Felder, and P. Zweifel (2007), 'Population Ageing and Health Expenditure: A School of "Red Herring"'?, *Health Economics*, 16, S1109–26.

Westerhout, E., and F. Pellikaan (2005), 'Can We Afford to Live Longer in Better Health?', *Netherlands Bureau for Economic Policy Analysis*, Document No. 85, June.

World Bank (2006), *World Development Indicators*, New York: Oxford University Press.

Yang, Z., E. C. Norton, and S. C. Stearns (2003), 'Longevity and Health Care Expenditures: The Real Reasons Older People Spend More', *Journal of Gerontology B, Psychol Social Science*, 58B(1), S1–10.

Yashin, A. (2003), 'Recent Demographic Findings Stimulating the Development of Ageing Research', in EC Workshop on Ageing, Genetics and Demography, Bologna, Jan. 2003, European Forum on Population Ageing Research.

Zhang, J., and J. Zhang (2001), 'Longevity and Economic Growth in a Dynastic Family Model with an Annuity Market', *Economics Letters*, 72, 269–77.

————and R. Lee (2001), 'Mortality Decline and Long-Run Economic Growth', *Journal of Public Economics*, 80, 485–507.

——————(2003), 'Rising Longevity, Education, Savings, and Growth', *Journal of Development Economics*, 70, 103–17.

Zweifel, P., S. Felder, and M. Meiers (1999), 'Ageing of the Population and Health Care Expenditure: A Red Herring?' *Health Economics*, 8, 485–96.

————A. Werblow (2004), 'Population Ageing and Health Care Expenditures: New Evidence on the Red Herring', *The Geneva Papers on Risk and Insurance*, 29(4), 652–66.

Comments

Axel Börsch-Supan

This is a veritable epos rather than a conventional report. I enjoyed reading it a lot as it represents an admirable collection of results and analyses, pieced together to form a holistic view of how health expenditures influence not only health and longevity, but also economic performance and economic growth. The ambition of the authors is to understand, and ultimately influence, the volume, costs, and outcomes of the health-care systems in the OECD countries. Given this ambition, it is not surprising that the report is a maze of interrelated topics (see Figure C1.1; the numbers in parentheses refer to the chapters/sections of the report).

The main weakness of this epos is the evidence on which it stands, in particular for Europe. The weak empirical base will be a continuing theme in the following discussion. This is not the authors' fault. Rather, it reflects the Achilles' heel of the European research infrastructure to date: we lack micro-data that would enable researchers to view health and economic outcomes jointly and comprehensively. Although advances are being made, in particular through the Survey of Health, Aging and Retirement in Europe (SHARE) and its older sisters, the US Health and Retirement Study (HRS) and the English Longitudinal Study on Ageing (ELSA), these data sets do not yet provide the longitudinal dimension needed for causal analysis. One can only hope that the sponsors of these data sets will take a long view in supporting these infrastructures such that they can become fruitful for enterprises such as this.

The discussion is structured as follows. I will first summarize the story-line in an attempt to make the a-maze-ing architecture of the epos a bit more transparent. I will do so by dissecting Figure C1.1 under several headings (see Figures C1.2 through C1.5). I will then critically review selected key themes.

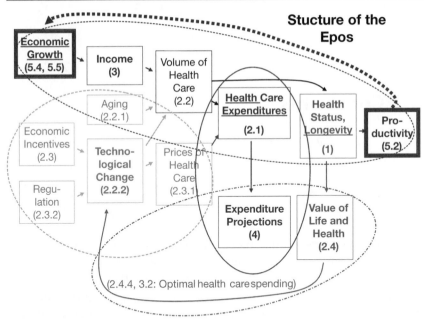

Figure C1.1. Structure of the epos

The core of the report is depicted in Figure C1.2. It represents a causal chain that starts with income driving the volume of health-care services provided, which in turn drive health-care expenditures and health out-comes such as functional status, morbidity, and mortality rates. This one-directional view is the conventional view which has been pursued by OECD researchers for quite a while. The authors go an important step further—important for both science and policy—by adding the other

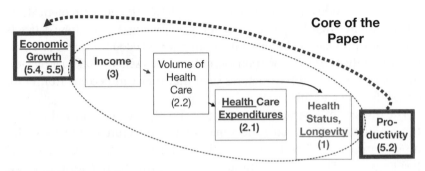

Figure C1.2. Core of the report

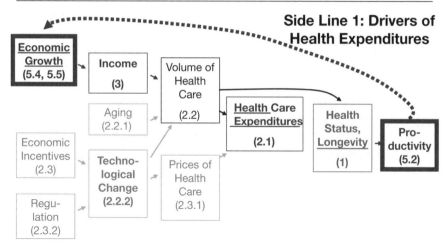

Figure C1.3. Sideline 1: drivers of health expenditures

causal direction to the correlation between socio-economic status and health (see the dashed line in Figure C1.2). Good health outcomes increase labour force activities and the productivity of the workforce, thus economic growth and income.

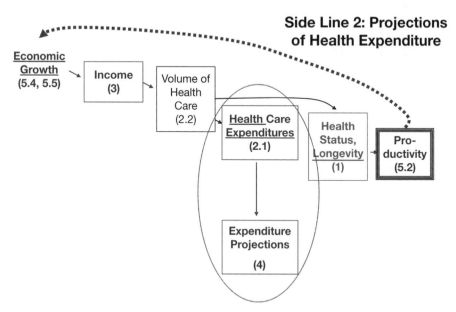

Figure C1.4. Sideline 2: projections of health expenditures

The authors then attach a host of separate points, empirical titbits, and several explicit sidelines to the core story of health care and economic activity. While these are all interesting and somehow related to the core story, this 'collection approach' often makes the report hard to follow, and at times the brevity (and the superficiality implied by the brevity) frustrates this reader. In fact, many stories are worth a separate paper (and some have been). Let me focus on a clearly identifiable set of three such additional stories which are linked to each other in a natural way. They address (a) possible drivers, (b) future projections, and (c) the optimal size of health-care expenditures. They are attached to the core line of the report as depicted in Figures C1.3 through C1.5.

In the first topic (see Figure C1.3), the authors investigate drivers of health expenditures other than income—mainly ageing and technology, the latter itself driven by economic incentives and regulation. The authors carefully distinguish effects on the volume of health care from effects on the price of health care.

The second topic features projections of future health-care expenditures (see Figure C1.4, depicting how Chapter 4 fits into the overall story-line).

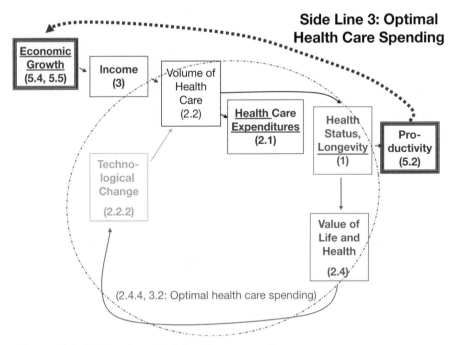

Figure C1.5. Sideline 3: optimal health-care spending

These expenditure projections are a typical and much-needed output regularly provided by the OECD.

The third set of arguments addresses the intellectually exciting topic of optimal health-care expenditures. The authors provide a framework, in which the value of life and health is the objective which is being optimized by allocating health-care technology. Figure C1.5 shows the authors' interpretation as a feedback cycle which runs from health outcomes and their societal value to an optimal rate of technological progress.

Now let me discuss these four key elements of the report in more detail, starting with the core story-line depicted in Figure C1.2, with its bi-directional causality between income and health. The reverse causality is an important feature from a scientific point of view since it implies that one needs much more careful analyses of international comparisons of health expenditures and income levels than are often found in the literature. Naïve cross-national regressions are biased due to simultaneity. The huge range of estimated income elasticities found in the literature may be interpreted as a symptom of this bias. The econometric analyses in Chapter 3, unfortunately, do not really avoid these consequences, although taking first differences certainly helps.

The political aspect of reverse causation strikes me as particularly noteworthy. It calls for a fundamental rethinking of what health-care policy and health system reform should be all about: investments in the future ability to work, and investment in the future productivity of labour. This is in contrast to the prevailing focus of many health-care reforms which are often purely cost-cutting exercises in which costs are minimized without much consideration for the damage done by underproviding health care. As with pension reform, the art is not to simply cut public health care down to sustainable levels, but to add functioning secondary and tertiary pillars of private health-care provision that fill the 'health gap'. There is, at least so far, little in the way of a blueprint as to how to design multi-pillar health-care systems.

An important element in both a scientific and a political respect is education. Its role is underrepresented in this epos, and in particular in the core story-line of health care and economic activity. We observe huge 'gradients' of health and socio-economic status, to a large extent, although by no means exclusively, driven by a similar gradient in education. The report misses the opportunity to point out that health and education are complements as investments for future economic activity. Education, through its influence on health behaviour, improves health outcomes.

117

This can be clearly seen in Figure C1.6, taken from a SHARE analysis by Mackenbach *et al.* (2005): Diabetes and lung diseases show the biggest socio-economic gradient; they are to a large extent driven by diet and smoking behaviour. In turn, good health appears to be one factor in improving the education process. It seems to be a worthy cause for the OECD to emphasize this mutual strengthening.

The first sideline to the core topic (see Figure C1.3) analyses technology and other drivers of health expenditures to lay the foundation for the expenditure projections in Chapter 4 of the report. I find this the weakest part of the report because the empirical base is so meagre. Most arguments are based on Brigitte Dormont and her co-authors' study, which included some 3,400 individuals in 1992 and some 5,000 individuals in 2000 in France. This simply does not represent what has happened over the last few decades in the OECD.

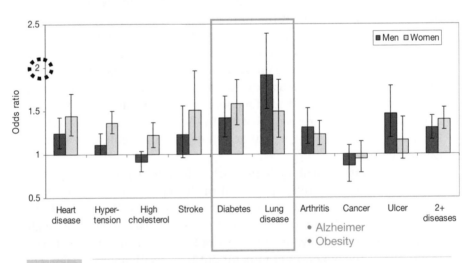

Figure C1.6. The role of health behaviour and education

Source: Mannheim Research Institute for the Economics of Aging.

Moreover, technological progress has been more subtle than described in the report, with its focus on product innovation. In addition, there has been process innovation, which has made some diseases much cheaper to cure. Sometimes, process and product are tightly linked (e.g. stents). Even more important is the influence of regulation on technology diffusion. Sometimes, it has pushed certain techniques way beyond efficient usage (e.g. mammography in Germany); sometimes it has hindered the introduction of efficient procedures (e.g. laparoscopy in Germany), as pointed out by Börsch-Supan (1996), summarizing a large-scale study of health-care productivity by the McKinsey Global Institute.

In general, I am missing the aspect of governance of, and government involvement in, the health-care sector. There is a striking lack of correlation between health-care expenditure and ultimate health outcomes, for example, measured as healthy life expectancy (see Figure C1.7). In some countries, health expenditures and health outcomes are in line: for

Input			Output	
15.0	United States		73.6	Japan
11.5	Switzerland		72.8	Switzerland
11.1	Germany		71.8	Sweden
10.5	Iceland		71.6	Australia
10.3	Norway		71.3	France
10.1	France		71.2	Iceland
9.9	Canada		71.0	Italy
9.9	Greece		71.0	Austria
9.8	Netherlands		70.9	Spain
9.6	Belgium		70.8	Norway
9.6	Portugal		70.6	Luxembourg
9.4	Sweden		70.4	Greece
9.3	Australia		70.3	New Zealand
9.0	Denmark		70.2	Germany
8.4	Italy		70.1	Finland
8.1	New Zealand		70.1	Denmark
7.9	Japan		69.9	Netherlands
7.7	Spain		69.9	Canada
7.7	United Kingdo		69.7	Belgium
7.5	Austria		69.6	United Kingdo
7.5	Czech Republ		69.0	Ireland
7.4	Finland		67.6	United States
7.4	Ireland		66.8	Portugal
6.9	Luxembourg		66.6	Czech Repub
6.5	Poland		64.3	Poland

Figure C1.7. Health expenditures (% GDP) and healthy life expectancy

Source: OECD (2005); WHO (2006).

example, high in Switzerland and low in Poland. But other countries have good outcomes at low expenditures (e.g. Japan, Sweden) or feature a relatively low healthy life expectancy in spite of very high health expenditures (most strikingly the US, but also e.g. Germany). One explanation lies in the confounding effects of health policy that drives expenditures up in some countries, given technology, and keeps them in check in other countries. The analysis in the report puts too little emphasis on these policy differences.

This critique naturally also applies to the health expenditure projections later in the report, which brings me to the second extra topic, shown in Figure C1.4. Different policies will have different impacts on future cost increases, and they should be part of a structural model as envisaged by the authors.

The potential impact of a morbidity compression in these projections is only briefly alluded to. While we know very little about it, morbidity compression has all the ingredients to make current projection attempts an empty exercise. According to a recent NIA analysis, current disability rates in the US are falling faster than costs are rising. The OECD's attempt to shed light on this in Europe has more or less failed due to the lack of good data. It is shocking on what weak foundations health expenditure projections and health-care policy must be based.

This then also renders the ambitious final story-line, though a scientific feast, a somewhat theoretical exercise (see Figure C1.5). If we do not really understand the influence of governance and government policy on health-care technology development, how can we provide a practically usable optimal health-care spending model? Do not misunderstand me: I think that the authors' attempt is a great innovation and should be pursued further. However, this attempt should be helped by providing better data now and in the future.

The optimization model in Section 2.4 also lacks the above-mentioned governance problems and the reason for strong government involvement: asymmetric information, moral hazard on the part of patients (too little care for themselves) and providers (supply-induced demand). The optimal input of health-care technology is not at all a matter of how undistorted markets find an optimum between capital input and health outcomes. Market distortions and government interference are crucial features of the market for health care, and since distortions are intrinsic to health-care demand and supply, it is unthinkable, at least to this reviewer, how one can manage without government interference now and in the future. Hence, all these features need to be key features of economic modelling of the health-care sector.

Let me summarize: this is an amazing collection of facts and modelling approaches, put together in a veritable epos. The authors should be congratulated upon their holistic view, and in particular for making the point that health care is, like education, an investment in the future ability to do productive work. While the analysis in this report would benefit from better modelling of government influence on health-care markets, but especially from a better base of micro-data in Europe, this policy message should be listened to in all OECD countries working on health-care reform.

Comments

Vincenzo Galasso

Nowadays, the typical economist seems to consider population ageing more as a curse than as a blessing. In the last decades, people have certainly come to live longer and healthier lives. But, in the public debate, these fortunate outcomes have often been overshadowed by some unfortunate economic implications. Everywhere population ageing has put unfunded pension systems under financial distress, labour markets will soon have to deal with an aged labour force, and there have even been studies predicting large stock market shocks when the baby-boom generation retires and hence start selling their financial assets.

The report on 'Health Expenditures, Longevity and Growth' by Dormont *et al.*, however, takes quite a different route. With rapid population ageing, health spending is suggested to have important *positive* effects on economic growth. To pursue this argument, the authors provide quite a comprehensive study of the complex interrelations among health spending, longevity and health status, medical innovation and economic growth.

To summarize, their large body of evidence is conducive—according to the authors—to envisioning a virtuous circle between health spending and economic growth. Figure C2.1 provides a brief description of this virtuous circle, which is also displayed—somewhat differently—at Figure 1 in the report. Let me start by describing the circle from the upper-left corner of Figure C2.1. Health spending has two main positive effects. On the one hand, more health care reduces mortality and morbidity. Individuals thus enjoy an increase in longevity and a better health status. In a nutshell, health care leads to healthy ageing. But more health care also means more medical innovation. These new medical treatments are crucial in the healthy ageing process just described. Yet, the report suggests also an

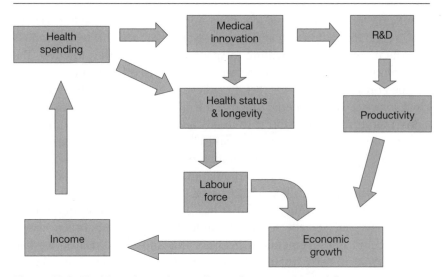

Figure C2.1. Health and spending and growth: a virtuous circle?

additional—more subtle—effect. Innovations in the medical and pharmaceutical sectors may spill over to other sectors, thereby leading to technological progress in other areas too. Moving now to the centre-right side of Figure C2.1, health spending has come to have a positive effect on the labour force as well as on productivity. Healthier workers will presumably be able (and willing) to work longer years—in order words, to retire later—and will also be more productive; while technological progress spilling over from medical R&D to the other sectors of the economy will increase overall productivity. These mechanisms provide the link running from health spending to economic growth. To close the virtuous circle—thereby moving from the lower-right corner back to the upper-left corner of Figure C2.1—one needs to establish the feedback from economic growth—and thus higher income—to more health spending. The authors dedicate a great deal of their report to addressing this issue. They conclude that higher income leads to proportionally more health spending, since individuals perceive health spending as a superior good: the richer they are, the more of it they want to buy. Once having estimated the income elasticity of public and private health-care spending, they hence continue by providing some projections of health-care spending.

I found the idea of a virtuous circle between health care and growth—in developed economies—very innovative and quite fascinating. Yet, when contrasted with the existing literature on the economic effects of ageing, the picture portrayed in this report sounds just *too good to be true*. Health care is good for your health and for your wallet. And the thicker the wallets get, the more people are willing to spend on their health. Moreover, the projections suggest that the expected large increase in health care is fully justified on welfare grounds. Yet, to believe in the existence of a virtuous circle, one needs to properly establish the different links in Figure C2.1.

My task in this discussion is to briefly address three of these links that may need some more discussion—and perhaps some further tightening. I will start by examining the determinants of health-care spending. Why has health spending increased so dramatically in the last few decades? The answer to this question is crucial to establishing the feedback from economic growth (or income) to further health spending. The second link to be analysed concerns the seemingly understood relation between health spending and improvements in health status and longevity. Do we live longer thanks to better medical treatments? Or is it perhaps due to better health habits? The third issue to be further investigated relates to some of the effects of health care on economic growth put forward in the report. Does a healthier, but older labour force retire later and/or become more productive? Do medical innovations and R&D actually spill over to other sectors, hence leading to higher growth?

What Drives Health-Care Spending?

Most developed countries have experienced a large increase in health-care spending. In the US, public spending on health care has risen from less than 0.5% of GDP in the 1960s to around 5% in 2005 (data from CPO: Budget of the United States Government). The conventional wisdom seems to point to the ageing process as the main culprit for this massive increase. Elderly people are the main beneficiaries of health care. According to Hagist and Kotlikoff (2005), people aged 65 to 74 receive five times more benefits than individuals of less than 64 years. As the population grows older, health spending is hence bound to increase due to the expansion in the number of beneficiaries.

Yet, things are not quite as simple as they seem. Health spending—as well as pension spending—has increased more than the share of the elderly in the population, thereby suggesting that health care (and pension) benefits per elderly individual have also increased. In the US, the ratio between health spending over GDP and the share of the elderly (people aged 65 years old or more) in the population has experienced a nine-fold increase from the 1960s to today. At the very least, ageing is hence not the only—or even the main—cause of the dramatic rise in health-care spending.

The report provides a valuable contribution to explaining these facts. The authors argue that the positive relation between health-care spending and individual age is mainly driven by 'proximity to death' spending. As shown in Figure 2.5, using data from Yang *et al.* (2003), at any age (above 55), health spending is strongly concentrated in the last year prior to death. Regardless of their age, if severely ill, individuals use health care more intensively. The bulk of health-care spending occurs in these contingencies. For those individuals who are still alive in the next year—and hence were not severely ill—health spending is much lower. However, this is indeed increasing with age: even when in relatively good shape, the older an individual gets, the more health care, such as medicines, she will need.

If 'proximity to death' spending is responsible for most of the health bill, ageing may actually reduce health-care spending, albeit temporarily. The reduction in mortality enjoyed by most countries in the last decades amounts to a postponement in the time of death for several elderly individuals. For these people, the bulk of their lifetime health spending, occurring one year prior to death, will also be postponed. This effect should be counterweighted by the increase in the share of elderly people in the population, which should also lead to more spending, as shown by the lower line in Figure 2.5. All in all, the conventional wisdom seems mistaken. Ageing is unlikely to be responsible for the spectacular rise in health spending. What is to blame—or to bless—then?

Countries such as the US are spending more in health care per elderly person. Is this due to the higher prices of the new, more expensive medical treatments, as argued by Newhouse (1992)? The report endorses the view that the increase in health spending is mainly driven by a large expansion in medical practices for given morbidity. Over time, the existence of better treatments for some given illnesses has led to a large diffusion of innovative procedures, whereas the quality-adjusted costs of care have remained stable, as suggested by Cutler and McClellan (1996) for the case of heart attack treatments.

Yet, this explanation raises two further questions. Why are these new medical technologies so widely used, in spite of their cost? And why has there been so much recent effort to develop these new treatments?

The latter question has an easy economic answer. The incentive of the R&D sector to develop new technologies stems from the—so far correct—expectation that they will be adopted. In the US, the expansion in health insurance coverage and even more the introduction in the 1960s of Medicare and Medicaid have contributed to creating a larger market for medical innovations. R&D firms have correctly reacted to these market incentives.

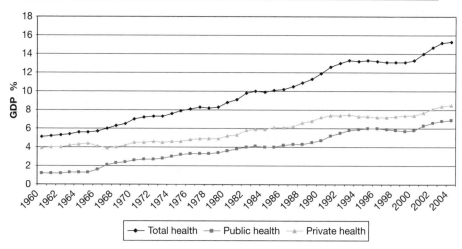

Figure C2.2. Public and private health spending

But why were these two public systems introduced in the 1960s and why has private health insurance coverage increased? In other words, why are so many more public and private resources devoted to health care than two or three decades ago? As shown in Figure C2.2, the growth in private and public health spending in the US is quite substantial.

The report endorses the answer provided in a recent paper by Hall and Jones (2007), who argue that health care is a superior good. As individuals get richer, they choose to spend a larger proportion of their income on health care. This could explain the increase in private health spending, but also in public health, if one is ready to believe that policy-makers are effectively adjusting public health spending to these individual preferences.

Yet, the report is silent on other possible explanations for the increase in health spending. An interesting hypothesis is presented by Philipson and Becker (1998). They argue that the increase in the generosity of public pensions may induce the elderly to increase their private health-care spending. This is because the existence of an annuity—the old-age pension—raises the value of longevity. In other words, thanks to a generous pension, individuals can afford to live longer and thus spend more money on health care.

Discussing this proposal by Philipson and Becker (1998) and other alternative explanations is more than an intellectual curiosity. In the interesting projections on future health spending provided in the report, the residual component—that is, after having controlled for demographic determinants and income—plays an uncomfortably large role. Testing additional explanations may help to refine these projections.

Does Health Spending Lead to Better Health and Higher Longevity?

A second important connecting knot in the virtuous circle between health spending and economic growth is represented by the impact of public and private health care on individuals' health status and longevity. Does more health care lead to healthy ageing? The discussion in the report suggests a definite yes! The evidence surveyed in Section 2.3.2 of Chapter 2 leads the authors to conclude that health spending is largely responsible for the increase in longevity and the compression of morbidity experienced in the US in the last decades: health care does lead to healthy ageing.

It is uncontroversial that individuals' health conditions have largely improved in the last few decades. People live longer and, perhaps, enjoy better health. But can all these health improvements be mainly attributed to medical care and doctors?

Evidence in the epidemiological literature highlights the prominent role of medical care. As shown in Figure C2.3, which uses data from the US Department of Health and Human Services, the leading cause of the large reduction in old-age mortality is lower mortality from cardiovascular diseases. And in this area, medical care has worked wonders. Cutler *et al.* (1999) estimated that medical improvements in primary prevention, acute management, and secondary prevention accounted for nearly half of the reduction in mortality from heart diseases. Yet, Cutler (2004), who again attributes most of the drop

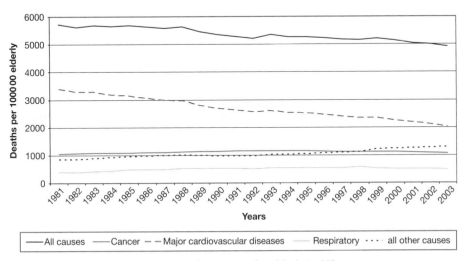

Figure C2.3. Mortality rate by leading causes for elderly in US

in cardiovascular disease mortality to medical advances, also suggests that the other major factor is the reduction in smoking.

This evidence points to the fact that individual health conditions may depend not only on the availability and access to medical care, but also on individuals' health-related behaviour. Living conditions, working environments, eating habits, smoking behaviour are all important determinants of individuals' health, which has been shown to depend on individuals' income and education (see Deaton, 2002, 2003, and Cutler *et al.*, 2006). A well-established fact in the health literature is that high-income individuals live longer. According to Rogot *et al.* (1992), for instance, the longevity at age 65 for a male in the highest income group is expected to be four years higher than for a male in the lowest income group.

If medical care—and in particular the extension of medical treatments—were the main determinants of the drop in mortality, one should expect this difference in mortality across income groups to be reduced. More access to better medical care should be beneficial in particular to low-income individuals, who presumably had initially less access to expensive medical treatments. Yet, while mortality rates have typically decreased for all socio-economic groups, the magnitude of this effect has differed. Relative mortality differences—measured as the ratio between mortality rates at low- and high-income levels—have indeed widened over the last three decades. This evidence may represent an alarm bell. Why are rich people doing better than poor people in reducing mortality? Perhaps this is because some of the reduction in mortality is to be attributed to changes in individual health-related behaviour, which has occurred more rapidly among high-income individuals. For instance, after the initial warning by the General Surgeon on the risk of smoking in the 1960s, high-income and better educated individuals have been quicker to quit smoking. Evidence on eating behaviour suggests similar considerations.

An even more pessimistic view of the differences in health status between low- and high-income individuals arises if one steps aside from the 'healthy ageing' hypothesis and considers only the improvements in longevity which relate to 'good' years—that is, years that are expected to be free of illnesses. As shown in Figure C2.4, a study by Mackenbach (2006) estimates that the differences in health status across income groups become even more extreme if one concentrates on healthy life expectancy.

The existence of a health gradient, that is, a difference in health status across socio-economic groups, that has increased over time, despite the overall reduction in mortality, suggests that more medical care may not be the only—or even the most relevant—determinant of the health

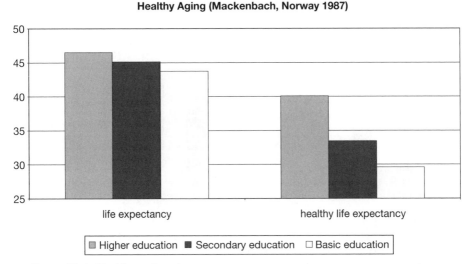

Figure C2.4. Health gradient

improvements enjoyed in the last 30 years. A further tightening up of the link running from health spending to healthy ageing would hence help.

Cashing on Better Health?

Having established the link from more health care to healthy ageing, the report suggests several channels leading from health spending to economic growth. Some aspects have been widely debated in the economic literature. Living longer and healthier lives, individuals have more time to devote to working activities. This increase in their working career should also provide them with better incentives to invest in human capital, as they will be able to obtain the returns from this investment—for instance, in terms of higher wages—over a longer time horizon. Moreover, healthier workers should be more productive. In the authors' view, healthy ageing should thus lead to a larger and more productive labour force.

Although these theoretical arguments sound very reasonable, the empirical evidence on labour force participation of the last few decades is quite alarming. People do live longer, but work much less than they used to do 30 years ago. Moreover, this long-term trend differs somewhat across countries, but is present everywhere. Yet, in the last five years, some countries have experienced an increase in the retirement age, which might suggest a reversion of the trend. This is certainly good news. But

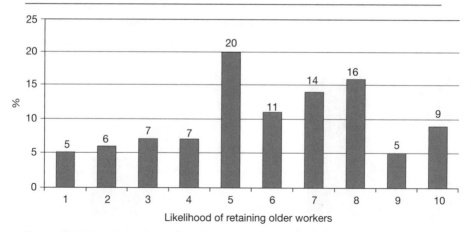

Figure C2.5. Employers' taste for elderly workers

Note: Retaining older workers is defined as creating job opportunities for at least half of workers who wish to work two to four years longer than the firms traditional retirement age.

Source: Andrew D. Eschtruth, Steven A. Saas, and Jean-Pierre Aubry *Employers Lukewarm About Retaining Older workers, Work Opportunities for Older Americans* Series 10, May 2007 © 2007, by trustees of Boston College. Reproduced with kind permission of the authors and the Center for Retirement Research, Boston College.

how big should the magnitude of the increase in the retirement age be to have a significant effect on the labour force and thus to countervail the ageing process?

Table C2.1 shows the effective median retirement age, and the old-age and the pension dependency ratios for six OECD countries in 2000 and their forecasted values for 2050. The former ratio is given by the ratio of the share of individuals aged 65 years or more over the share of people aged 16 to 64. The latter ratio instead divides the population between retirees (at the numerator) and workers (at the denominator) according to the effective retirement age. Due to population ageing, both dependency ratios will increase significantly from 2000 to 2050. The last column of Table C2.1 calculates the effective retirement age that would be needed in 2050 to counterbalance the ageing effect. The size of the increase is very large: from 5 years in the US to 12 years in Italy and Spain.

Will workers be willing to modify their retirement behaviour so dramatically? And, perhaps more importantly, will firms be willing to demand the working services of these elderly workers? As shown in Figure C2.5, employers in the US seem overall willing to retain their elderly workers. Will the same situation apply to other countries—such as Italy or Spain—characterized by more regulated labour markets and by a more stringent pay scale based on seniority?

130

Table C2.1. Ageing and retirement

Country	Old age dependency ratio		Effective retirement age	Pension dependency ratio		Required retirement age
	2000	2050	2000	2000	2050	2050
France	25.9	48.8	58	40.4	76.1	68
Germany	25.0	51.5	61	36.0	67.7	70
Italy	27.9	64.5	59	44.0	91.7	71
Spain	26.0	63.4	61	34.2	80.2	73
UK	25.3	44.3	63	29.2	50.9	71
US	20.5	36.3	63	23.4	41.5	68

Perhaps, these questions are beyond the scope of this report. But they are relevant to addressing one of the fundamental links running from healthy ageing to greater economic growth through a larger and better labour force.

Finally, a warning is needed on the relationship between income and health care. While the existence of a positive association between income and longevity is well established, some controversy remains on the direction of causality. Among other connecting links, the virtuous circle between health care and economic growth described in Figure C2.1 requires higher income to lead to more health spending. Yet, does this positive relation between income and health care stem from health affecting individual working opportunities—and hence income—or from income providing a protective effect on health? A broad overview of the existing literature suggests that both directions of causality are indeed at work (see Smith, 1999).

References

Cutler, D. (2004), *Your Money or Your Life*, Oxford: Oxford University Press.

—— A. Deaton, and A. Lleras-Muney (2006), 'The Determinants of Mortality', NBER Working Paper No. 11903.

——and M. McClellan (1996), 'The Determinants of Technological Change in Hearth Attack Treatment', NBER Working Paper No. 5751.

—— —— and J. P. Newhouse (1999), 'The Costs and Benefits of Intensive Treatment for Cardiovascular Disease', in J. E. Triplett (ed.), *Measuring the Price of Medical Services*, Washington: The Brookings Institute.

——and E. Richardson (1997), 'Measuring the Health of the United States Population', Brookings Papers on Economic Activity, Microeconomics, 217–72.

Deaton, A. (2002), 'Policy Implications of the Gradient of Health and Wealth', *Health Affairs*, 21(2), 13–30.

Deaton, A. (2003), 'Health, Inequality and Economic Development', *Journal of Economic Literature*, 41 (March), 113–58.

Eschtruth, A. D., S. A. Sass, and J.-P. Aubry (2007), 'Employers Lukewarm about Retaining Older Workers', Work Opportunities for Older Americans Series 10.

Hagist, C., and L. J. Kotlikoff (2005), 'Who's Going Broke? Rising Health Care Costs in Ten OECD Countries', *Milken Institute Review*.

Hall, R. E., and C. I. Jones (2007), 'The Value of Life and the Rise in Health Spending', *Quarterly Journal of Economics*, 39–72.

Mackenbach, J. (2006), 'Health Inequalities: Europe in Profile', European Union Report.

Newhouse, J. P. (1992), 'Medical Care Costs: How Much Welfare Loss?', *Journal of Economic Perspectives*, 6(3), 3–21.

Philipson, T., and G. Becker (1998), 'Old-Age Longevity and Mortality-Contingent Claims', *Journal of Political Economy*, 106(3), 551–73.

Rogot, E., Sorlie, P. D., Johnson, N. J., and Schmitt, C. (1992), 'A Mortality Study of 1.3 Million Persons by Demographic, Social, and Economic Factors: 1979–1985 Follow-up', NIH, Bethesda.

Smith, J. (1999), 'Healthy Bodies and Thick Wallets: The Dual Relation between Health and Economic Status', *Journal of Economic Perspectives*, 13(2), 145–66.

Yang, Z., E. C. Norton, and S. C. Stearns (2003), 'The Real Reasons Older People Spend More', *Journal of Gerontology B, Psychol Soc Sci*, 58(1): S1–S10.

Part II

Age and Productivity

Pekka Ilmakunnas, Jan van Ours,
Vegard Skirbekk, and Matthias Weiss

Introduction

Our study deals with the relationship between population ageing and productivity at the level of the individual and the level of the firm. We contribute to the discussion on this relationship in two ways. First, we present a 'grand view', in which we discuss the various components of productivity in detail and look at long-term historical developments, where we take changing economic structures into account. Second, we present results from an empirical analysis of a variety of productivity measures. Our main findings are the following. Productivity is multidimensional and age affects various skills differently. The productivity effects of ageing depend on the extent to which age-induced changes in cognitive and non-cognitive abilities are relevant for work performance. In the past century, the structure of work has changed a lot and therefore the relationship between age and productivity is also changing. Our empirical analysis shows that younger workers tend to have a higher number of absences, while older workers are absent less often but have longer durations of absences. The overall effect of age on absenteeism is concave. Sick leave increases with age up to the age of 45 and flattens out afterwards. Age has an effect not only at the individual level. More age diversity within a group of workers leads to more individual absence. Rotation of older workers to tasks that are less physically demanding may improve the perceived working capacity and may even improve actual productivity. Productivity at work is monotonously decreasing with age but this decline in productivity can be compensated if workers remain in the same plant and accumulate job-specific experience. So tenure is good for productivity ('intensive margin') but not for absenteeism ('extensive margin'). From our analysis, we conclude that individual productivity deteriorates if no investments are made to keep human capital up-to-date. The main lesson from our study is that labour market behaviour is more important than demographic changes. And labour market behaviour can be influenced through flexibility in mandatory retirement ages, human resource management, employment protection legislation, and wage policies. All in all, we think that the potential negative effects of ageing on productivity should not be underestimated. Nevertheless, they should not be exaggerated either. The decline of productivity with age is partly endogenous and subject to policy influence. The way productivity is affected by age is not just an exogenous phenomenon but is also influenced by choice.

7

Setting the Stage

In most, if not all, countries, the population is ageing. Population ageing affects labour market performance in two ways. First, ageing will cause a decline in the relative size of the economically active population. This is a matter of both numbers and incentives. If an ageing population requires more transfers from employees to retirees—marginal—taxes may go up and individuals may reduce their working hours or withdraw from the labour force. Second, ageing may affect productivity levels if older workers are less productive than prime-age workers. This study focuses on the relationship between age and productivity in order to investigate whether there is indeed reason to worry about the negative effects of population ageing on labour market performance.

Age and labour force participation are clearly related. Figure 7.1 shows the familiar inverse-U-shaped relationship between age and labour force participation. Although across various regions in the world the pattern is very similar, there are also clear differences. In Europe, labour force participation starts to decline earlier than in Japan and the US.

The population in the EU countries is ageing rapidly. Between 2004 and 2050 the working-age population (15 to 64) in the EU-15 countries is predicted to decrease by 13%, while over the same period the elderly population (65+) will increase by 75% (Carone *et al.*, 2005). In absolute terms, the working-age population will decrease by 34 million, while the elderly population will increase by 49 million. Carone *et al.* (2005) distinguish three time periods at the aggregate EU-25 level. First, 2004–11 is a window of opportunity when both the working-age population and the number of employed workers increase. Second, during 2012–17, rising employment rates offset the decline in the working-age population when the baby-boom generation enters retirement. Third, from 2018 onwards, the effect of ageing dominates, by which time the trend increase in female

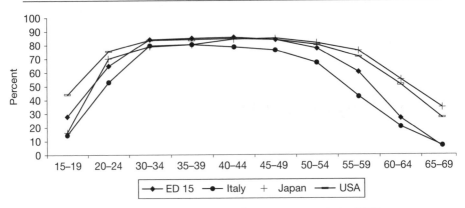

Figure 7.1. Labour force participation rates by age across regions, 2003

Source: OECD (2005), 'Economic Policy Reforms Going for Growth 2005', p. 156, available at <http://www.oecd.org/economics/goingforgrowth>.

employment rates will have worked itself out and the employment rate of older workers is also projected to reach a steady state.

Figure 7.2 shows the evolution of the working-age population in Western Europe (both genders, ages 15–79). A considerable proportion of the ageing is due to the large cohorts born around 1960. The strongest impact from ageing baby-boomers will be around 2030. Thereafter the age structure will be flatter, but still older than today. A potentially much stronger effect on the ageing of the workforce is caused by increasing labour force

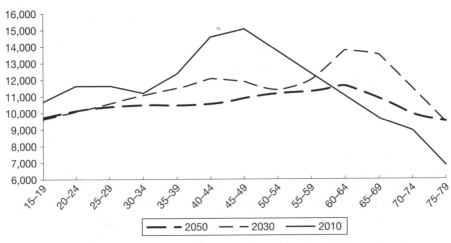

Figure 7.2. Population structure of Western Europe, 2010–2050 (in 1000s)

Source: UN (2005).

participation rates at higher ages. The net effect of later retirement ages and population ageing is workforce ageing, particularly in the medium term (2030), and to a lesser extent in the longer term (2050). Both population ageing as well as later retirement ages result in longer working lives, with an increase in the proportion of elderly workers.

Although ageing is a common phenomenon, there are substantial differences in the magnitude of the ageing problem between countries. Table 7.1 classifies a number of OECD countries according to the participation rate of older workers in 2000 and the changes in the old-age dependency ratio over the period 2000–50. The table indicates that some countries face much bigger problems than others. Problems are potentially largest in Greece, Italy, Poland, Spain, and the Slovak Republic. In these countries, the old-age dependency ratio will increase considerably until 2050, while the labour force participation of older workers is low.

Countries have a different position if only because they differ widely in participation rates of elderly workers. In 2003, the female participation rate for the age category 60 to 64 ranged from about 7% in Austria and Belgium to 82.4% in Iceland; for the age category 55–9, the range was from 27% in Belgium to about 80% in Sweden and 86.5% in Iceland. For males, the differences are not that big, but still substantial. Participation rates for the age category 60 to 64 ranged from 15.2% in France to 88.7% in Iceland; and for the age category 55–9, from 53.4% in Belgium to 90% in Sweden and 93.4% in Iceland. Figures 7.3 and 7.4 give a graphical representation of these cross-country differences.

Some countries do relatively well in terms of labour force participation rates for both age groups 50–4 and 60–4. Other countries have age-specific

Table 7.1. The size of the challenge of population ageing, selected countries

Participation	Increase in old-age dependency ratio, 2000–2050		
50–64, 2000	Moderate	Large	Very large
High	Denmark, Iceland, Norway, Sweden, Switzerland, U.S.	Canada, New Zealand	Japan
Average	Netherlands, U.K.	Australia, Finland, France, Germany, Ireland	Czech Republic, Portugal
Low	Belgium, Turkey	Austria, Hungary	Greece, Italy, Poland, Spain, Slovak Republic

Note: Old-age dependency ratio = Population age 65+ / Population 20–64.
Source: OECD (2006).

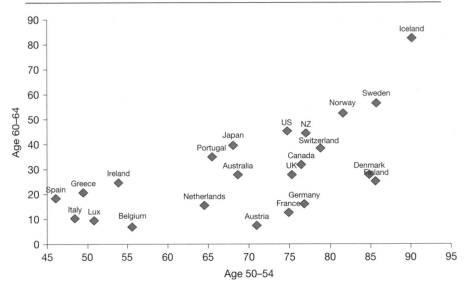

Figure 7.3. Participation rates, 2003—females (%)
Source: OECD Labour Force Statistics.

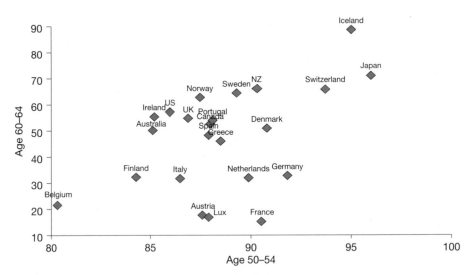

Figure 7.4. Participation rates, 2003—males (%)
Source: OECD Labour Force Statistics.

problems, which are most likely related to their attractive early retirement schemes. Whereas in the 50–4 age group they do better than other countries, they do worse in the 60–4 age group. Finally, there are countries that have a general problem of low participation rates for workers of 50+.

In some countries, early retirement schemes play a dominant role in the explanation for older workers' low labour force participation rates. An important argument in the discussion on early retirement schemes is that these will reduce youth unemployment. This argument is based on the erroneous assumption that there is a 'lump of labour' that may be redistributed from old workers to young workers without costs. Boldrin *et al.* (1999) show that there is no positive relationship between youth unemployment and the retirement age, that is, early retirement by older workers does not induce lower youth unemployment. Nevertheless, in some countries, people have strong opinions on this issue. According to the World Value Survey in the 1990s, on average 65–70% of the Italian and Spanish population of 15 years and older agreed with the statement that 'older people should be forced to retire when jobs are scarce'. In Sweden and the US, the percentage of people agreeing with this statement was about 15. As shown in Figure 7.5, there is a negative cross-country correlation between the percentage of people that agrees with the statement and the employment rate of elderly workers. The relationship is clear, but the causality is not. It could be that people in Italy and Spain decide to retire early in line with the common perception, while people in Sweden and the US do not—also according to the common perception. However, it is also possible that the common opinion is shaped to rationalize the situation concerning the employment rates of elderly workers.

Early retirement schemes are a rather recent phenomenon, but the reduction of the retirement age is a long-term phenomenon. For the purpose of illustration, Figure 7.6 shows the main developments in Italy concerning ages of labour market entry and exit for different groups of workers. The upper panel of Figure 7.6 shows developments for men, the bottom panel those for women. As shown, there are not many differences between men and women. In each case, the top three lines concern ages of exit for different educational groups; the bottom three lines concern ages of entry for different educational groups of workers.

For both bundles of lines, the order is in line with the level of educational attainment: the lowest line represents the lowest educational level, the highest line corresponds to the highest level of education. As shown, the age-of-entry lines are rather flat, indicating that there is hardly any change across various birth cohorts. The age-of-labour-market-exit lines are all downward sloping, indicating that more recent birth cohorts have left the labour market at a

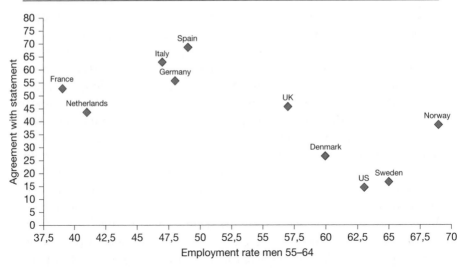

Figure 7.5. Employment rate, men aged 55–64 (1994) and agreement with statement 'older people should be forced to retire when jobs are scarce' (1990–1999), (%) per cent
Source: World Value Survey, OECD Employment Outlook.

younger age. Taken together, these developments imply that the duration of labour market attachment has been reduced quite substantially. Figure 7.6 also shows that the differences between workers with a different educational level are bigger for age of labour market entry than they are for age of labour market exit. Hence, the duration of labour market attachment is inversely related to the educational level of the worker; the lower the educational level, the higher the duration of labour market attachment. Table 7.2 summarizes for five countries the main evolution in ages of labour market entry and exit and the resulting duration of labour market attachment. By and large, the developments in all countries are very similar. Finally, Figure 7.7 represents the evolution of labour market attachment for men, for two birth cohorts—1915–19 and 1940–45—and for three educational levels. Irrespective of gender and education, there is a big drop in the duration of labour market attachment.

All in all, the length of working lives in Europe has shrunk mainly due to an earlier exit from the labour market.[1] Since health has increased a lot, most of the years spent in retirement appear to be years of healthy life. Historically, healthy retirement is uncommon as is illustrated in Figure 7.8.

---

[1] Recently, a trend reversal in the timing of retirement is visible in a number of countries. Some countries have legislated increases in their statutory retirement ages. Nevertheless, it will take some time until the consequences of early retirement schemes have faded away. Brugiavini and Peracchi (2005) also point to a later age of labour market entrance which reduces working life.

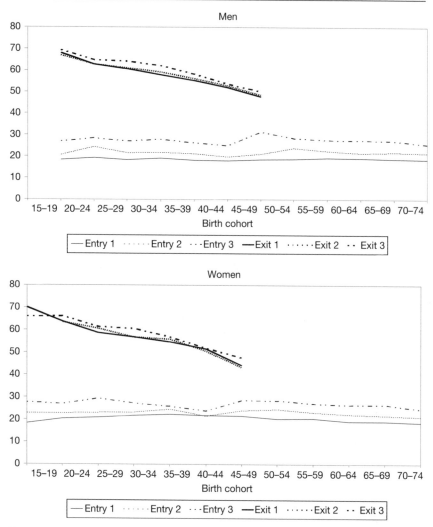

Figure 7.6. Age of labour market entry and exit by birth cohort and educational attainment, Italy

Notes: Educational attainment: 1 = Primary education, 2 = Secondary education, 3 = Tertiary education.
Source: European Community Household Panel.

Table 7.2. Age of labour market entry and exit and duration of labour market attachment by educational level and birth cohort

Men	Birth cohort	Entry by education			Exit by education			Duration (years)		
		1	2	3	1	2	3	1	2	3
Finland	1915–19	14.7	16.3	23.5	67.1	64.6	68.2	52.4	48.3	44.7
	1940–45	16.2	17.3	20.7	51.8	50.9	51.7	35.6	33.6	31.0
France	1915–19	14.0	18.5	24.6	65.7	66.2	67.6	51.7	47.7	43.0
	1940–45	16.1	16.9	24.0	49.9	50.0	51.0	33.8	33.1	27.0
Germany	1915–19	15.3	19.1	21.4	62.6	63.9	64.5	47.3	44.8	43.1
	1940–45	16.8	17.5	20.5	51.2	53.1	54.6	34.4	35.6	34.1
Italy	1915–19	18.2	20.6	27.0	68.1	67.0	69.5	49.9	46.4	42.5
	1940–45	18.0	19.8	25.0	52.0	52.8	53.6	34.0	33.0	28.6
UK	1915–19	14.9	15.4	19.1	65.7	65.1	65.6	50.8	49.7	46.5
	1940–45	17.1	17.8	19.1	50.8	52.3	53.4	33.7	34.5	34.3
Women										
Finland	1915–19	18.6	17.5	20.7	65.4	70.8	63.5	46.8	53.3	42.8
	1940–45	17.4	17.9	22.3	51.6	53.9	54.6	34.2	36.0	32.3
France	1915–19	16.5	18.1	17.1	65.4	64.2	70.5	48.9	46.1	53.4
	1940–45	17.0	18.0	22.1	46.4	47.7	45.6	29.4	29.7	23.5
Germany	1915–19	17.2	18.2	19.2	64.1	64.2	63.6	46.9	46.0	44.4
	1940–45	18.0	17.4	20.7	48.7	51.3	51.9	30.7	33.9	31.2
Italy	1915–19	18.3	22.7	27.7	70.1	63.6	66.0	51.8	40.9	38.3
	1940–45	21.6	21.5	23.8	51.5	50.5	51.8	29.9	29.0	28.0
UK	1915–19	15.2	17.7	18.2	66.1	67.5	67.8	50.9	49.8	49.6
	1940–45	16.0	17.7	19.4	52.1	52.1	53.2	36.1	34.4	33.8

Notes: Educational attainment: 1 = Primary education, 2 = Secondary education, 3 = Tertiary education.

Source: European Community Household Panel.

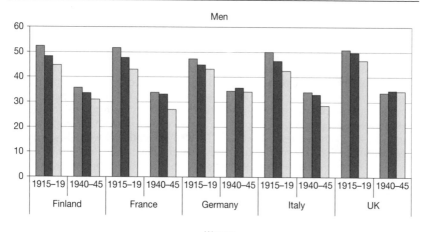

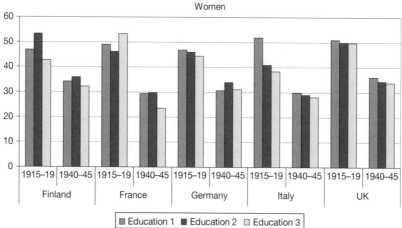

■ Education 1 ■ Education 2 □ Education 3

Figure 7.7. Duration of labour market attachment by country, birth cohort, and educational attainment

Notes: Educational attainment: 1 = Primary education, 2 = Secondary education, 3 = Tertiary education.

Source: European Community Household Panel.

Figure 7.8 shows the population size and labour force participation by age for both genders in Norway in 1801 and 2001.[2] Whereas in 2001 labour force participation is absent from age category 71–5 onwards, in 1801 the

[2] Labour force participation rates for the 1801 census (which encompassed the whole Norwegian population) is calculated by categorizing the following groups belonging to the labour force: farm-workers, fishermen, seamen, craftsmen, soldiers, public officials, clergy, day-workers, medical workers, and traders. Individuals registered as pensioners, retired farm-workers, those workers who are partially or fully unable to fully sustain themselves and are dependent on an allowance are not considered to be part of the labour force.

BOX 7.1 LUMP OF LABOUR FALLACY

The lump of labour fallacy relies on the assumption that the amount of work in a labour market is fixed and can be redistributed across workers without any costs. Historically, the term originated to rebut the idea that reducing the number of hours workers are allowed to work in a work day would in turn reduce unemployment.[1] Another famous example is the discussion in 1950s about the effects of automation, which it was believed would lead to mass unemployment. As the derisive name suggests, it's an idea economists view with contempt, yet the fallacy makes a comeback whenever the economy is sluggish. In the recent past, the assumption of a 'lump of labour' has been used to advocate that older workers should retire earlier, making room for young unemployed workers to enter employment. To illustrate the basis of the fallacy we assume a labour market with homogeneous labour, decreasing marginal labour productivity, a standard Cobb-Douglas production technology, product price equal to 1, and firms maximizing profits. Then, the quantity produced equals:

$$y = Ak^{1-\alpha}l^{\alpha} \tag{7.1}$$

where k is the amount of capital used, l the amount of labour and A and α are parameters of the production function. Firms maximize profits $\pi = y - wl - rk$, where w represents the wage and r the capital costs. From this maximization follows labour demand:

$$l^d = (w/\alpha A)^{1-\alpha}k \tag{7.2}$$

If capital and labour supply i are exogenously fixed, wages are endogenously determined ($w = w^*$) and the labour market clears, there is no unemployment. Unemployment may arise from the existence of a minimum wage $w_{min} > w^*$; then the unemployment rate equals:

$$u = (l^s/l^d)/l^s = 1 - (w_{min}/\alpha A)^{1-\alpha}k/l^s \tag{7.3}$$

In this model, it is clear that an exogenous reduction in the labour supply—such as early retirement for older workers—would reduce the unemployment rate, bringing young unemployed workers into work. In the simple model, the lump of labour fallacy is based on the assumption of exogenous capital. If capital is endogenous, the demand for capital is determined in a similar way to the demand for labour:

$$k^d = \left(r/\left((1-\alpha)A\right)\right)^{\alpha}l \tag{7.4}$$

Then, labour and capital demand are jointly determined. If capital supply depends on the size of labour supply, $k^s = \mathcal{P}\,\kappa(r^*)$, where $\kappa(r^*)$ is the savings rate at the equilibrium capital price, then equation (7.3) can be rewritten as:

$$u = (l^s - l^d)/l^s = 1 - (w_{min}/\alpha A)^{1-\alpha}\kappa(r*) \tag{7.5}$$

From equation (7.5), it is clear that the unemployment rate no longer depends on labour supply. If labour supply is reduced, initially unemployment may go down, but because of the smaller labour force, savings are reduced, and therefore capital use is reduced as well, and in the end the unemployment rate is unchanged.

[1] Lührmann and Weiss (2007) show that longer working hours may actually reduce unemployment.

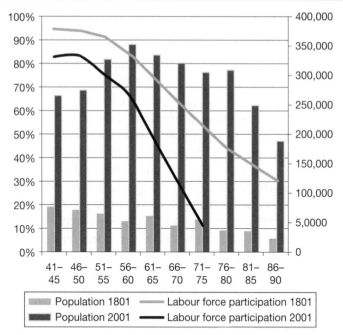

Figure 7.8. Labour force participation rates and population size, Norway, 1801 and 2001, ages 41–90, both genders

Source: Bull (2006), Digitalarkivet (2007), and Statistics Norway (2007).

labour force participation rate was as high as 40% for individuals aged 71–5. Of course, this high labour force participation by older workers had to do with the absence of labour market institutions such as old-age pensions. Nevertheless, the structural changes in the labour market over past decades, particularly the shift from physical to cognitive skills required, could have been accompanied by a strengthening of old-age labour market attachment. Even if speed, flexibility, and the ability to learn weakens with age, this does not imply that one becomes unable to work, as was the case where work involved tough physical demands, and the weakening of attachment to the workforce on the part of older workers is unnecessary.

So, whereas over many decades the working life of individuals was reduced due to the reduction in the retirement age, in the near future a reversal of this trend is necessary from a demographic point of view. An important element of the discussion on this is the perceived relationship between age and productivity. At the level of the individual worker, ageing is assumed to affect productivity. Older workers are thought to be

147

more reliable, to have fewer workplace accidents, to be less likely to quit, and to have more experience than younger workers. These factors cause a positive correlation between age and productivity. However, older workers are also thought to have more absences from work, to have lower flexibility in accepting new assignments, and to be less suitable for training. These factors cause a negative correlation between age and productivity. As a stylized fact, individual labour productivity is assumed to decline after some age between 40 and 50. However, such a concave relationship between age and productivity is not a well-established fact. It is possible that future technological and organizational changes will affect the relationship between age and productivity. Knowledge about the relationship between age and productivity is also extremely important because the current policy in most, if not all, EU countries is to try to increase labour force participation by elderly workers. This will be easier if productivity does not strongly decline with age. Hence the focus of our report.

Our report contributes to the body of knowledge on the relationship between age and productivity. It is set up as follows. Chapter 8 presents the 'grand view', that is, the general framework to understand the relationship between age and productivity. Productivity is complex and multidimensional, with physical strength, experience, and cognitive abilities being important elements. While experience increases and physical strength reduces with age, the relationship between cognitive abilities and age is less clear. There are different types of cognitive abilities. Crystallized abilities such as verbal abilities are independent of age or even increase with age. Fluid cognitive abilities—speed and memory—tend to deteriorate with age. Apart from age effect, cohort effects matter too. Younger cohorts of individuals on average have better health and better mental performance. Furthermore, the nature of labour demand is changing. In new jobs, physical strength is important. Chapter 9 to 11 present empirical analyses based on Finnish and German data. Chapter 9 deals with an empirical analysis of the relationship between age and absenteeism, the extensive margin of productivity. The analysis shows that absenteeism increases with age. Older workers are less likely to be absent, but once they are absent, they take more time off. Age diversity at the team level tends to increase individual absence rates. Chapter 10 presents an analysis of working capacity, a subjective measure of productivity. Age turns out to have a negative effect on working capacity, but the fall over the life cycle is not dramatic. Chapter 11 deals with the intensive margin of productivity, productivity at the team level and at the plant level. The results on the team-level analysis are that age has a negative effect on productivity, but tenure has a positive effect of about the same magnitude. The empirical analysis at the plant level does not show that there is a robust connection between age and productivity. Age diversity at the team level has a negative effect on productivity. Chapter 12 concludes and discusses policy implications.

8

The Grand View on Age and Productivity

8.1 Introduction

In 1842, Belgian researcher Adolphe Quetelet published what is possibly the very first curve describing the relationship between age and various measures of productivity. Quetelet suggested that individuals write the best literary work in their late twenties to late forties, while criminal activity is most intense between ages 20 and 25 (see Figure 8.1).

Perhaps the most interesting part of his work is Quetelet's argument that abilities are not necessarily constant. He argues that *strength increases at all ages for every subsequent generation* (also in Figure 8.1). The point that the age-productivity relation is not fixed but likely to change over time has seldom been taken into account by subsequent research; also recent studies have tended to neglect this dimension.

We investigate the shape and peak of the relationship between age and productivity and under what circumstances specific age-productivity profiles exist. We start by reviewing the main approaches used to estimate productivity by age: supervisors' evaluations, measuring the quantity and quality produced, analyses of large-scale employer-employee data sets, and studies of age-earnings structures. Thereafter, we discuss potential causes of job performance variation by age, and how changes in abilities and health by age and variations in workplace requirements are likely to alter age-variation in productivity over time.

8.2 Age-Variation in Productivity

Investigations into productivity differences by age are frequently based on managers' ratings of employees in a firm. On average, these ratings indicate

150

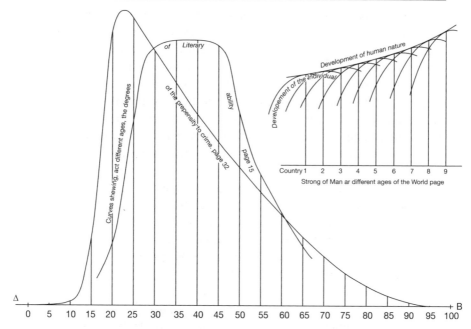

Figure 8.1. Quetelet's (1842) age variations in literary and criminal productivity

a relatively flat relation between age and productivity (McEvoy and Cascio, 1989; Warr, 1994), though variation is high. These estimates may, however, be biased if managers' hold discriminatory views of older or younger workers. Moreover, employers may inflate their evaluation of older workers as a reward for past achievement or for being loyal to the firm (Levy, 2003; Salthouse and Maurer, 1996).

Directly measuring the quantity and quality of work produced can be done for production processes where an individual's work effort is readily observable, such as in piece-rate work. Several studies identify decreased productivity from around 50 years of age (Kutscher and Walker, 1960; US Department of Labor, 1957). The proportion of the population working in piece-rate or assembly-line work is, however, small and declining, which can make findings from this approach less representative for the average worker. Moreover, the limited time available to investigate the workers could skew the age-performance estimates (as some groups of individuals may be able to maintain a high rate of production only for the short duration they are observed and may on average have lower productivity).

A third approach is to estimate individual productivity from employer-employee data sets (e.g. Gelderblom, 2006; Hægeland and Klette, 1998; for an overview see Skirbekk, 2004), which tend to find a hump-shaped relationship between job performance and age. A key strength of these estimates is the large samples that can encompass almost all workers in certain industries; several of the samples that have been used include millions of individuals and thousands of firms. However, bias may come from the fact that many important determinants of the firm's value-added, such as a firm's capital levels, are either omitted or poorly measured. Moreover, a young age structure may be the result of, rather than the reason for, a firm's success—firms that go well tend to hire more, and new employees are often young.

Earnings are sometimes used to study age-variation in productivity. However, wages are often determined by factors other than individual contribution to the firm's value-added, including the role of unions, uncertainty about new workers' productivity, and delayed payment contracts where performance while being young results in higher earnings for those still employed while they are older (Agell and Lundborg, 1995; Freeman, 1992; Harris and Holmstrom, 1982; Hutchens, 1989).

Age-earnings profiles can, however, provide information on productivity profiles in situations where wages reflect actual productivity. Lazear and Moore (1984) find that the self-employed tend to have little wage variation over the life cycle, while salary workers have increasing wages throughout their career. This suggests that productivity remains constant during the working life—and the higher wages of older salary workers are due to seniority-based earnings systems rather than to higher productivity. A study by Boot (1995) describes age-earnings profiles for British cotton workers in the first half of the 19th century, where there were few regulations in the labour market. For the physically demanding work analysed, men reached their peak earnings in their early thirties, and wages decreased substantially from around 40 years of age.

Burnette (2006) investigates wage differentials between male and female agricultural and factory workers during the 19th century in Britain. She finds that male and female wages were more similar in the years after labour market entrance (which at the time often took place before the early teens). However, at later ages, as gender differences in physical strength and stamina become evident, the male wage advantage emerged. Boot's (1995) study of Lancashire cotton workers identifies similar sex differences in age-earnings profiles, which are almost identical for the first years in the workforce until early adulthood—where men earn more.

8.3 Determinants of Performance Differences by Age and Occupation

All the approaches to measuring age-variation in productivity discussed in the previous section are subject to various problems that can lead to bias and decrease the generalizability of the findings. Moreover, most of these studies do not address why productivity should vary or be constant by age. Investigating causes of productivity variation can allow a better understanding of how age relates to work performance. Identifying which causal factors determine productivity and the relative importance of these causes under various settings could help reveal how the age-productivity curve differs over time and across work tasks.

Individual productivity is complex and multidimensional. It relates to a number of characteristics of the individual and the work environment (illustrated in Figure 8.2). Several characteristics that relate to productivity differ by age groups, including communication skills, information-processing speed, strength and endurance, health, self-discipline, flexibility, administrative and strategic capacities, mathematical proficiency, vocabulary size, education, motivation, energy, and job experience.

The variation in the type of skill required in the workplace is likely to cause differences in the age-productivity pattern across occupations. Skirbekk (2008) presents productivity variation by age based on age-variation

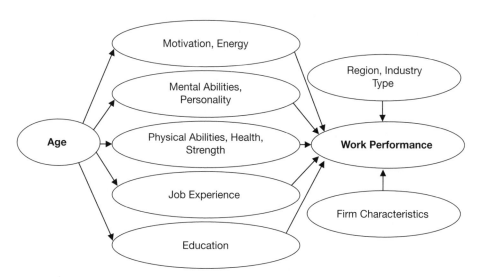

Figure 8.2. Some causes of age-variation in productivity

in ability levels. Figure 8.3(a) presents age-variation in mathematical skills, ability to discriminate between visual stimuli, leadership skills, hand movement, and body coordination from a US Department of Labor survey. The estimated effect of experience is based on surveys indicating that up to ten years of experience is associated with productivity gains (Figure 8.3(a)). Figure 8.3(b) indicates the importance of various abilities in the labour market—which determines their relative influence on productivity.

Based on these assumptions, work performance follows an inverse-U-shaped pattern, where the peak is around ages 35–44 where the gains from experience outweigh the impact of deteriorating cognitive and physical abilities (see Figure 8.4(a)). The shape of the curve differs over time and between jobs due to changes in the labour market importance of the abilities. If skill demand only values management and experience skills, the productivity variation may be similar to the solid line in Figure 8.4(b), while the dashed line reflects differences in job performance if only numerical and analytical skills matter.

Lehman (1953) describes achievements by age for scientists and artists. He finds that performance peaks at ages 30–9, with output 40–70% higher than at ages 50–9 in a variety of disciplines, including mathematics, chemistry, medicine, genetics, entomology, psychology, and physics. In some cases, longevity is controlled for by only considering those who survived to older ages, and this does slightly increase estimated output among older individuals, but does not alter the general shape of the curve. When quality of output is not controlled for (peer review, quality of journal), the age-productivity profile is more flat, suggesting quality diminishes, but

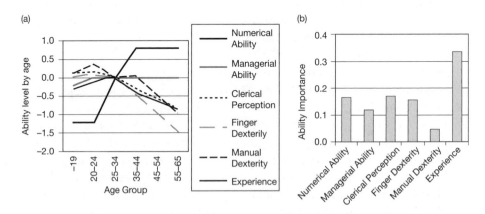

Figure 8.3. Age variation in abilities and their labour market importance
Source: Skirbekk (2007).

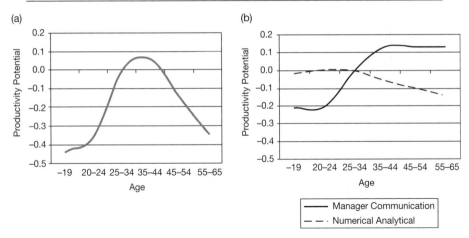

Figure 8.4. Productivity variation over the life cycle
Source: Skirbekk (2007).

quantity decreases less. A young peak in the age-performance curve in the sciences is also found by Stephan and Levin (1988) and Bratsberg *et al.* (2003).

For professions where communication skills, social network, and management capabilities are important, top positions tend to be held by more senior individuals (Lehman, 1953). Political leaders, supreme-court judges, university directors, heads of trusts, and those with the highest incomes tend to be in their late fifties or older. The modal age of religious leaders, including the pope and heads of American churches, is above 70 years— contrasting the age patterns for founders of religions, who tend to be in their thirties.

Time stress may be another area where young age could be an advantage. Welford (1958) finds that in professions with strong time requirements, most workers are relatively young (20–45 years), while in professions not involving time stress the age distribution of workers is more flat.

Miller (1999) analyses writers, painters, and musicians, finding that the peak ages for these types of creative output tend to be in the thirties and forties. However, female authors are found to be slightly more productive in their fifties than at earlier ages. On the other hand, Lehman (1953) finds that when quality is adjusted for, the peak productivity for female writers is at ages 30–9.

Some areas of cognitive change over the life cycle are similar among men and women, while it is different for other areas. Longitudinal data from Maitland *et al.* (2000) suggest that gender differences do exist—women always outperform men on *verbal recall* and *perceptual speed* in the younger and middle-age group, whereas men consistently outperformed women on *spatial orientation*.

8.4 Changes in Job Performance over Time

An individual's productivity level can depend on his or her characteristics (such as education, age, motivation, and skills). However, the individual's marginal contribution to the firm's value-added is also determined by how important various individual skills are in the work process, how the work is organized, and how the individual interacts with other workers, and firm-level factors such as technology and capital levels, all of which are factors that change over time.

Technological development and increased global trade lead to changes in the demand for skills. For European countries, where labour costs are generally high, labour-intensive production of goods and services has increasingly shifted to other world regions. Moreover, new technologies and new working techniques imply a decreased need for manual labour and an increase in the demand for highly skilled workers. In effect, strength requirements tend to decrease over time, while the need to learn new skills increases (Acemoglu 2002).

Long-term employment shifts between industries and changes to the relative wage levels of unskilled and skilled employees reveal that physical strength and bodily co-ordination have become less important in the workplace, while cognitive abilities, in particular analytic, numerical, and communication skills are increasingly important (Howell and Wolff, 1991; Juhn *et al.*, 1993; Phelps Brown and Hopkins, 1955; Spitz, 2004). The productivity of older workers relative to the young increases only insofar as the lower relevance of physical strength is not replaced by increasing requirements for cognitive abilities that decline more over the life cycle.

Increasing emphasis is likely to be put on the ability to acquire new knowledge as the workplace is rapidly changing. This may adversely affect the relative productivity of senior employees, as many studies have shown that the ability to remember and learn new skills decreases with age (Smith, 1996). In industries where there is rapid change in skill and knowledge requirements, and where technological shocks make acquired competencies obsolete, early retirement is common and the productivity peak is found to be early in the working life (Ahituv and Zeira, 2000; Bartel and Sicherman, 1993; Dalton and Thompson, 1971).

Job experience is an important determinant of productivity that can be related to higher productivity of senior employees. Studies show that more experienced employees use more efficient working strategies (De la Mare and Shepherd, 1958; Salthouse, 1984). However, at some point it also acknowledged that additional experience no longer improves job performance in most professions, meaning that the marginal productivity is zero. Ericsson and Lehmann (1996) argue that it takes roughly ten years to achieve expert competence where strategic and analytic competence is important, which is supported by findings from a variety of job domains, ranging from livestock evaluation and x-ray analysis to scientific performance in the medical and natural sciences (Phelps and Shanteau, 1978; Lesgold, 1984; Raskin, 1936).

If the way work tasks are carried out remains constant, accumulated experience continues to benefit employees' performance throughout the working life. If new working techniques and new technologies are introduced, acquired experience could become less relevant, while the need to learn something new becomes more relevant. Some cognitive abilities increase to a relatively late age or remain stable throughout the working life, such as vocabulary size and verbal abilities. These cognitive abilities are often termed *crystallized abilities*. Other cognitive abilities that are termed fluid abilities—such as speed and memory—deteriorate strongly with age (Cattel, 1963; Horn and Cattell, 1963).

Variations in the importance of different abilities in the labour market (depending on job) can lead to very different age-productivity patterns. Figure 8.5(a) illustrates a setting where high importance is given to fluid abilities (which decline strongly by age). If crystallized abilities and experience are of lesser relative importance, this leads to a relatively young peak in job performance, as shown in Figure 8.5(b). A low importance accorded to acquired experience and a high demand for the ability to acquire new knowledge can be the case in occupations where the rate of technological change is high.

Figure 8.5(c) gives an example of an occupation where accumulated experience is the most important trait, while fluid abilities and crystallized abilities are less important. This means that productivity remains high towards the end of the working life, as shown in Figure 8.5(d). The productivity peak late in the working life can be representative of situations where accumulated experience remains relevant throughout one's career—which may be the case for industries with low rates of technological change or for historical periods. Older workers' productivity will decline only insofar as

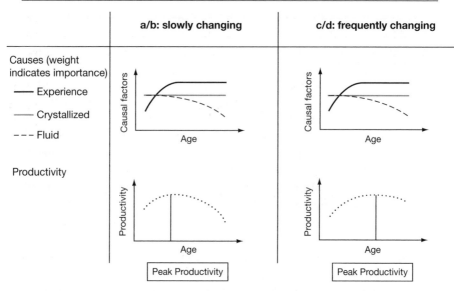

Figure 8.5. Productivity, slowly and frequently changing job tasks

the cognitive and non-cognitive traits that deteriorate are relevant for the type of work task performed.

We analysed age-variation in four cognitive ability types—memory, verbal fluency, numeracy, recall—using the SHARE survey, which describes variation in cognitive abilities over the life course (Börsch-Supan and Jürges, 2005). The data come from European countries that are grouped into three regional groups: northern (Denmark, Sweden), continental (Austria, France, Germany, Netherlands, Switzerland), southern (Greece, Italy, Spain). For reasons of comparison, we normalized the cognitive abilities of people aged 50–4 to be equal to 100. Figure 8.6(a) shows that after age 55 cognitive abilities decrease faster for males than for females, while after age 60 the decline is stronger for females. Figure 8.6(b) suggests that the decline of cognitive abilities with age is strongest in southern countries and weakest in northern countries.

Figure 8.7 shows evidence from cognitive tests from the US (Park et al., 2002) showing the very different paths age-variation in cognitive skills tends to have—where verbal knowledge increases, while other cognitive abilities decrease over the life cycle. Age-related declines have been documented both using longitudinal studies (Deary et al., 2000) and in earlier cross-sectional studies (Welford, 1958).

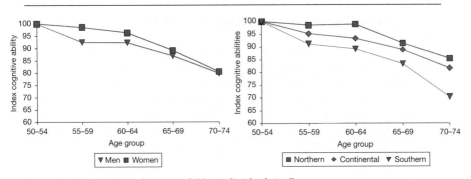

Figure 8.6. Cognitive changes of 50+ individuals in Europe

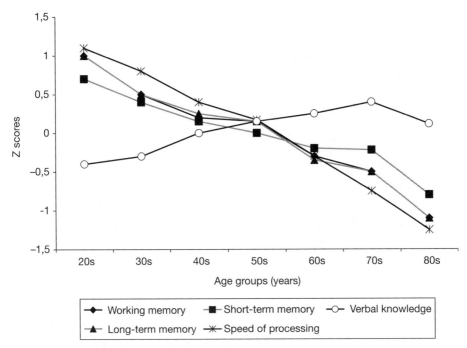

Figure 8.7. Age variation in various cognitive skills
Source: Park *et al.* (2002).

The relation between age and cognitive functioning is, however, not constant over time. Recent evidence put forward by Romeu Gordo (2005) uses the Health and Retirement Survey data set and finds that every subsequent cohort tends to have a higher cognitive performance at ages 50–9, 60–9, and 70–9. With better mental performance, which is a key determinant of labour market success, older individuals will increasingly maintain productivity until later ages.

Education is closely correlated with labour market participation and performance, and increasing school levels can lead to increased cognitive capacities and work productivity among senior individuals. Education levels have risen rapidly for the elderly population in Europe over recent decades. From 1970–2000, the education of the average man aged 50–64 years increased in Italy from 4.2 to 8.2 years, while in France it increased from 4.8 to 8.4 years, and in Sweden it increased from 5.1 to 10 years, according to data on age-specific education levels (Lutz *et al.*, 2007). Improvements in educational levels are likely to be one of the key causes why cognitive abilities (typically measured by IQ tests for young males in military selection) have improved over time (Flynn, 1987; Neisser, 1997).

Physical strength and health are also closely related to work performance and decline over the life cycle. Average muscle strength decreases by roughly 10% per decade for ages 20–60, decreases by approximately 15% each decade for ages 60–80, and 30% each decade after age 80. Maximum oxygen uptake also decreases, which could decrease endurance and work capacity. De Zwart *et al.* (1995) find that aerobic capacity peaks in the twenties, and declines by around 1% per year thereafter. Moreover, flexibility reduces as one grows older, which makes it difficult to adopt several working positions at older ages (Bosek *et al.*, 2005).

Costa (2000) finds a decrease of chronic disease rates by 66% from the early 1900s to the 1970s and 1980s among men aged 50–74, and Romeu Gordo (2005) identifies a continued decrease in disability levels throughout the 1990s. Costa argues that 29% of the observed decline in chronic disease rates in the 20th century was caused by a shift to non-manual work and a reduction in the physical load, and that this shift was responsible for 75% of the decline in back problems. Using data on cohorts born in 1924–47 from the Health and Retirement Survey, Romeu Gordo (2005) shows that the number of age-specific disabilities roughly halved for the more recent cohorts during the 1990s and beyond. During the 20th century, US male life expectancy increased by 61% from 46 to 74 years (CDC, 2006). This suggests that the increase in life expectancy did in fact lead to longer healthier lives.

Over time, health levels have improved at adult and older ages. Longevity has increased during the last two centuries, and currently in industrialized countries, life expectancy increases by roughly 1.5 years per decade (Oeppen and Vaupel, 2002; UN, 2005). Most studies into age-specific disability trends find that the decrease in mortality rates is mainly reflected in longer healthy lives (Crimmins *et al.*, 1997; Manton *et al.*, 1997; Lee, 2003; Romeu Gordo, 2005; Schoeni *et al.*, 2001).

While age-specific health levels improve, health requirements in the workplace reduced due to new technologies and more efficient organization of work are likely to create a strong positive effect on the elderly's work potential. Individuals with reduced mobility, even those dependent on wheelchairs, are decreasingly disadvantaged in the workplace as computer work and reduced physical requirements makes it possible to work with disadvantages that in earlier times forced individuals to exit the workplace.

In addition to reduced physical demands in the workplace, there has also been a reduction in the length of the working day. A reduced number of working hours implies longer time to recover from a hard day's workload. Ausubel and Grubler (1995) find that in France, Germany, the UK, USA, and Japan, the number of hours worked per year declined by at least a third from 1850 to 1987. This is likely to imply a substantial reduction in work-related health and strength requirements, and a further increase in the productivity potential of the elderly population.

8.5 Conclusions on the Grand View

It is not easy to establish the relationship between age and productivity for at least two reasons. First, individual productivity is complex and multidimensional. Second, the relationship between age and productivity is not fixed but is changing over time.

Individual productivity relates to a number of characteristics of the individual and the work environment. Individual characteristics such as experience, motivation, mental abilities, and physical abilities differ between age groups. Accumulated experience benefits employees' performance throughout the working life. However, physical strength and health are reduced over the life cycle. The net effect of the age-specific productivity determinants depends on how individual skills are used in the work process, how the work is organized, and how the individual interacts with other workers and firm-level factors such as technology and capital levels. The variation in the type of skill required in the workplace is likely to cause differences in the age-productivity pattern across occupations.

A further complication in assessing the importance of the age effect on productivity is the change over time in the relationship between age and productivity. This is due to both changes in the demand for skills and changes in individual characteristics across generations. New technologies and new working techniques imply a decreased need for manual labour and an increase in the demand for highly skilled workers. Physical strength and bodily co-ordination have become less important in the workplace, while cognitive abilities, in particular analytic, numerical, and communication skills are increasingly important. With better mental performance, which is a key determinant of labour market success, older individuals will increasingly maintain productivity until later ages. Over time, health levels have improved at adult and older ages. Improved age-specific mental and physical health levels are likely to create a strong positive effect on the elderly's work potential.

9

Age and Absenteeism

9.1 Introduction

As discussed in the introductory chapter, as the large cohort of baby-boomers becomes older, the age composition of workers changes dramatically. For example in Germany, by 2010, the largest age group in the workforce will be the 50-year olds (and by 2020, the 58-year olds). Similar numbers apply to other developed countries. With this evolution in mind, it is important to have a better understanding of the relationship between workers' age and their productivity. Sick leave is an important detriment to productivity: after all, when a person is absent from work, his productivity on that particular day is zero. Absences can potentially lead to a substantial loss of actual working time and thereby impose substantial costs on both firms and co-workers, because they often require reorganization of work. Therefore, a better understanding of the relationship between age and sick leave is essential.

The literature on absenteeism consists of two strands: one is concerned with the effects of individual characteristics of workers (gender, age, wage, education, health status, marital status, number of children) on their absenteeism.[1] The other strand considers the role of the work environment (work conditions and risks, control mechanisms, firm size, contracts) and the incentives that workers face (e.g. sick-pay arrangements, variations in absenteeism in different phases of the business cycle).[2] What has—to the best of our knowledge—not been studied yet is the link between team

---

[1] Economists, as well as psychologists, have contributed to this literature strand. See e.g. Hedges (1973), Leigh (1983), Paringer (1983), Eyal *et al.* (1994), Bridges and Mumford (2001), Flabbi and Ichino (2001), Ichino and Moretti (2006), and the surveys by Steers and Rhodes (1978) and Brown and Sessions (1996).

[2] This literature strand consists of several economics papers; see e.g. Allen (1981b, 1981a), Leigh (1981), Barmby *et al.* (1991, 1995, 2002), Askildsen *et al.* (2000), Henrekson and Persson

composition and absenteeism. There is a literature in psychology that finds a negative relation between workers' job satisfaction and their absenteeism (see e.g. Steers and Rhodes, 1978; Farrell and Stamm, 1988; Scott and Taylor, 1985; and Kohler and Mathieu, 1993). Other studies, in turn, found that job satisfaction is affected by team-mates' characteristics (Spector, 1997).[3]

In this chapter, we explore absenteeism using two different kinds of data. One is a unique data set of workers in a German truck assembly plant where we can identify workers who work together in a team on a daily basis. Thus, we are able to relate the probability of absence of a worker to characteristics of the work team. Characteristics of the work team in this study include team size, and measures of diversity with respect to age, nationality, education, and age. The second data set is a Finnish survey based on a representative sample of persons in paid employment. Besides working conditions, personal characteristics, and work experience, it includes information on the number and duration of absences.

It should be noted at this point that—even though 'sickness' is reported as the reason for absence in both of the data sets—other factors like motivation and pressure certainly have an effect (see Steers and Rhodes, 1978). The 'decision' to call in sick is the result of a process that is influenced by all three factors: health, motivation, and pressure/control. If motivation and pressure/control are weak, 'less sickness is needed' to actually call in sick. In addition, motivation (job satisfaction, etc.) and pressure can affect workers' health and thereby indirectly affect absenteeism.

9.2 Age and Sick Leaves in Work Teams

9.2.1 Assembly Line Data

We make use of a unique data set from an assembly plant of a German car manufacturer.[4] At this plant, work teams assemble cars on a production line. The assembly line is split into 50 workplaces at which teams of 10 to 15 workers work together. We have information on the daily composition

---

(2004), Ichino and Riphahn (2004, 2005), and Andrén (2005). There is also an extensive literature in the field of occupational health; see e.g. Vahtera *et al.* (2001).

[3] Mathieu and Kohler (1990), Harrison and Shaffer (1994), and Martocchio (1994) study the role of a person's co-workers' absenteeism in her own absence behaviour and find a positive relationship.

[4] This chapter reports the first results from a study that is described in more detail in Weiss (2007b). For details on the data set, see Appendix III.

of these work teams on any workday in 2003 through 2004 and on the personal characteristics of the workers such as age, gender, education, nationality, and job tenure. In addition, the data contain information about whether or not a worker is in her regular team. A detailed description of the data can be found in Appendix III.

Absence Rates The average rate of absence due to sickness is 5.5%.[5] There is variation over time and across workers as can be seen from Figure 9.1. The daily absence rate is defined as the percentage of workers on a given day who are absent due to sickness. The distribution of the daily absence rate is given in the left-hand panel of Figure 9.1. The individual absence rate is defined as the percentage of days on which an individual has been absent. The distribution of individual absence rates is given in the right-hand panel of Figure 9.1. Absence rates also vary quite substantially across age groups. On average, absence due to sickness increases with age (see the left-hand panel of Figure 9.2). The next section will reveal whether this relation still holds in a multivariate setting. The right-hand panel of Figure 9.2 shows that absence rates also vary substantially within age groups[6].

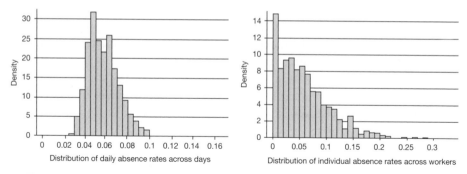

Figure 9.1. Distribution of absence rates due to sickness

[5] In the remainder of the chapter, we refer to absence due to sickness whenever we use the terms 'absence', 'sick leave', or 'sick days'.

[6] According to German labour law, employees have a right to continue to receive full pay at the beginning of a spell of sickness absence. If the employment relationship has lasted for more than a month, there is full pay for the first six weeks of the spell of sickness. After the continuation of payment ceases, the employee receives income-related sick-pay compensation from statutory sickness insurance. This compensation amounts to 70% of gross salary. The replacement rate in terms of net earnings is around 75%. Sick-pay lasts for at most 78 weeks for one and the same sickness. In principle, employees have to show a doctor's certificate in the case of sickness that lasts for more than three days. But in many firms, this rule is implemented rather laxly in the case of short absences.

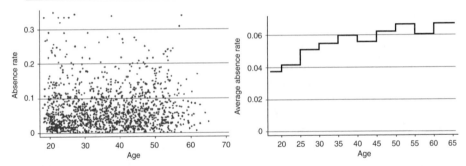

Figure 9.2. Individual absence rates vs. individual age and average absence rates due to sickness by age group

9.2.2 Results with the Assembly Line Data

We use day-to-day variations across 2,271 workers during 2003 and 2004 (429 work days) to estimate the effects of individual and team characteristics on absence due to sickness using a logit specification. Appendix III contains additional information on some of the variables. The results are reported in Table 9.1.

Age Absenteeism increases with age up to the age group of 35–40 years only. For some older age groups, absenteeism is even lower. More interestingly, age diversity in the work team also increases the probability of calling in sick. This result calls into question the currently ubiquitous call for age-diverse teams. An explanation for this result might be that age diversity impedes communication and leads to lower group cohesiveness. This in turn can affect the motivation to show up at work.

Job Tenure The effect of job tenure is less clear. There is no monotonic relation and the results are not very robust. This may reflect counteracting effects: longer tenure is usually associated with stronger identification with the employer, more responsibility (see Baumgartel and Sobol, 1959), and more interesting tasks (see Nicholson *et al.*, 1977). These factors should reduce absenteeism. On the other hand, longer job tenure also often implies better job security and—maybe—more boredom/less enthusiasm. These factors would lead to more absenteeism. The combination of these positive and negative effects may lead to mixed results overall. Diversity with respect to job tenure clearly reduces absenteeism. Diversity with respect to job tenure facilitates the assignment of tasks and roles within a team so that

Table 9.1. Regression results

Dependent variable: absence due to sickness (dummy, logit specification)

Age groups				Job tenure groups			
20–25 years	0.027		(0.021)	5–10 years	0.034	***	(0.0079)
25–30 years	0.090	***	(0.021)	10–15 years	−0.017	*	(0.0101)
30–35 years	0.087	***	(0.021)	15–20 years	0.079	***	(0.0110)
35–40 years	0.121	***	(0.021)	20–25 years	−0.009		(0.0121)
40–45 years	0.089	***	(0.022)	25–30 years	0.003		(0.0135)
45–50 years	0.141	***	(0.022)	30–35 years	0.065	***	(0.0149)
50–55 years	0.155	***	(0.023)	35–40 years	0.153	***	(0.0275)
55–60 years	0.098	***	(0.026)				
60–65 years	0.108	***	(0.033)				
Age diversity	0.110	***	(0.023)	Tenure diversity	−0.312	***	(0.0193)
Years of schooling							
11–12 years	0.0041		(0.0066)	Female	0.066	***	(0.015)
13–14 years	−0.0276	***	(0.0075)	Female share	−0.689	***	(0.049)
15–20 years	−0.0004		(0.0102)	External	−0.56	***	(0.015)
Sch. diversity	−0.298	***	(0.0294)	External share	0.98	***	(0.030)
Team size	−0.0433	***	(0.0030)	Diversity w.r.t nat'lity	0.024		(0.020)
(team size)^2	0.0020	***	(0.0001)				
pseudo R^2	0.019						

Notes: No. of observations: 370,942, unbalanced panel of 1,898 workers in 100 teams on 429 days.
Reference category for age groups: 15–20 years, reference category for job tenure: 0–5 years, reference category for schooling years: 9–10 years. Standard errors in parentheses.

conflicts and rivalry are avoided. This conflict-alleviating effect may lead to lower absenteeism.

Education The effect of years of schooling on absence is U-shaped. Absenteeism is lowest among workers with 13 to 14 years of schooling. These are usually workers with a medium school degree and vocational training. As most tasks at the assembly line do not require higher education, better skilled workers may well be overqualified, which reduces job satisfaction. Job satisfaction has been found to be an important factor in absenteeism (Steers and Rhodes, 1978). Workers with lower education may be assigned less responsible or less interesting tasks, so that their job satisfaction also suffers. Diversity with respect to education leads to lower absenteeism. The reason for this effect may be similar to the one for diversity with respect to job tenure.

Gender Women are more likely to be sick. In contrast, a higher female share in work teams enhances attendance of team members. This is interesting because the absence-reducing external effect of a higher female share neutralizes (even slightly overcompensates) the effect that women themselves are absent more often.

External Workers Each worker is assigned to one team as her 'regular' team. But—due to fluctuations in team composition as a result of sick leave or vacation or fluctuations in workload—workers work outside their regular team 6% of the time on average. Being external to the team reduces the probability of sick leave. However, the share of externals in the team increases sick days.

Nationality Workers' nationality has no significant effect on sick leave (not reported in the table). Diversity with respect to nationality does not have a significant effect either.

Team Size Team size has a U-shaped effect on absence. The optimal team size is 11 workers. This result has also been found in other studies and is related to lower group cohesiveness, higher task specialization, and poorer communication in larger teams (Indik, 1965; Porter and Lawler, 1965). If teams are too small, personal conflicts may be more severe.

9.3 Age and Absenteeism in a Representative Survey of Employees

9.3.1 *Quality of Working Life Survey*

We use the Finnish Quality of Working Life Survey (QWLS) from 2003. This is a representative sample of employed individuals. The main emphasis in the survey is on the respondents' subjective views with respect to their working conditions, as well as perceived job satisfaction. Besides working conditions, QWLS includes information on the respondents' personal characteristics and work experience. The data source is explained in more detail in Appendix III.

Sickness absences are documented in the QWLS with four questions that relate to absences within the last 12 months: (1) the number of absences that have lasted 1–3 days; (2) the number of absences that have lasted 4–9 days; (3) the number of absences that have lasted at least 10 days; and (4) the annual number of days in absences that have lasted at least 10 days. Based on these questions, we can form alternative indicators of absenteeism. One is the incidence of absence, that is, whether the individual has had any absences. The second is the total number of cases of absenteeism a person has had. The third is the total number of days absent from work. We approximate this as (number of absences of 1–3 days)*2 + (number of absences of 4–9 days)*6.5 + number of days in absences of at least 10 days. This can be calculated for all individuals or alternatively for only those who have had absences, that is, for whom the number of days is not zero. Fourth, we can measure the duration of a typical absence as the ratio of total number of days absent divided by the total number of cases of absenteeism. This is calculated for those individuals who have actually been absent from work at least once.

Sickness absences are self-reported, but there is no particular reason to believe that employees give systematically biased answers to this particular question, because the employers do not know their identity. A major advantage of information recorded in the QWLS data set is that it also covers short sickness absences that are not recorded by the Social Insurance Institution which pays out sickness benefits to the affected employees. Short sickness absences do not entitle employees to payment of sickness benefits, but they obtain normal pay from the employer.[7] Including all spells is important, because most sickness absences are short. On the other hand, for longer absences, the respondents have a tendency to give the number of days rounded to figures like 40, 50, and so on, which are easier to choose if the actual number cannot be recalled. This may slightly bias the results on the duration of absences.

Figure 9.3 shows the distribution of the number of absences. This is very skewed, with a high share of individuals with zero absences. Figure 9.4 shows the connection between age and absenteeism, with age groups defined as five-year intervals, expect for the lowest (which is 18–20) and the highest (which is 61–4). The upper right-hand panel presents the share of individuals who have had at least one absence by age group. The share is

---

[7] According to Finnish labour law, employees have a right to full pay at the beginning of a spell of sickness absence. If the employment relationship has lasted over a month, there is full pay for the day the sickness started and for nine following working days. When the employment relationship is shorter, the employee receives 50% of pay. After the period with pay, the employee receives income-related compensation from statutory sickness insurance. This compensation can be granted for 60 working days at a time and for a maximum of 300 working days. The replacement rate is 70% of earnings (net of social security payments) up to a limit, 40% of the part of earnings that exceeds the limit, and 25% of the part of earnings exceeding another, higher limit. In many sectoral contracts, the period of full pay is extended for those with long tenure. In these cases, the employer gets the sickness insurance compensation for the extended period. In principle, the employees have to show a doctor's certificate in the case of sickness, but the exact rules vary in sectoral contracts or firm-level agreements. Therefore, in many firms, no certificate is needed in the case of short absences.

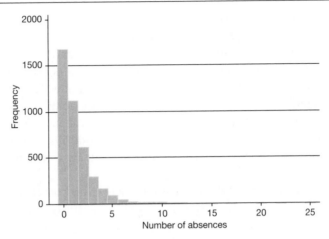

Figure 9.3. Distribution of the number of absences within the last 12 months

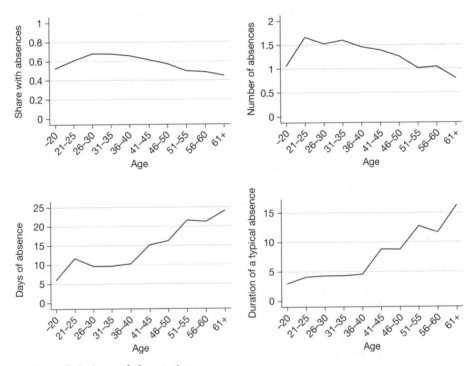

Figure 9.4. Age and absenteeism

highest for ages 26 to 40 and then starts to fall with age. The upper right-hand panel of the figure shows the average annual number of absences by age group. In the up to 20 age group, the average number of absences is one; it increases to 1.6 in the next age group, and falls to under one in the oldest age group. If we took into account only those who have absences, that is, leaving zero observations out, the differences between age groups would be smaller and the numbers higher. All in all, this descriptive analysis shows that the oldest age groups tend to have fewer absences.

The annual days of absence by age group are shown in the lower left-hand panel of Figure 9.4 This includes only persons with absences, so zero observations, that is, those who have not been absent from work at all, are excluded. The youngest employees tend to have few and very short absences, so their total number of days away from work is small. The oldest ones, on the other hand, although they have a small number of absences, tend to have a high number of days absent. Finally, the lower right-hand panel presents the days of duration of a typical (non-zero) absence. This varies from three days among the youngest ones to over two weeks in the oldest age group.

Figure 9.5 presents the same graphs as in Figure 9.4, but drawn separately for men and women. The youngest and the oldest females are more likely to have absences than men in the same age groups, but from the early twenties to early fifties, the incidence of absenteeism is relatively similar. A similar pattern is seen in the annual number of absences. However, in the total number of days absent (for persons who actually have absences), there is not much difference between the genders. Finally, men in their fifties tend to have especially long absences, but for older men the duration of absences falls. For women in their fifties, the duration of absences is shorter than for men in the same age group, whereas for the oldest group of women, the absence duration is higher than for men. This may be a selection effect: men tend to get serious illnesses earlier than women and those men who suffer more from illnesses make an early exit from the labour force.

The QWLS survey includes a question on whether the respondents have had an accident at work during the last 12 months that has led to an absence. There are only 201 individuals (4.9%) who have had such an accident. The incidence of accidents also varies greatly between different types of work. Figure 9.6 shows the share of individuals who have had an accident by age group separately for blue-collar and white-collar employees. Due to the small number of observations, we use wider age groups than in the previous figures. There is some indication that in blue-collar

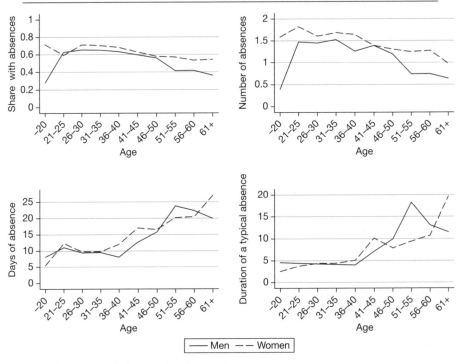

Figure 9.5. Age and absenteeism by gender

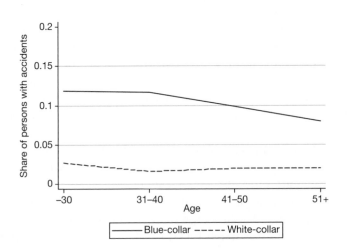

Figure 9.6. Age and accidents

occupations the probability of accidents starts to fall when employees reach their thirties. In white-collar occupations, accidents are rare and start to fall at an earlier age. This shows that accidents may be one factor behind the higher number of absences in the younger age group, but do not contribute to the longer absences of the older employees.

9.3.2 Results with the Survey Data

We start by examining who has days of absence in the first place, that is, we study the probability of having absences.[8] In the results that are reported here, we have used age group indicators. Using a polynomial of age gave insignificant effects on the higher powers of age, so we do not report those results. Besides age, we include a set of explanatory variables, which are as follows. There is an indicator for females, indicators for four educational levels (comprehensive education (reference category), upper secondary or vocational education, polytechnic or lower university degree, and higher university degree), logarithm of monthly pay (mid-point of self-reported monthly wage category), and indicators of occupation (10 occupational groups) to control for possible differences between jobs. To control for more specific differences in jobs we include plant-size indicators (less than 10 employees (reference group), 10–49, 50–249, and 250 or over), indicators for at least one clear factor of hazard, harm, and uncertainty at the work-place,[9] and an indicator for shift work. Absenteeism is likely to be associated with various disamenities involved in a job. The survey includes information on job satisfaction, which is often used to explain absenteeism in the psychological literature. However, since job satisfaction is highly negatively correlated with bad working conditions, we do not include it in the estimated models. In addition, we also include indicators for temporary contract and part-time work, and industry indicators (12 industries).

In a second model, we add an indicator for health, which is a dummy variable for having a medically diagnosed illness, and a score of self-assessed working capacity on the scale 0 to 10. (We examine the relationship between age and this measure of working capacity in the next chapter.) Since health and working capacity decline with age, when we control for

---

[8] Böckerman and Ilmakunnas (2006b) examine the determination of absences using the 1997 QWLS. They do not, however, consider age effects in detail, but concentrate on the interactions of work disamenities and job satisfaction with the incidence and number of absences.

[9] See Böckerman and Ilmakunnas (2006a) for an explanation of how these measures were formed.

Table 9.2. Results on the probability of absences and the number of absences

| | Probability of absences | | Number of absences | |
	Probit	Probit	Poisson	Poisson
Age –20	Reference group	Reference group	Reference group	Reference group
Age 21–25	0.01	0.004	0.26	0.21
	(0.06)	(0.06)	(0.18)	(0.18)
Age 26–30	0.06	0.04	0.15	0.09
	(0.06)	(0.06)	(0.18)	(0.18)
Age 31–35	0.03	0.01	0.14	0.05
	(0.06)	(0.06)	(0.18)	(0.18)
Age 36–40	0.01	−0.03	0.02	−0.10
	(0.06)	(0.06)	(0.18)	(0.18)
Age 41–45	−0.04	−0.09	−0.04	−0.20
	(0.06)	(0.06)	(0.18)	(0.18)
Age 46–50	−0.10	−0.16	−0.17	−0.38
	(0.06)*	(0.06)***	(0.18)	(0.18)**
Age 51–55	−0.18	−0.26	−0.40	−0.65
	(0.06)***	(0.06)***	(0.18)**	(0.18)***
Age 56–60	−0.17	−0.27	−0.33	−0.61
	(0.06)***	(0.06)***	(0.19)*	(0.19)***
Age 61–	−0.16	−0.26	−0.46	−0.77
	(0.08)**	(0.08)***	(0.23)**	(0.23)***
Illness		0.10		0.30
		(0.02)***		(0.05)***
Working		−0.05		
Capacity		(0.01)***		(0.013)
N	4042	4037	4038	4033

Notes: Robust standard errors in parentheses. Significance: *** 1%, ** 5%, * 10%. The first and second column show marginal effects on the probability of absences. Unreported variables include logarithm of monthly pay and indicators for gender, educational level, occupation, plant size, harms, hazards, and uncertainty at the workplace, shift work, temporary contract, part-time work, and industry.

these factors, we should get a pure age effect on absences. The first two columns of Table 9.2 show the marginal effects of the explanatory age group variables on the probability of having absences, based on a probit model. The figures show the difference in the probability of having absences, compared to the reference group, those in the up to 20 age group.[10] The first column shows the results from a probit model without health and working capacity and the second column the results from a model that includes them. Among the younger age groups, the differences are not significant, but those over 50 are significantly less likely to have absences than the reference group. When health and working capacity are controlled

---

[10] The effects of the age group indicators are differences in probabilities for the age group in question and the reference group, evaluated by setting all other age group indicators to zero and all the other variables to their mean values.

for, the marginal effects of the age indicators drop, that is, with similar health and working capacity, the older age groups are even less likely to have absences. Without controlling for health, those over 50 years old are 16–18% less likely to have absences than the youngest age group; controlling for health, the difference is 26–7%. Chronic illness itself increases the likelihood of absences by 10% and an increase in the working capacity by one point in the scale 0 to 10 decreases the likelihood by 5%.

We briefly summarize the results on the other variables without showing the results in the table. Female employees are 9% more likely to have absences. Education has no impact, but the level of income has a positive influence. Part-timers have fewer absences, which is understandable since in the case of minor illnesses, they are less likely to have to be absent from work than full-time employees. Absences are least likely in the smallest plants, where it would be more difficult to make up for the lost input of an absent worker, whereas in larger workplaces, it is easier to distribute the work to other employees. Working conditions really matter: harms, hazards, and uncertainty at the workplace have a strongly significant positive effect on the likelihood of having absences.

Next we consider the relationship between age and the number of absences.[11] Since the number of absences can only be zero or an integer number, we have used a Poisson regression model. The results are reported in the last two columns of Table 9.2. There are significant age effects only in the age groups above 40 years, where age reduces the number of absences. Controlling for health and working capacity reduces the coefficients of the age group variables considerably.[12]

The other effects are similar in direction to those in the probit model. There are, however, some interesting differences in the significance of the variables. Those with the highest level of education have a lower number of absences, whereas their probability of having absences did not differ significantly from those with a lower level of education. Also, temporary workers have fewer absences. This can be explained by their incentives to perform well to obtain an extension to their contract.

---

[11] The number of observations in columns 3 and 4 is slightly lower than in columns 1 and 2. This is caused by a few individuals, who answer in the survey that they have had absences, but whose number of absences has been coded as zero or as a missing value. We have included them in the probit estimations, but not in the Poisson estimations.

[12] If the model is estimated with ordinary least squares regression, the results are not much different from those shown in the table. If the regression is run only for those who have absences, the age effects are no longer significant.

Table 9.3. Results on the duration of absences

	Total days of absence		Duration of a typical absence	
	OLS	OLS	OLS	OLS
Age –20	Reference group	Reference group	Reference group	Reference group
Age 21–25	9.50	6.51	3.38	1.92
	(2.58)***	(2.60)**	(1.33)**	(1.37)
Age 26–30	7.75	5.06	3.84	2.53
	(2.56)***	(2.53)**	(1.56)**	(1.59)
Age 31–35	7.11	2.60	3.42	1.24
	(2.64)***	(2.61)	(1.63)**	(1.71)
Age 36–40	7.64	2.51	3.72	1.26
	(2.75)***	(2.72)	(1.67)**	(1.75)
Age 41–45	12.16	5.99	7.97	5.01
	(2.87)***	(2.82)**	(1.89)***	(1.91)***
Age 46–50	13.60	5.87	8.11	4.39
	(3.33)***	(3.08)*	(2.36)***	(2.28)*
Age 51–55	16.96	6.60	11.21	6.35
	(3.33)***	(2.93)**	(2.13)***	(1.80)***
Age 56–60	16.42	6.25	10.08	5.37
	(3.56)***	(3.61)*	(2.51)***	(2.62)**
Age 61–	18.88	6.74	13.37	7.65
	(5.05)***	(4.85)	(3.92)***	(4.03)*
Illness		3.93		1.79
		(0.97)***		(0.67)***
Working capacity		−5.90		−2.85
		(0.87)***		(0.77)***
R-squared	0.08	0.19	0.06	0.11
N	2400	2396	2394	2390

Notes: Robust standard errors in parentheses. Significance: *** 1%, ** 5%, * 10%. Unreported variables include logarithm of monthly pay and indicators for gender, educational level, occupation, plant size, harms, hazards, and uncertainty at the workplace, shift work, temporary contract, part-time work, and industry.

Table 9.3. shows least squares regression models for the duration of absences. The results are shown for the total annual days of absence and the duration of a typical absence. In both cases, we use in the regression only those individuals who have had absences. We can consider our approach as a two-part model where the first part is the probit estimation for the probability of absences and the second part is the separate regression model for the duration of absences.[13] Two-part models can be justified

---

[13] With a high concentration of zeros, a tobit model would otherwise be appropriate, but the descriptive analysis indicated that age might have different impacts on the likelihood of absences and the duration of absences. Two-part models (see e.g. Cameron and Trivedi, 2005) are often used in health-related applications, like visits to a doctor. Our application bears a close resemblance to these. An alternative would be to use a selection model. However, it is difficult to divide the variables into those that influence only the likelihood of absences, but not their duration and those that potentially affect both. Therefore our two-part model is a practical alternative.

especially in situations where the processes that determine the two parts are likely to be different. In our case, the age-absenteeism relationship seems to be different when the incidence and duration of absences are examined.

Age increases the annual days of absence. For example, those in the age group 60+ have 18 days more absences than those in the reference group up to 20. When health is controlled for (column 2), the age effects fall, especially in the older age groups, and are no longer significant for those in their thirties and the oldest age group. Now those over 50 have six days more absences than a person in the youngest group with similar health and working capacity. Having chronic illness increases the annual days of absences by four days, and one point increase in the index of working capacity decreases absences by six days.

To summarize the other results in the estimation with positive number of absences, there is no gender effect, days of absence decrease with education, and harms, hazards, and uncertainty at the workplace increase the annual days absent from work. However, when illness is controlled for, the job disamenities are no longer significant.

The results on the duration of a typical absence are shown in the third and fourth columns of Table 9.3. There is a clear positive age effect. In the oldest age group, the duration of a typical absence is ten days longer than in the reference group of those 20 years or below. When chronic illness and working capacity are controlled for, there are no longer significant differences between the youngest age groups. However, the difference between the oldest and youngest age group is still almost eight days. Chronic illness increases the duration of a typical absence by two days and a one point increase in working capacity decreases it by three days.

The other results, not included in the table, show that there are no gender or wage effects, but education and plant size reduce the duration of absences. Job disamenities do not have significant impacts when illness and working capacity are controlled for. Although poor working conditions give rise to many absences, they are typically short. Interestingly, income has a positive impact on the duration of a typical absence. This implies that higher income makes it more affordable to be absent from work, although with high income the cost of being absent is higher.

9.4 Conclusions on Absenteeism

We have presented evidence on the connection between age and absenteeism from two different data sets. First, we explored a unique data set that has information on day-to-day variation in the composition of work teams. This variation was used to identify the effects of individual and team characteristics on individuals' probability to call in sick. The probability of sick leave for workers in work teams is shown to be higher the more age-diverse their work team is. Diversity with respect to other characteristics (job tenure, education, and nationality) does not seem to play a role. The effect of age on absenteeism is concave. Sick leave increases with age up to the age of 45 and flattens out afterwards. Despite a vast literature on absenteeism in disciplines as diverse as economics, managerial sciences, psychology, and medicine, the relation between sick leave and team composition has not been studied yet. This chapter is a first step. More research in this direction is needed to better understand these effects.

The findings from the cross-sectional survey data, on the other hand, show that age has very different kinds of effects on the incidence and duration of absences. Younger employees tend to have a higher number of absences. The probability of having absences and the number of absences start to fall when employees are in their late thirties and absences are clearly less common in the older age groups. This result is in line with that found with the assembly-line data. However, when older employees are absent from work, the durations of the absences are long.

We have not directly measured how the absences affect productivity (besides the fact that the productivity of the absent employee is zero). The productivity effects at the work unit or firm level depend on the firms' ability to adjust their processes to short versus long absences. The ability to adjust may be different in small firms with few co-workers to make up the work of the absent employee and in large firms with larger work groups. In assessing the results, we must bear in mind that there is probably some selectivity in the absenteeism data: those (most likely older employees) who would have been more prone to having very long absences have already exited employment.

10

Age and Working Capacity

10.1 Introduction

As discussed before in Chapter 2, it is difficult to obtain data on the productivity of individuals. In economic research, supervisor ratings have been used as measures of the productivity of individuals (see Medoff and Abraham, 1980, and Flabbi and Ichino, 2001, among others). In psychology and medicine, the relationship between age and performance has been studied using various tests and experiments (see e.g. McEvoy and Cascio, 1989, and Waldman and Avolio, 1986). As a general measure of work ability, the Work Ability Index (WAI) has been developed, which combines information on several self-reported aspects like work ability, health, absences, subjective optimism, etc. (Tuomi *et al.*, 1998; Ilmarinen, 2001).

Although these kinds of data sources give direct measures of productivity, they are not always based on representative samples of the whole population. We will use a data set that gives indirect information on productivity from a representative sample of persons in paid employment. Our indirect measure of productivity is a self-assessed measure of working capacity.[1] There are, of course, problems with subjective measures. For example, it is unlikely that all individuals use the same kind of scale in their assessment. Since we have only cross-section data, we cannot control for this. By including many variables describing the characteristics of the individuals and their jobs, we may, however, be able to control for factors that influence how individuals view their working capacity. For example, workers who face unpleasant working conditions may be more inclined to report that their working capacity is low.

---

[1] This can be regarded as one aspect of the WAI, although the wording of the question in the QWLS survey that we are using is not the same as in the WAI, where each individual compares her work ability to her best work ability ever. Our analysis of absenteeism in Chapter 9 studied another particular aspect of WAI.

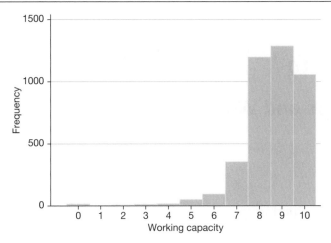

Figure 10.1. Distribution of working capacity

We use the Finnish Quality of Working Life Survey (QWLS) from 2003. This data set was already used in the previous chapter and the data source is explained in more detail in the Appendix III. We are interested in examining how the subjective assessment of work capacity is related to age. In the survey, the question on working capacity takes the form: 'Assuming that your top working capacity would score 10 points while your total inability to work would score zero, how many points would you give to your working capacity at the moment?' We will interpret this as a self-assessed measure of productivity. Figure 10.1 presents a histogram of the index of working capacity. The figure shows clearly that the respondents tend to give fairly high scores to their working capacity. Those giving low figures, even zero, are in a clear minority. This indicates that we are not likely to find very dramatic age effects.

10.2 Results on Age and Working Capacity

In a first look at the relationship between age and working capacity, we plot the working capacity index against age in Figure 10.2. As the measure of working capacity is categorical, a normal scatter-plot would not illustrate it well. We therefore use a plot where some randomness ('jitter') has been added to the observations. This makes it easier to see big concentrations of dots in the figure. Especially at younger ages, the distribution of working capacity scores is concentrated on the highest values. With age, the

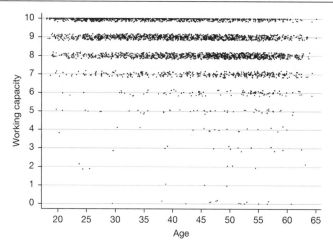

Figure 10.2. Working capacity and age

distribution spreads and there are relatively fewer observations with the highest working capacity among the oldest employees. In the empirical analysis, we will use age groups defined as five-year intervals. In the youngest age group up to age 20, the median self-assessed working capacity is 9.5 (i.e. there is a tie between 9 and 10). With age, the median falls and it is 8 from age group 46–50 onwards. The mean value of the working capacity index falls from 9.2 in the up to 20 age group to 8 in the 61+ age group.

When assessing the figure, we must bear in mind that in the older age groups many individuals have already retired and therefore are no longer in the population from which the sample is drawn. The average effective retirement age in Finland is 59 years, since many individuals take some form of early exit from the labour force, in particular disability pension, unemployment pension, or individual early retirement.[2] For example, in QWLS, the age 61+ group includes only 96 individuals, whereas the 56–60 group has 425 individuals. It is likely that many of those who have retired early have had health problems. The disability pension is clearly related to a reduced working capacity. There is also some evidence that poor heath is related to the risk of becoming unemployed (see Böckerman and Ilmakunnas, 2007, for Finnish evidence), so too the unemployment pension may be connected with poor

---

[2] The official retirement age in Finland has been 65. In many public sector jobs, it was 63, but has been increased to 65. In recent pension reforms, these rules have been changed so that individuals can now more flexibly choose their retirement age and have a subjective right to stay until age of 68.

working capacity. When those who use these early exit channels drop out of the data, those who remain have relatively good health for a person of their age.[3] This leads to a sample selection problem. The figure therefore tends to overestimate the working capacity of the oldest age groups, compared to a situation where all individuals were forced to work until the age 65.

To investigate the connection between age and working capacity further, we estimate models where the working capacity score is explained by age and the characteristics of the individual and the workplace. We start by treating the working capacity scores as cardinal measures. That is, we treat the figures as ordinary numbers, which implies that the respondents consider score 10 to be twice as good as score 5, for example. It is unlikely that the respondents understand the scores in this way, but this is a good starting point when we try to uncover the age-productivity relationship. Later we relax this assumption and treat the scores as ordinal measures.

Since the relationship between age and working capacity may be non-linear, we have examined various ways of taking the non-linearity into account. Including powers of age in an ordinary least squares regression model for working capacity showed that we obtain significant coefficients only for the linear term, that is, age itself. However, when we used age-group indicators, the results show that the age effect is not quite linear. We therefore present the results only for the age-group variables.[4] In the first model of Table 10.1, age-group indicators, personal characteristics, and job characteristics explain working capacity.

The other explanatory variables are as follows. There is an indicator for females, since both the actual working capacity and the subjective perception of it may vary by gender. There are indicators for educational levels, logarithm of monthly pay, and indicators of occupations to control for possible differences in the type of working capacity that is required in different types of jobs. High-skill jobs require less physical working capacity than low-skill jobs, for example. To control for more specific differences in jobs, we include plant-size indicators, indicators for at least one clear factor of hazard, harm, and uncertainty at the workplace, and an indicator for shift work. The perception of working capacity is likely to be connected to various disamenities involved in the job. Dangers encountered in the work

---

[3] Ilmakunnas and Ilmakunnas (2006) show that among the individuals in the QWLS sample, the working capacity index itself does not explain willingness to extend working life beyond the age 63. However, having a diagnosed chronic illness has a significant negative effect.

[4] We also used a semi-parametric method, partial linear regression (see Yatchew, 2003). The conclusion was that the drop in working capacity is relatively linear in age, irrespective of the included control variables.

and feel of uncertainty, for example, may negatively impact how workers feel they are able to perform their work tasks. Finally, we include an indicator for teamwork. Work practices may influence how employees experience their ability to cope with their tasks. In particular, in teams, the work can be divided so that the older employees can have tasks where, for example, reduced physical abilities do not matter. The survey has a question about the proportion of time that individuals work in teams. We form an indicator for working in teams at least 75% of the time.[5]

In the second model of Table 10.1, we add an indicator for having a medically diagnosed illness. Age itself need not be the factor that reduces productivity, but rather the things that come with age, like deteriorated health. Therefore inclusion of the illness variable gives us a better measure of a 'pure' age effect on working capacity.

The working capacity index drops steadily with age, although the age impact is not exactly linear. The reference group to which the other age groups are compared is age 20 or below. The biggest drop compared to the previous group happens in the 46–50 age group. The inclusion of the illness indicator decreases the absolute values of the coefficients of the age-group variables, but their pattern stays the same. This shows that the decline of working capacity is not only related to serious illnesses, but there is a 'pure' negative age effect as well. If we use age as a continuous variable (the results are not shown in the table), we can conclude that one additional year of age reduces the working capacity index by 0.03 points, or 0.3 points in ten years. When the health indicator is added, the age impact becomes slightly smaller. Chronic illness itself reduces the perceived working capacity by half a point on the scale 0 to 10.[6]

We briefly summarize the results on the other explanatory variables without reporting their coefficients in the table.[7] Females have better working capacity. Those with higher pay have better working capacity, but after controlling for wage, education plays no role. Employees of plants that are

---

[5] This includes alternatives 'almost all of the time' and 'approximately ¾ of the time'. In addition to these variables, we tried some other explanatory variables, for example industry indicators, tenure, and an indicator for part-time work. These were, however, clearly insignificant and have been dropped from the estimations.

[6] As the distribution of the working capacity values is concentrated close to the upper limit 10, we also used a tobit model to investigate the robustness of the results. The conclusions on the impacts of the variables were fairly similar to those from the OLS estimation and are therefore not reported here.

[7] The results regarding age are not much affected by the particular set of control variables included. If we first estimate the model with only personal characteristics, and then also with job characteristics, the age coefficients remain practically the same. Only the inclusion of the health indicator has a larger impact on the results.

in the middle-size groups (10–49 and 59–499) have lower working capacity than those who work in the smallest or largest plants. The largest workplaces may be able to rotate tasks so that employees find jobs that fit better their possibly lowered working capacity. An alternative explanation is that in the largest firms, those with lower working capacity have already exited. The largest employers have incentives for laying off employees who may face a disability risk, since in case of disability large Finnish firms have to cover the disability pension until the normal retirement age.

Working conditions clearly play an important role, as harms, hazards, and uncertainty at the workplace have strong negative effects on self-assessed working capacity. It is unclear, however, whether this is a true productivity-reducing effect or whether it rather reflects job dissatisfaction.[8] Shift work has a positive effect. It may be that individuals with better working capacity are more likely to end up in jobs that involve shift work. Finally, teamwork has a significant positive effect on working capacity. This supports the view that 'high performance' work practices can improve productivity.

It is possible that the relationship between age and working capacity is quite different in different fields or occupations. To investigate this possibility we have estimated the model separately for the industry sector (defined to include mining, manufacturing, public utilities, and construction) and the service sector (private and public services). The results are in columns 3 and 4 of Table 10.1. We have also estimated the model separately for blue-collar and white-collar employees. These results are in columns 5 and 6 of the table.[9] In these models, the health indicator is included, so the results should be compared with those in column 2. The estimates clearly show that in the industrial sector and in blue-collar occupations the decline in self-assessed working capacity is stronger. Industrial employees over 60 years old have 2 points lower working capacity than the reference group of those aged 20 years or under. In the service sector, the difference is 1 point. The oldest group of blue-collar workers has 1.3 points lower working capacity than the youngest blue-collar group. Also the negative health effects are somewhat stronger in the industry sector and for blue-collar workers than in services and for white-collar employees. Concerning the results not reported in the table, it can be mentioned that

---

[8] Böckerman and Ilmakunnas (2006a) show that harms, hazard, and uncertainty have clear negative effects on job satisfaction.
[9] Those working in agriculture or forestry or where industry is unknown are left out when the model is estimated for the industry and service sectors. Further, occupation indicators are not included in the models reported in columns 3–6 of Table 10.1, since some occupations are relatively uncommon in subsets of the data.

females have better self-assessed working capacity in the industry sector and in blue-collar occupations and teamwork has a positive impact in services and among blue-collar workers.

The results show that women have better working capacity. However, the gender difference may also be age-related. We therefore also estimate the model separately for men and women. The results are shown in columns 7 and 8 of Table 10.1. Up to age group 31–5, both genders show a similar decline in working capacity. After that, the development diverges. Especially from age group 46–50, males' working capacity clearly declines faster than that of the females.

So far we have treated the working capacity as a cardinal measure. Now we allow it to be an ordinal measure, which is, of course, a more realistic assumption. To model the relationships, we use ordered probit regression. The purpose is to model how the explanatory factors affect the probability of being at one of the score levels (from 0 to 10). Since there are 11 possible scores, it is not easy to summarize the results. We do not present the results in the table, but instead show in Figure 10.3 how age and the probability of high working capacity are related. We define 'high' to include values 9 and 10 of the working capacity index.

The age effects are illustrated in Figure 10.3, which shows the probability of high working capacity at various age levels. The indicator of chronic illness is included as a variable in the model and the probabilities are calculated separately for the cases where this indicator equals one and zero.[10] There is a steady fall with age in the probability of having high working capacity. For example, when there is no chronic illness, the age group over 60 has over 40% lower probability of having high working capacity than the group aged 20 years or under. Having chronic illness decreases the probability at all age levels. In age groups over 30, the drop is roughly 15%. If the indicator of illness is not included in the estimated model, working capacity drops more with age than in Figure 10.3. This shows that when chronic illness is taken into account, the 'pure' age effect is slightly less dramatic.

The results on the explanatory variables are very similar to those from the ordinary least squares results, where working capacity was treated as a cardinal measure. Facing harms, hazards, or uncertainty reduces the probability of top working capacity by roughly 10% each and teamwork increases

---

[10] The probabilities are calculated for each age group by setting the indicators for the other age groups equal to zero, the other variables to their mean values, and the indicator for chronic illness to zero or one in the two cases.

Table 10.1. Models for working capacity

	Dependent variable—working capacity								Wage
	All	All	Industry	Services	Blue-collar	White-collar	Men	Women	All
Age –20	Reference group	Reference group	Reference group	Reference group	Reference group	Reference group	Reference group	Reference group	Reference group
Age 21–25	−0.20 (0.14)	−0.19 (0.14)	−0.64 (0.31)**	0.04 (0.17)	−0.09 (0.21)	−0.27 (0.19)	−0.26 (0.25)	−0.21 (0.16)	0.17 (0.04)***
Age 26–30	−0.25 (0.14)*	−0.25 (0.14)*	−0.57 (0.29)*	−0.12 (0.17)	−0.13 (0.21)	−0.31 (0.18)*	−0.29 (0.24)	−0.29 (0.17)	0.23 (0.04)***
Age 31–35	−0.51 (0.14)***	−0.49 (0.14)***	−0.86 (0.29)***	−0.30 (0.17)	−0.39 (0.20)	−0.54 (0.18)***	−0.52 (0.24)*	−0.53 (0.17)*	0.29 (0.04)***
Age 36–40	−0.56 (0.14)***	−0.52 (0.14)***	−0.73 (0.29)**	−0.42 (0.17)**	−0.40 (0.22)*	−0.59 (0.18)***	−0.46 (0.24)*	−0.65 (0.16)***	0.34 (0.04)***
Age 41–45	−0.68 (0.14)***	−0.61 (0.14)***	−0.93 (0.29)***	−0.47 (0.17)***	−0.50 (0.21)**	−0.66 (0.18)***	−0.74 (0.24)***	−0.56 (0.16)***	0.35 (0.04)***
Age 46–50	−0.95 (0.14)***	−0.87 (0.14)***	−1.29 (0.30)***	−0.69 (0.17)***	−0.91 (0.21)***	−0.86 (0.18)***	−1.12 (0.24)***	−0.72 (0.16)***	0.33 (0.04)***
Age 51–55	−1.10 (0.14)***	−0.98 (0.14)***	−1.31 (0.29)***	−0.83 (0.18)***	−0.95 (0.21)***	−1.00 (0.18)***	−1.12 (0.25)***	−0.91 (0.16)***	0.35 (0.04)***
Age 56–60	−1.27 (0.14)***	−1.13 (0.15)***	−1.57 (0.31)***	−0.87 (0.17)***	−1.21 (0.22)***	−1.07 (0.18)***	−1.41 (0.26)***	−0.95 (0.16)***	0.36 (0.04)***
Age 61–	−1.36 (0.21)***	−1.24 (0.20)***	−2.01 (0.64)***	−1.02 (0.22)***	−1.32 (0.39)***	−1.19 (0.22)***	−1.48 (0.34)***	−1.04 (0.23)***	0.31 (0.06)***
Illness	−0.50 (0.05)***	−0.50 (0.05)***	−0.59 (0.09)***	−0.48 (0.06)***	−0.53 (0.08)***	−0.47 (0.06)***	−0.48 (0.07)***	−0.50 (0.07)***	−0.02 (0.01)**
N	4031	4028	1068	2710	1401	2634	1909	2119	4003
R-squared	0.15	0.18	0.22	0.16	0.20	0.15	0.21	0.17	0.60

Notes: OLS estimates. Robust standard errors in parentheses. Significance: *** 1%, ** 5%, * 10%. Unreported control variables are indicators for gender, educational levels, plant-size categories, shift work, teamwork, harms, hazards, and uncertainty, as well as logarithm of earnings. The models with all individuals, and with men and women separately, also include occupation indicators. Harms, hazards, and uncertainty are excluded from the wage model.

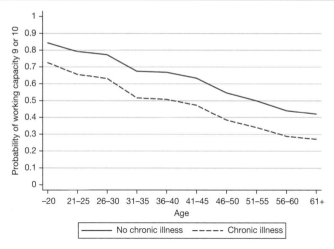

Figure 10.3. Age and probablility of high working capacity

the probability by 4%. If age is included in the ordered probit model as a continuous variable and not as age-group indicators, one additional year of age decreases the probability of having top working capacity by roughly 1%.

From the firm's point of view, the profitability of employing individuals of different ages depends not only on their productivity, but also on their wage. The QWLS includes information on self-reported monthly income. This is based on a question where respondents choose one of 20 wage intervals. We have used logarithms of the midpoints of the intervals as our income measure. In the lowest wage group, we have used the upper limit of the group and in the highest wage group the lower limit of the group. Estimates of the age effects in the wage model are shown in the last column of Table 10.1. Besides the age-group variables and chronic illness, the wage model includes indicators for gender, educational level, length of tenure, occupation, plant size category, shift work, and teamwork. In addition, monthly working hours are included as a continuous variable.

There is a clear increase in wage by age until the late thirties, then the wage profile is relatively flat and in the oldest age group there is a slight decline. This kind of inverted-U-shaped pattern is consistent with many cross-sectional studies of wages. The fall in the oldest age group may reflect a selectivity effect: higher paid individuals may have already retired. Also overtime and piece-rate payments may decrease with age. In any case, the pattern of wages is quite different from that of self-assessed working capacity. Whether the working capacity measure accurately reflects productivity or not, there is a clear discrepancy between the development of the variables with age. This difference is likely to persist even with a more accurate measure of productivity.

10.3 Conclusions on Working Capacity

To summarize the findings, there is clear evidence that employees' own assessment of their working capacity falls with age, while there is no corresponding decline in wages by age. However, the fall in working capacity is not dramatic, as the majority of the older age groups still consider their working capacity to be relatively high on a scale from 0 to 10. Age affects working capacity, as least to the extent that the employees themselves think so. It is unclear, however, to what extent this shows up in lower actual productivity. It is also not possible to indicate whether the fall in working capacity is related to physical or mental factors. However, at least if chronic illnesses are taken into account, there is still a fall in perceived working capacity. Lowered working capacity is related to the tasks that the employees have. Rotation of older employees to tasks that are less physically demanding, for example in work teams, may improve perceived working capacity and even improve actual productivity.

Our analysis shows that in jobs where more physical strength has traditionally been needed, that is, in the industry sector and in blue-collar occupations, perceived working capacity drops faster with age. If technological change leads to an increasing trend away from these kinds of occupations, it is possible that ageing will have less effect on productivity.

When evaluating the results, we must bear in mind that there is a potentially very important selection issue, as those more prone to have very low working capacity are most likely to have already exited employment. In this sense, our findings may overestimate the productivity of older employees.

11

Age and Productivity: An Analysis at the Plant and the Team Level

11.1 Introduction

As discussed at length in Chapter 2, estimating age-productivity profiles is difficult because good measures of productivity are rare. Studies in medicine, psychology, and gerontology have analysed how different abilities and skills (muscle strength, sight, retentiveness, and other cognitive abilities) evolve over the life cycle. Measures of economic productivity are harder to come by.

Since individual-level productivity measures are available only in very special cases, a field of research has emerged, where linked employer–employee data sets are used for analysing the impact of workforce characteristics, including age, plant- or firm-level productivity, and wage (e.g. Hellerstein *et al.*, 1999; Haltiwanger *et al.*, 2007; Ilmakunnas and Maliranta, 2005; Daveri and Maliranta, 2007). Linked data sets are such that individuals can be linked to their workplaces. This is possible on a large scale in countries that have personal identity numbers for all citizens and records on their employment relationships or through membership of some social security systems (like the unemployment insurance in the US). On a smaller scale, this can be done through specific surveys where both the firms and a sample of employees are interviewed, or by using personnel records of single firms.

Using the links between employees and employers, it is possible to form measures of the age structure of the workforce in each establishment and/or firm. In the research in this field, various measures of age structure have been used. One is to use the average age of the employees. For example, Ilmakunnas *et al.* (2004) use average age and its square, and the standard deviation of age, to explain plant-level total factor productivity. Average age is used also by Malmberg *et al.* (2005), and Daveri and Maliranta (2007) use average potential experience, which is closely related to age. The squared terms are included to allow the age-productivity relationship to be non-linear, either U- or inverted-U-shaped. Higher powers of average age are sometimes included to allow for more complicated non-linearities.

Another approach has been to use the shares of employees in various age groups. Applications of this method include Hellerstein *et al.* (1999), Hæge-land and Klette (1999), and Ilmakunnas and Maliranta (2005), among others. Yet another way to infer age effects on productivity with linked data sets is to use information on hiring and separation rates by age groups. Ilmakunnas and Maliranta (2007) have suggested this 'flow approach'. In this study, we use average age (and its square) as the measure of plant-age structure.

The research with linked data sets has mostly dealt with comparisons of productivity and wage profiles to test different theories of wage formation. The age issue has not been the sole concern, as the influence of various other workforce characteristics has been examined. The results in this literature are not quite conclusive, but there is some evidence from various countries that firm productivity tends to have an inverted-U-shaped relationship with age, while average wage is increasing in age (for a survey, see Skirbekk, 2004). On the other hand, in recent work, Daveri and Maliranta (2007) show that the productivity effects may differ greatly across industries even within the same country. The possible decline in productivity with age would not be a great concern if it were accompanied by a corresponding change in wage. One purpose of this chapter is to compare productivity and wage profiles by age.

A drawback of most studies of the firm-level age-productivity connection is that they do not pay much attention to how the structure of the workforce is determined. This structure does not come out of the blue, but is likely to be influenced by firms' choices. If there are unobservable factors, like management skill, they may affect both the productivity of the plants and the structure of the workforce. This can be taken into account by using panel data on plants, which allows elimination of the unobservable factors. There may also be reverse causality. If the firm knows that its low produc-tivity plants are going to exit in the future, most likely very few new (and young) employees are hired, which leads to a negative relationship between employee age and productivity. Some of the studies on ageing and produc-tivity have therefore used instrumental variables to account for this (e.g. Aubert and Crépon, 2003; Malmberg *et al.*, 2005; Daveri and Maliranta, 2007), mostly using lagged values of the variables as instruments. Our intention is to use instrumental variables based on the age structure of employees in the plants when they are established.

In these kinds of studies, the interaction of the age effects with other workforce characteristics has rarely been studied. The usual approach is to control for the education and seniority structure of the workplace when the age effects are examined. Our purpose is to examine in more detail the role of workforce diversity for plant-level productivity.

It may be that older workers are able to compensate for their lower physical productivity by experience. They may also be able to transfer tacit knowledge to younger, less experienced employees. We therefore examine the role of age-experience diversity, that is, whether it matters for productivity that workplaces have young employees working together with older ones, rather than being segregated into 'old only' or 'young only' workplaces. The second kind of diversity that we will examine is age-education diversity. This relates to age-skill composition. This kind of diversity is likely to change over time, when there is technological change and also because of changes in the educational structure of the available labour supply.

In this chapter, we present and compare results from two studies that analyse the same research questions with different data sets. The research questions are:

1. How does productivity evolve with age?
2. How does workforce diversity with respect to age and other characteristics affect productivity?
3. How does the age-wage relationship differ from the age-productivity relationship?

The first study analyses data on productivity at the level of work teams in one single plant. The tasks in this plant are rather homogeneous and age-productivity profiles can be estimated fairly precisely. But the results cannot be generalized to other parts of the economy. The other study analyses the Finnish Linked Employer-Employee Data (FLEED), which provide information on productivity at the plant level for the Finnish economy. At this aggregate level, age-productivity profiles are obviously cruder. On the other hand, the results apply to a large part of the entire Finnish economy[1] and can easily be generalized to other developed economies. The linked data also make it possible to compare productivity and wage profiles by age.

---

[1] The data encompass the whole business sector, but we use data on plants in mining, manufacturing, energy, and construction.

11.2 Econometric Analysis of Age and Productivity

11.2.1 *Age and Team-Level Productivity at DaimlerChrysler*

This subsection reports first results from the econometric analysis of the relation between age and productivity using a unique data set that we have compiled from an assembly plant of DaimlerChrysler.[2] At this plant, trucks are assembled by work teams on an assembly line. The quantity of output is determined by the speed of the assembly line. If work teams differ in productivity, this is not going to show up in differences in the quantity of output because the assembly line has the same speed for all teams. But production quality differs across work teams as they can make errors.

A 'quality inspector' at the end of the assembly line records these errors. The quality inspector is able to assign every error to the workplace where it happened. At any time, there is exactly one work team at any workplace. Every error is given a weight (between 5 and 95) that specifies the severity of the error.

From this data set, we know which team has made how many errors of which severity on any day between January 2003 and December 2004. We observe 100 work teams at 50 workplaces on roughly 500 days. The number of teams is double the number of workplaces because on every day, there is an early and a late shift. Our productivity measure is the sum of errors per team per day where the errors are rated with their respective weights. As larger teams work more and therefore make potentially more errors, we divide this sum by the number of workers in the team. For example, if a team with seven workers makes two errors on a day with weights 5 and 30, the sum of error weights is 35 in that team on that day. Our (inverse) productivity measure for this team for this day takes the value $35/7 = 5$.

The information on errors is matched with personnel data that inform us about the daily composition of the work teams, personal characteristics of the workers such as age, sex, education, nationality, job tenure, and whether or not a worker is in her regular team.

Our observation unit is a team-day. We try three different specifications to capture the effect of average team age: two-year age dummies, age splines, and a third-degree age polynomial. As it turns out, they yield very similar results. The results from the dummy-specification are reported in Table 11.1.

---

[2] This chapter reports the first results from a study that is described in more detail in Börsch-Supan *et al.* (2007). For details on the data set, see Appendix III.

Table 11.1. Regression results

Dependent variable: error intensity (measured as the sum of error weights per person)

Age						
26–28 years	0.142		(0.169)	0.355	*	(0.186)
28–30 years	0.143		(0.157)	0.396	**	(0.178)
30–32 years	0.191		(0.154)	0.482	***	(0.179)
32–34 years	0.167		(0.152)	0.469	***	(0.180)
34–36 years	0.161		(0.152)	0.446	**	(0.181)
36–38 years	0.21		(0.152)	0.489	***	(0.185)
38–40 years	0.209		(0.156)	0.459	**	(0.182)
40–42 years	0.166		(0.155)	0.398	**	(0.184)
42–44 years	0.213		(0.154)	0.443	**	(0.184)
44–46 years	0.221		(0.156)	0.465	**	(0.186)
46–48 years	0.197		(0.159)	0.467	**	(0.194)
48–51 years	0.175		(0.174)	0.499	**	(0.207)
Diversity	0.927	***	(0.168)	0.991	***	(0.143)
Job tenure						
2–4 yrs	—		—	−0.413	**	(0.186)
4–6 yrs	—		—	−0.594	***	(0.913)
6–8 yrs	—		—	−0.599	***	(0.190)
8–10 yrs	—		—	−0.591	***	(0.187)
10–12 yrs	—		—	−0.539	***	(0.197)
12–14 yrs	—		—	−0.519	***	(0.195)
14–16 yrs	—		—	−0.483	**	(0.198)
16–18 yrs	—		—	−0.431	**	(0.200)
18–20 yrs	—		—	−0.486	**	(0.200)
20–22 yrs	—		—	−0.473	**	(0.150)
22–24 yrs	—		—	−0.503	**	(0.207)
24–30 yrs	—		—	−0.615	***	(0.212)
Diversity	—		—	−0.149	**	(0.007)
R^2	0.1029			0.1047		

Notes: No. of observations: 48,315 (unbalanced panel of 100 work teams on 524 work days).
Reference category for age dummies: 23–26 years, reference category for tenure dummies: less than 2 years. Standard errors in parentheses.

The left-hand column reports the results of a regression that does not control for job tenure. Age is insignificant. Older work teams make no more and no fewer errors than younger work teams. This insignificance may result from the counteracting effects of increasing experience on the one hand and decreasing physical and mental fitness on the other. The right-hand column displays the results from a regression that controls for job tenure as a measure of experience. Now, almost all other age groups make significantly more errors than the reference age group of 23–6-year-olds. The increase between these age groups is only sometimes significant. The potentially counteracting effect of average job tenure on errors is also only partly significant.

For job tenure below six years, an increase in job tenure (i.e. the difference between the coefficients on two adjacent dummies) has a significantly negative effect on errors (at the 5% significance level). However, for job tenure between 10 and 16 years, we find a significant positive effect on errors (at the 5% level). The results regarding age diversity are discussed in Section 11.3.1. Control variables include a dummy for an early shift, education measured in years of schooling, the share of women in the team, the share of workers who do not belong to the team regularly, team size, diversity with respect to nationality, the share of French, the share of Turkish, and the share of German workers, and weekday dummies. The share of women is also interacted with average team age. Our findings suggest that in younger work teams, a higher female share leads to more errors, while in older work teams, the reverse holds. As the data do not contain information on who in the work team actually made the error, we are not able to say whether it is the women who make the errors or whether it is the men who get distracted by the women. If this latter interpretation is true, than older workers are less easily distracted by the presence of women than younger workers.

In summary, our findings suggest that productivity is decreasing with age. However, the effect of job tenure has the opposite sign and similar magnitude. If workers remain in the same plant, they can compensate for the negative age effect by accumulating job-specific experience.

11.2.2 Age and Plant-Level Productivity in Finnish Industry

For the plant-level econometric analysis of the relation between age and productivity, we use data drawn from the Finnish Linked Employer–Employee Data (FLEED), 1990–2002, which include information on plants and the employees who can be linked to their employer. The Finnish system of registers covers the whole population and all firms and their plants. Information on the workplace of the individuals at the end of the year allows linking of the registers. We explain the data set in more detail in Appendix III. In this study, we concentrate on industrial plants, which we define to include mining, manufacturing, energy, and construction. One reason for restricting attention to this sector is that we do not have data on capital stock for most of the plants in the service sector. We need this information for calculating our measure of productivity, total factor productivity (TFP). The measure is explained in more detail in Box 11.1.

Box 11.1 TOTAL FACTOR PRODUCTIVITY

Total factor productivity measures the contribution of all factors of production. We measure output by value-added Y, labour input by hours worked H, and the other input is capital K. Total factor productivity is defined as $TFP = Y/H^{a}K^{1-a}$, that is, output divided by an 'aggregated' input. This will be used in logarithmic form $\log(TFP) = \log(Y/H) - (1-a)\log(K/H)$, where Y/H is value-added per hours worked and K/H is capital input per hours worked. To obtain an estimate of the effects of average employee age and other employee characteristics on TFP, one could regress $\log(Y/H)$ on $\log(K/H)$ and the plant-age structure variables. However, we construct a measure of total factor productivity directly rather than estimate a production function. The weight a is calculated separately for each of the Finnish two-digit industries by taking averages over time of the ratios of labour cost to value-added in the OECD STAN database. This approach of calculating the TFP directly rather than estimating a production function follows Barrington and Troske (2001), Daveri and Maliranta (2007), and Ilmakunnas and Maliranta (2005), among others. We avoid, among other specification issues in production function estimation, the problem that with panel data one often obtains unreasonably low capital input coefficients (Griliches and Mairesse, 1998). If the regression models for $\log(TFP)$ include year dummy variables interacted with industry dummy variables, the TFP measure needs not be deflated, since this amounts to the same as deflation with industry-specific price indices.

The explanatory variables are the employee characteristics, average age, and years of tenure (months of tenure divided by 12), and average education years. To allow for non-linearities, we add the squares of average age and tenure. The information on degrees has been transformed to years by using standard degree times to form the education variable. The other regressors are share of female employees and plant-size indicators to account for scale effects. In addition, we include in the regressions year dummy variables to take into account cyclical changes, industry indicators, and we further interact the year and industry indicators.

Average employee age and plant age are likely to be correlated (see the Appendix III). If older plants have older technology, a possible negative correlation between employee age and productivity can therefore be related to plant age and not necessarily to employee age per se. This emphasizes the importance of controlling plant vintages in statistical analyses of productivity. In fixed-effects estimation, this is not a problem, since the cohort is a characteristic of a plant that does not change over time.[3]

---

[3] There is information on regions, but in fixed-effects estimation these are not used, since they do not vary over time. Only in very few cases have there been changes of industry, so in practice not all industry effects can be identified.

Since the smallest plants can have very extreme age structures, we drop the smallest size class, 0 to 4 employees. As capital stock data are not available for all the plants, there is a further drop especially in the number of the smaller plants. This restriction cuts the tails of the age distribution further.

There has been a change in the coverage of the data, which may have an impact on the results. The capital stock, hours, and value-added data needed for calculating the *TFP* indicator originate from Industrial Statistics. As explained in the Appendix III, there is a break in this data source between 1994 and 1995. Many single-plant firms with below 20 employees are no longer included, whereas even some very small plants that belong to larger firms may now be included. We therefore concentrate on the period 1995–2002, but also present some results for the earlier period 1990–4. There is also another reason for investigating the sub-periods. In the early 1990s, there was an unprecedented deep recession in Finland, with a sharp increase in firm exits. After the recession, there has been a rapid recovery. Coinciding with the recession, there has been a strong structural change from 'traditional' industries towards high-technology industries. The break between 1994 and 1995 can therefore also be regarded as a break point between a period of recession and a period of recovery and growth.

We first analyse the productivity effects of changes in the age of employees within plants over time. The changes in the distribution of plant average employee ages show that there has been a slow, but steady increase in the mean of the distribution (see Appendix III). This has been the case also when a cohort of plants is followed over time, so that we would expect that the average age of employees within plants has increased.

The productivity model is estimated with fixed-plant effects, so the regression is run using the deviations of the variables from their plant-level means. The results on the key variables of interest are shown in Table 11.2. In the first column appear the results for plants with at least five employees for the period 1990–4. The age and tenure effects are not significantly different from zero. In the second column, we show the corresponding results for the later period 1995–2002. Now there is a negative effect from average tenure of employees. Since the squared tenure term has a positive coefficient, the effect has a U-shape, with a minimum at 14.6 years of average tenure. Since the average tenure is 7.9 years, actually most of the plants are in the declining range of the tenure-productivity curve. As there may be more noise in the data among the smaller plants, we repeated the estimations with plant size restricted to at least 20 employees (i.e. plants are included in those years when they are above this size limit). The third and fourth columns of the table show the results for the two time periods with this size restriction. In the earlier period, the average age term has a positive coefficient, which is, however, significant only at the 11% level, and the squared-age term has a negative and significant coefficient. Taken at face value, the estimates would imply that productivity peaks at 27.9 years of average age.[4] However, given that for most of the plants the average age is higher, they are in fact in the declining part of the productivity profile. In contrast, in the period 1995–2002, the age effect is significant and negative, but the squared term is insignificant. It seems that, especially in larger plants, the ageing of employees within the plants over time will have a negative impact on productivity. Since we have used fixed-plants effects, they also account for the plant cohorts, so the results are not affected by differences in plant age. For these larger plants, the tenure effect is negative in 1995–2002, but insignificant in the earlier period.

Since the results may be affected by selection if older plants with older employees and low productivity exit,[5] we have investigated the robustness of our findings by using two different subsets of the data. Column 5 of the table includes results for 'stable' plants, which we define to be those plants that are in the data set in all of the years 1995–2002, have the necessary information for calculating *TFP* in each year, and have at least five employees in all the years.[6] In this case, the results are purged of the effect of plants that exit and perhaps have an older workforce and low productivity. This subset includes 1,374 plants. The effects of average age and tenure are very similar to those in column 4. This implies that the exiting plants did not drive the negative age effects obtained using data on plants with at least 20 employees. The similarity of the results is understandable, since most of the 'stable' plants are relatively large. Still, the number of plants included is only roughly half of the number of plants in column 4.

In the last column of Table 11.2, we include only the 519 plants that have entered in the period 1995–2002 and may have a younger workforce and newer technology. In this case, we do not obtain significant age effects. Also the tenure effects are insignificant, which is understandable since all entering plants have low average tenure.

We briefly mention the main results on the variables not reported in the table. The coefficient of the average education years variable is not significant in 1995–2002, but obtains a negative and significant coefficient in

---

[4] An inverted U-shape is consistent with the results in Ilmakunnas *et al.* (2004) for the period 1988–94, but in their estimates the peak is at 40 years.

[5] For example, Olley and Pakes (1996) have emphasized the role of this kind of selection effect in the estimation of production functions.

[6] They may, however, have some missing values for the other variables.

Table 11.2. Fixed-effects estimates of productivity models

	Dependent variable log(TFP)					
	Plants with at least 5 employees, 1990–1994	Plants with at least 5 employees, 1995–2002	Plants with at least 20 employees, 1990–1994	Plants with at least 20 employees, 1995–2002	Plants with at least 5 employees, existing in 1995–2002	Entering plants, at least 5 employees, 1995–2002
Average age	-0.01	-0.04	0.06	-0.06	-0.06	-0.14
	(0.02)	(0.04)	(0.04)	(0.03)*	(0.04)*	(0.14)
Average age squared/100	-0.01	0.04	-0.10	0.07	0.07	0.17
	(0.03)	(0.05)	(0.05)**	(0.05)	(0.05)	(0.18)
Average tenure	-0.001	-0.04	-0.003	-0.02	-0.02	-0.01
	(0.002)	(0.01)***	(0.003)	(0.01)*	(0.01)*	(0.06)
Average tenure squared/100	0.003	0.13	0.01	0.05	0.07	-0.10
	(0.01)	(0.06)**	(0.01)	(0.05)	(0.05)	(0.20)
Observations	16387	16025	10759	14438	10738	1340
Number of plants	5228	3088	3210	2686	1374	519
R-squared (within)	0.04	0.02	0.06	0.02	0.03	0.16

Note: Cluster standard errors in parentheses. Significance: *** 1%, ** 5%, * 10%. Unreported variables: plant-size indicators, year and industry dummy variables and their interactions, share of female employees, average education years.

1990–94. This is consistent with earlier research (Daveri and Maliranta, 2007), which has found that lagged rather than current education seems to matter. The same is the case here: if we add lags of average education years, their coefficients are positive and significant. The share of females is not significant, and among the plant-size indicators, there is some evidence that the largest size classes have the highest productivity. However, since many plants do not change their size class over time, it is not surprising that not all of the size effects are significant in the fixed-effects estimation that is based on changes within plants over time.

The underlying assumption in the analysis so far has been that the structure of the workforce of the plants can be considered as exogenous. For example, there are no shocks that affect both the age structure and productivity at the same time. Further, the firms are assumed not to adjust the age structure of their workforce to improve productivity. If we relax these assumptions, it is necessary to use instrumental variables to purge the correlation of the age variable and the error term of the model. In previous work, lagged values of average age of employees have been used as instruments for current average age (e.g. Aubert and Crépon, 2003; Malmberg *et al.*, 2005; Daveri and Maliranta, 2007). However, lagged values are not necessarily very good instruments.

It is likely that the age of the workforce when a plant enters is more exogenous than the average age lagged a few periods. For example, studies by Haltiwanger *et al.* (1999, 2007) find that firms start with a certain workforce structure, for example in terms of average age, which only slowly evolves over time. Finding that, conditionally on the average age of employees at the time of entry, current age of employees predicts exits, Kuhn (2007) concluded that employee age can be interpreted to cause firm performance rather than vice versa.[7] He analysed plant survival, but the same argument can be applied to the analysis of productivity.

We will investigate the role of instrumental variables in the estimation of the productivity model for the period 1995–2002. Following the idea that the age structure at the time of entry matters, we form instrumental variables for current average age, which are interactions of average age at the time of entry with year dummies. We cannot use the average age at entry itself, since we use a fixed-effects model, that is, the variables are deviations

---

[7] The current average age of the workforce has also been used as an explanatory variable for plant survival in other studies, including Nurmi (2004) and Andersson and Vejsiu (2001). These studies show that the probability of plant exit increases with the age of the workforce. Also Malmberg *et al.* (2005) find that the share of employees over 50 increases the probability that a plant will close down.

from their means for each plant. The average age at entry is constant for a plant over time, so its deviation from its plant means would be zero. Still, the average age at entry varies across plants in any given year, and it increases over time across entry cohorts, because of the ageing of the available labour supply (see the Appendix III). Interacting it with the year dummy variables gives us variables that vary over time and across plants. As an alternative, we use average age lagged one and two periods as instruments. To simplify the analysis, we use just the average age of employees without the squared term to describe the age structure of the employees. When included, the squared term was not significant. In addition, to reduce the number of variables, we use deflated log(*TFP*) as the dependent variable and do not include the year-industry interactions that were used in the fixed-effects estimations to account for price changes.[8]

Since the age effects in Table 11.2 were strongest when the smallest plants were excluded, we concentrate on plants with at least 20 employees in 1995–2002. The main data restriction is the availability of information on the average age at plant entry, which restricts the analysis to plants that have entered in 1991 or later. The control variables are the same as in Table 11.2, but we did not include year or industry dummies as explanatory variables. Table 11.3 shows the results from three estimations, where the sample has been constrained to be the same. For the purpose of comparison, we also present the fixed-effects estimate, which is slightly smaller in absolute value than the coefficient of the linear age term in column 4 of Table 11.2. The two instrumental variables estimations give negative

Table 11.3. Instrumental variables estimates of the age effect

		Dependent variable real *log(TFP)*	
	Fixed effects	Fixed effects, IV	Fixed effects, IV
Average age	−0.04	−0.18	−0.18
	(0.01)**	(0.06)**	(0.04)***
Instruments		Average age lagged 1 and 2 years	Average age at time of entry interacted with year dummies

Notes: N = 1713, number of plants = 537. Plants with at least 20 employees included. Period is 1995–2002. Standard errors in parentheses. Significance: *** 1%, ** 5%, * 10%. Unreported variables: plant-size indicators, share of female employees, average education years, average tenure, average tenure squared. The dependent variable is deflated with industry-specific price indices.

[8] log(*TFP*) is deflated by industry-specific price indices computed from the nominal and real production series in the OECD STAN database.

coefficients that are much higher in absolute value than the fixed-effects estimate, but identical to each other. This indicates that the estimates of the age effect on productivity presented above may be biased towards zero. The parameter is more precisely estimated when age at entry is used as instrument than with lagged average age as instrument.

In the fixed-effects estimation, we do not observe plant-vintage effects on productivity, since for a given plant, its entry cohort is a time-invariant characteristic. To illustrate the importance of the vintage effects, we present cross-sectional evidence on the age-productivity connection. Since the relationship may be non-linear, we use a semi-parametric method, partial linear regression (see Yatchew, 2003).[9] Figure 11.1 shows for three years, 1990, 1995, and 2000, the cross-sectional age-productivity relationship for plants that have at least 20 employees. The upper panel of the figure shows the relationship for all of these plants and the lower panel the relationship for stable plants, that is, those that have existed for the whole period 1990–2002. In these figures, we control for average tenure and its square, average education years, share of females, plant size, industry, region, and plant cohort. We use deflated log(*TFP*) values, so the upward shift in the curves over time reflects productivity growth. The tails of the curves are based on relatively few observations and not too much attention should be paid to the shapes at low or high average ages. Therefore the extreme tails have been removed from the figure.

In the upper panel, the relationship has an inverted U-shape in 1990, with a peak at approximately 38 years, a U-shape in 1995, and in 2002 the relationship is more or less flat in the range of average ages where most of the plants are. These figures are consistent with what we found in the fixed-effects estimations. They show that over time the age-productivity connection has indeed changed, perhaps because of the big structural changes in the economy and the exit of low-productivity plants. In the lower panel, the entering and exiting plants are excluded and the basic shape of the curve stays very similar for all years. The relationship is inverted U-shaped, with a peak at roughly 44 years in 1990 and slightly higher in 1995. The productivity of the plants with a younger workforce has risen more over time, so in 2000 the curve is downward sloping. The figure indicates that part of the reason for a negative age effect on productivity may be a higher productivity growth rate in plants with a younger workforce.

---

[9] Productivity is regressed on the other variables except the age terms. A non-parametric smoothed curve is then fitted to the relationship between age and the residual from the first-step regression.

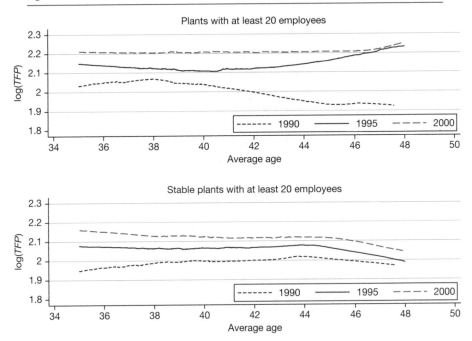

Figure 11.1. Non-linear age-productivity relationship in cross-sections

In Figure 11.2, we illustrate the importance of plant age in the assessment of the effects of employee age on productivity. We fit the non-linear cross-sectional relationship between average age of employees and log(*TFP*) in 2000 for three cases: average tenure and plant age (cohort) not controlled, plant age controlled, and both controlled. Again, only plants with at least 20 employees are included. With both plant vintage and employee tenure taken into account, the curve is rather flat. (This is the same as the curve for year 2000 in the upper panel of Figure 11.1.) The variables used have a clear impact on the shape. The curve is steepest, that is, the negative age effect is strongest, when neither average tenure nor plant vintage is controlled. Controlling for plant-age groups shifts the curve down for low average ages. When plant age is not included, the average employee age variable picks up the positive productivity impact of new technology in the youngest plants, and does not necessarily reflect decreasing productivity with age. When average tenure (and its square) are also controlled, the curve also shifts upward for higher average ages. These are cases where both tenure and age tend to be high, so if tenure is not taken into account, average age picks up both effects.

In summary, the results with plant-level data show that we cannot find a very robust connection between average age of employees and productivity,

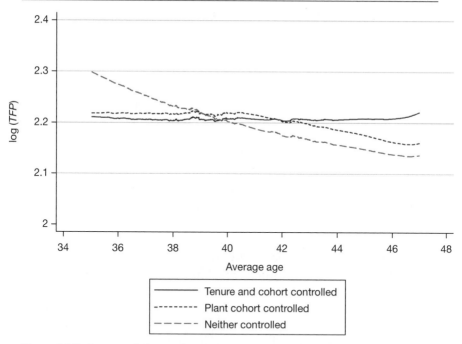

Figure 11.2. Impact of plant cohort on age-productivity relationship, 2000

as there is a change over time in the productivity profile. It is not clear what is behind the changed relationship. We can conjecture that the big structural change caused by the deep recession in Finland in the early 1990s has led to an industrial structure where low productivity plants have exited and the high-technology industries that have emerged show a different age-productivity connection than the previously dominant 'traditional' industries. At the same time, there has been a change in the average age of the workforce because of demographic developments. This may have contributed to the shift in the age-productivity profile. In the later period, 1995–2002, the evidence is more consistent that among the larger plants (over 20 employees), there is a negative effect of average age of employees on productivity. In small and young plants, there is no clear age-productivity connection.

11.3 Workforce Diversity and Productivity

In this section, we report regression results regarding the role of workforce diversity. Research on the age-productivity connection has not emphasized workforce diversity. Ilmakunnas *et al.* (2004), however, included standard deviations of employee characteristics to explain productivity. In other fields of research, arguments have been presented as to why a diverse labour input should be beneficial or harmful. In this connection, the diversity is mostly understood as skill diversity, which can be measured, for example, by the variation in the educational levels of the employees. One line of argument states that performance is determined by the 'weakest link'. An organization can reach its full productivity potential only if the employees have relatively similar skills, since employees with different kinds of skills cannot be substituted for each other. This argument has been labelled 'O-ring' theory (Kremer, 1993).[10] Another, opposite argument is that the full potential of an organization can be reached with a diversified labour input. For example, the performance may depend on a few key employees, who, however, need others to support them.[11]

Transferred to the age-productivity connection, these arguments would imply that a diversified age structure performs better than a homogeneous age composition, if workers of different ages are complementary. It has indeed been a popular argument that younger workers can learn from older ones. The O-ring argument would predict the reverse. There are some studies where the effects of age diversity have been examined. Hamilton *et al.* (2004) find that skill diversity enhances team productivity, but age diversity has a negative effect. Leonard *et al.* (2004) found that age diversity predicted low sales in retail stores.

However, age does not directly measure skills, but rather age connected with other employee characteristics. Older employees may have more outdated skills, but they may be able to compensate with longer experience, especially when the work involves firm-specific skills. Diversity of age-experience combinations may therefore be more relevant than just age

---

[10] This term is borrowed from the O-ring that was the cause of the destruction of a space shuttle.

[11] Other types of workforce diversity have been examined empirically in the work on wage dispersion and firm performance (Winter-Ebmer and Zweimüller, 1999; Hibbs and Locking, 2000, among others), where the issue is whether wage dispersion (measured by variance of wages or variance of wage equation residual) gives incentives or disincentives for working harder. Age dispersion has not been an issue in this context. Further, Iranzo *et al.* (2006) use person effects from a wage equation estimated with linked employer–employee data as a measure of skills and examine the role of skill dispersion on productivity. In yet another strand of the literature, Barrington and Troske (2001) examine the role of racial diversity on productivity. There is also work in organizational sociology, where the connection between organizational demography and performance has been investigated. Most of this work deals with tenure diversity (e.g. Carroll and Harrison, 1998) and the performance measure is often labour turnover.

diversity. Another possible diversity is in the age-education dimension. Education of employees itself may be beneficial for firm performance, but education obtained a long time ago may be less useful than more recent education. We can therefore argue that a workforce that is very diversified in the age-education dimension may be less productive than a workforce that is highly concentrated on young workers with a high level of recently acquired education.

11.3.1 *Age Diversity in Work Teams and Productivity*

This subsection presents results on the role of age diversity in work teams at an assembly plant of DaimlerChrysler.[12] The hypothesis that age diversity is good for performance because younger and older workers complement each other is clearly rejected by our data (see Table 11.1 in Subsection 11.2.1). The more age-diverse work teams are, the more errors they make. We have two explanations for this strong result. The first concerns communication: within teams, workers have to communicate as many tasks are done jointly. Communication across generations is probably more difficult than within generations. Another explanation draws on research in psychology and pedagogics, which finds that elderly workers' performance in on-the-job training is better when they are not mixed with younger workers. If younger and older workers are mixed (in training groups or in work teams), prejudices about the 'useless old' might become self-fulfilling prophecies.

Diversity with respect to nationality does not seem to have an effect. Probably, the French and Turkish workers in the plant speak German very well.[13]

11.3.2 *Age Diversity in Plants and Productivity*

In this subsection, we present results on the role of age and skill diversity in Finnish industrial plants. When analysing workforce diversity, we use two types of measures. First, we use coefficients of variation of workforce characteristics. The coefficient of variation of age is the standard deviation of employee ages within the plant divided by the average employee age. Similarly, we use coefficients of variation for tenure and education years.

---

[12] For details, see Weiss (2007a).

[13] It is noteworthy that, on most days, most teams have some nationality mix. In less than 1% of our observations do teams consist of only one nationality. This would certainly not be possible if language was a problem.

Second, we use diversity indices, suggested by Barrington and Troske (2001). They measure diversity in two dimensions at the same time. We use diversity indices to measure age-tenure diversity and age-education diversity. The diversity index is explained in Box 11.1.

We estimate productivity models that are similar to those in Table 11.2, but we now include diversity measures. The coefficients of variation are based on information on all employees in the plants, whereas the age-tenure and age-education diversity measures are calculated from data on a sample of individuals. However, in all cases, we include only plants where the total number of employees is at least 20 employees, since this was the group for which we found the strongest results in the previous section of this chapter.[14] The sample data include roughly one-third of the workforce of the plants (see Appendix III). To obtain enough observations that do not have a large number of zero cells, we restrict the analysis to plants that have at least 20 linked employees in the sample data. This means that the size limit for the total number of employees is roughly 60 employees. As an alternative, we use the limit of at least ten linked employees in the sample data, which corresponds roughly to plants with at least 30 employees. The set of plants in the analysis is therefore much smaller than in the other analyses.

Figure 11.3 shows in the upper-left panel a histogram of the age-tenure diversity index for all of the years combined and in the upper-right panel the development of its distribution over time in a boxplot. Both are shown for the case of at least 20 linked employees. The values of the diversity measures cover the whole range from zero to one. The mode of distribution of the age-tenure diversity is close to one-half, and there are clearly more observations with values close to one than very low values.[15] The time series shows a drop in diversity during the recession years in the early 1990s and a slightly increasing trend in diversity after that. The drop can most likely be attributed to reduced hiring of new employees during the cyclical downturn, which led to a drop in the share of young employees. Also separations in this period may have been more concentrated on the less senior employees.

The lower part of Figure 11.3 presents similar distributions for the age-education diversity measure. The age-education diversity has a much more skewed distribution, with most plants having an index value clearly

---

[14] Naturally, this does not reduce the number of observations in the case where we use plants with at least 20 employees in the sample data.

[15] There is a peak at the value 0.33, which is caused by plants that have zeros in two cells of the 2 x 2 matrix, and higher shares of employees in the other two cells than the baseline population. In this case, the sum in the numerator of the diversity index is equal to 2, so the index equals 1/3.

Box 11.2 DIVERSITY INDEX

When analysing age-tenure diversity, we divide the employees within plants into four cells according to the following matrix:

	'Young' Y (age 50 or less)	'Old' O (age over 50)
'Inexperienced' I (tenure under 3 years)	Y, I	O, I
'Experienced' E (tenure 3 years or more)	Y, E	O, E

The definitions of the age groups are 50 or below and over 50 (the terms 'young' and 'old' refer to relative, not absolute age), and the experience division is based on whether the employees have at least three years' tenure in their current workplace. To avoid too many empty cells, we use only 2 x 2 classifications of the employee characteristics. In terms of age-education diversity, the data are divided within plants into the following cells:

	'Young' Y (age 50 or less)	'Old' O (age over 50)
'Low education' L (Comprehensive or lower secondary education)	Y, L	O, L
'High education' H (Upper secondary or university education)	Y, H	O, H

The educational division is based on whether employees have a university or polytechnic degree as opposed to comprehensive or lower secondary education.
   We adopt an index of diversity suggested by Barrington and Troske (2001):

$$Diversity = \frac{\left(\sum_{i=1}^{D} Min\left(\frac{W_i}{B_i}, 1\right) \right) - 1}{D - 1}$$

where D is the number of cells into which the employees are divided according to the characteristics in question (in our case, $D = 4$), W_i is the share of the plant's workforce in cell i, and B_i is the corresponding share in the baseline population (in our case, all industrial plants for which we have data on individuals in our sample data). The index has the property that when the composition of the workforce in a plant corresponds to that in the underlying population, the index obtains the value 1 (i.e. in this case, the sum in the numerator is D, so both the numerator and denominator are equal to $D - 1$). When the workforce is less diversified, the index is below one, and in the extreme case where the whole workforce of a plant concentrated into one cell, the index equals zero (i.e. the sum in the numerator equals one).

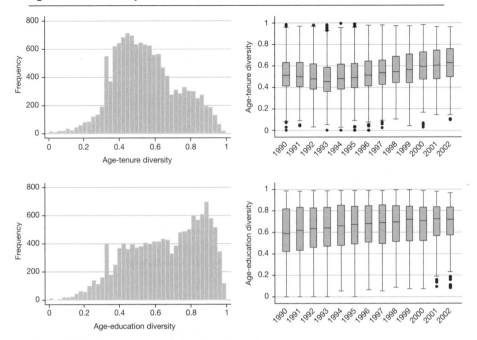

Figure 11.3. Distributions of the diversity indices

above one-half. In this dimension, the workplaces seem to be relatively diversified. Over time, there is an increasing trend in the index throughout the time period. This is a reflection of a higher educational level in younger age cohorts of employees, in combination with the on average lower educational level of older employees, leading to a more diversified workforce.

The median value of the plant-level coefficient of variation of employee ages fell slightly during the early 1990s, but after that the median has slowly increased (see the Appendix III). The reasons for this development are most likely the same as those behind the development of the age-tenure diversity index.

The results on productivity equations with workforce diversity measured are shown in Table 11.4. The first two columns present the results with coefficient of variation measures of diversity for two time periods. These results correspond to those in columns 3 and 4 of Table 11.2, but the number of observations is slightly lower because of some missing observations. Inclusion of the diversity measures renders the average age variable insignificant, which may be an indication of more age diversity in plants with high average age. There is an indication of a positive association between age diversity and productivity in both periods and of a negative relationship between education diversity and productivity in the later period. Tenure diversity is not significant in either period.

The third and fourth columns of Table 11.4 include the results for the two periods with diversity indices included and estimation restricted to plants with at least 20 linked employees in the sample data. In this case, the diversity measures are not significant. The age effect is similar to the age effects in Table 11.2, although the number of included plants is smaller. Finally, in the last two columns of Table 11.4, we show corresponding results when we include plants with at least ten linked employees in the sample data. In this case, we find a positive association between age-tenure diversity and productivity in the first period. This supports the view that different age-tenure combinations are complementary to each other in the workplace. Plants that have a balanced mixture of firm-specific skills and employees of various ages seem to perform better. However, in the second period, the coefficient of the diversity measure is close to zero.

Comparing the results to Figure 11.3, we see that the age-tenure diversity index was positively related to productivity in the period where diversity was on average falling. That is, during the recession, those plants that faced falling productivity also had falling diversity. This hints at possible reverse causality between the variables; firms in difficulties perhaps laid off younger employees, thereby creating a less diversified workforce.

The results do not show much of a role for age-education diversity. The diversity index does not obtain a significant coefficient in any of the estimations. The coefficient of variation of education is significant only in the second period, with a negative sign.

11.4 Productivity and Wage Effects of Age

So far we have examined only the age-productivity connection. The Finnish linked employer-employee data include information on the earnings of the individuals, making it possible also to study the age-earnings relationship. We could do this at the level of individuals, but since the productivity analysis is conducted at the plant level, we study plant average wages. There is information on the annual earnings of individuals, as well as on months worked. We can therefore measure average monthly earnings at the individual level, and linking the individuals in the sample data, we obtain a plant-level measure of average monthly wages. Since there is no information on individual hours worked, there is likely to be some measurement

Table 11.4. Fixed-effects estimation results with workforce diversity measures

	Dependent variable log(TFP)					
	1990–1994	1995–2002	1990–1994	1995–2002	1990–1994	1995–2002
Average age	0.03	−0.05	0.03	−0.14	−0.002	−0.10
	(0.05)	(0.04)	(0.10)	(0.07)**	(0.06)	(0.05)*
Average age squared/100	−0.05	0.07	−0.09	0.17	−0.03	0.12
	(0.06)	(0.05)	(0.13)	(0.08)**	(0.08)	(0.06)*
Average tenure	−0.01	−0.02	−0.01	0.02	−0.004	−0.02
	(0.003)**	(0.01)	(0.004)***	(0.02)	(0.003)	(0.02)
Average tenure Squared/100	0.03	0.05	0.03	−0.08	0.01	0.03
	(0.01)**	(0.05)	(0.02)*	(0.08)	(0.01)	(0.08)
Average education	−0.05	0.02	−0.16	0.04	−0.11	0.03
	(0.04)	(0.02)	(0.06)***	(0.04)	(0.04)***	(0.03)
Coefficient of Variation of age	1.12	0.45				
	(0.36)***	(0.26)*				
Coefficient of Variation of tenure	0.01	0.08				
	(0.01)	(0.06)				
Coefficient of Variation of education	−0.26	−0.64				
	(0.54)	(0.38)*				
Age-tenure diversity			0.09	0.01	0.12	0.02
			(0.07)	(0.04)	(0.05)**	(0.03)
Age-education Diversity			0.02	−0.02	0.05	−0.04
			(0.08)	(0.06)	(0.06)	(0.04)
Linked employees			20–	20–	10–	10–
N	9,557	14,422	4,963	7,547	8,165	11,995
Number of plants	3,093	2,683	1,431	1,360	2,418	2,227
R-squared (within)	0.10	0.05	0.16	0.08	0.11	0.06

Notes: Cluster standard errors in parentheses. Plants with at least 20 employees included. Significance: *** 1%, ** 5%, * 10%. Unreported control variables: plant-size indicators, year and industry dummy variables and their interactions, share of female employees.

error in the wage variable.[16] We therefore leave out the tails of the wage distribution and restrict attention to plants where average monthly earnings are at least 500 euros and at most 6,000 euros. Further, we concentrate on plants where total number of employees is at least 20 and there are either at least 20 or at least ten linked employees in the sample data (i.e. employees for whom we have earnings data). We estimate models for the logarithm of average wage, which we explain by the same variables as we used in the productivity models, namely, average age and its square, average tenure and its square, average education years, share of females, as well as industry and year dummy variables and their interactions (to deflate the earnings variable). To make the comparison to the productivity results as transparent as possible, we estimate a model for total factor productivity for the same set of plants that are included in the estimation of the wage model.[17]

The fixed-effects estimation results for the period 1995–2002 are shown in Table 11.5. The productivity effects of age in columns 1 and 3 are roughly similar to the results in Table 11.4, where the number of plants is somewhat higher. The age effect is U-shaped, with a minimum at 42 years, using the estimates in column 1. This again corresponds to the shape of the cross-sectional result in Figure 11.1. The tenure variables are insignificant. Although productivity is increasing at higher average ages, the productivity level of a plant with average age in the mid-forties does not reach that of the same plant when average age was in mid-thirties. In contrast to these results, the connection between average age and average wage is inverted U-shaped, with a peak at 46 years using the figures in column 2 (47 years based on estimates in column 4). Given that there are relatively few plants with average age of employees higher than this, average wage is in practice increasing in age for the relevant range of the variables. In addition to this, there is evidence of a small tenure effect on wage. Therefore, in the range of variables that we actually observe in the data, the wage development is quite different from the development of productivity.

Among the results not reported in the table, we may note that a one-year increase in average education years increases the average wage by 11%, but has no significant productivity impact. One percentage point increase in

---

[16] An additional measurement error is caused by the fact that earnings may originate from several employment relationships, whereas the link to plants is based only on the employment relationship at the end of the year.

[17] The biggest drop in the number of observations is caused by lack of data on capital stock in many plants. Therefore we estimate the productivity model first and then restrict estimation of the wage model to the same sample.

Table 11.5. Fixed-effects estimation results for productivity and average wage

	Dependent variable			
	log(TFP)	log(wage)	log(TFP)	log(wage)
	1995–2002	1995–2002	1995–2002	1995–2002
Average age	−0.14	0.06	−0.10	0.05
	(0.07)**	(0.01)***	(0.05)*	(0.01)***
Average age	0.17	−0.07	0.12	−0.06
squared/100	(0.08)**	(0.01)***	(0.06)*	(0.01)***
Average tenure	0.02	0.003	−0.02	0.004
	(0.02)	(0.003)	(0.02)	(0.002)**
Average tenure	−0.08	0.02	0.03	0.02
squared/100	(0.08)	(0.01)*	(0.06)	(0.01)
Linked employees	20 –	20 –	10 –	10 –
N	7,542	7,542	11,978	11,978
Number of plants	1,360	1,360	2,225	2,225
R-squared (within)	0.08	0.59	0.06	0.51

Notes: Cluster standard errors in parentheses. Plants with at least 20 employees included. Significance: *** 1%, ** 5%, * 10%. Unreported control variables: plant-size indicators, year and industry dummy variables and their interactions, share of female employees, average education years.

the share of female employees decreases the average wage by 0.28%, but there is no corresponding effect on productivity.[18]

11.5 Conclusions on Age and Productivity

We have presented evidence on the relationship between the age structure of the workforce and productivity from two different data sets. The data on team-level productivity at an assembly plant of DaimlerChrysler suggest that productivity is monotonously decreasing with age. However, to some extent, this decline in productivity can be compensated for if workers remain in the same plant and accumulate job-specific experience.

The results from the data on plant-level productivity are less clear-cut. This is not surprising, given that the study embraces sectors as diverse as mining, manufacturing, energy, and construction. As discussed in Chapter 8, different skills and abilities decay with age, while experience

[18] This can be interpreted so that average female wages are 28% below average male wages. It is shown in Ilmakunnas and Maliranta (2005) that the share of female employees is negatively related to productivity, but this connection disappears in fixed-effects estimation, where time-invariant unobservable plant differences are taken into account. See also Haltiwanger *et al.* (1999, 2007) for related results.

naturally increases with age. The importance of these different skills and abilities and experience varies across different jobs and tasks. Accordingly, age-productivity profiles vary across different jobs and tasks. There is weak evidence that in the early 1990s, the industry-wide age-productivity profile was hump-shaped, which is consistent with earlier evidence. On the other hand, in the late 1990s and early 2000s, the profile was declining with age. A cross-section inspection reveals the age-productivity profile to be rather flat in the 2000s. An explanation for these changes might be the big structural change in the Finnish economy caused by the deep recession in the early 1990s and the exit of low-productivity plants. An examination of plants that have survived for the whole period gives more evidence for a hump-shaped pattern in the early 1990s that was changing over time to a declining pattern, as plants with a younger workforce have had a higher productivity growth rate.

Regarding the role of workforce diversity, the evidence from the two data sets seems inconsistent. The data from DaimlerChrysler suggest that age diversity has adverse effects on productivity, while using the Finnish plant-level data, age diversity is positively related to productivity, at least when measured by the coefficient of variation of employee ages. This seeming contradiction can be ascribed to the different observation units. The DaimlerChrysler data measure productivity of work teams. This is the level where teamwork takes place. At the team level, age diversity is bad for performance. The Finnish data measure productivity at the plant level. Age diversity at the plant level may mean that in some parts of the plant (e.g. management), there are many older (wise, experienced) workers, while in other parts (e.g. production), there are many younger (fit, flexible) workers. Complementarity at the firm level may well be consistent with non-complementarity at the team level.

Another explanation may be that the tasks at the assembly line at DaimlerChrysler are rather homogeneous, so that the advantages of diversity are not important, while the disadvantages of diversity (impeded communication, etc.) are important. In other parts of the economy (included in the Finnish data), complementarities between different age groups (even at the team level) may be more important.

The results from the plant-level data show that plant age and employee age are connected. If plant age is not taken into account when a cross-section of plants is examined, old technology in old plants would erroneously be interpreted as decreased productivity because of employee ageing. This is an important issue when productivities in several plants are compared. When studying assembly lines in a single plant, the vintage effect is not relevant.

We have also studied the connection between age and wages. A rather consistent result from the earlier studies in this area is that wages tend to increase with age or tenure irrespective of the shape of the age-productivity profile. This is also what we found. From the point of view of the effects of ageing on firms' competitiveness, it is not only productivity that matters, but also the relationship between productivity and wage profiles by age. Clearly, wage-setting systems may lead to a discrepancy in the development of productivity and wage, which gives firms incentives to concentrate possible lay-offs among older employees.

12

Conclusions and Policy Implications

Population ageing occurs in every OECD country because birth rates are low and people live longer. Population ageing is a phenomenon that can be foreseen for decades. Not only is the labour force ageing, it is also the case that the length of working lives is declining, because workers retire earlier than they used to retire. There is some uncertainty with respect to the exact demographic developments but other than that, there is nothing unexpected. The main question addressed in our study is how population ageing will affect productivity.

Basically, from an economic point of view, the effects of population can be studied at three levels: economy, firm, and individual worker. Not much is known about the way ageing affects productivity at the level of the economy. Ageing has an unambiguous effect on the age structure of the population: the number of old-age individuals increases relative to young and prime-age individuals. Ageing will affect the size and composition of the workforce, but also labour demand. An important question is whether older workers are good substitutes for younger workers. If workers of different ages are imperfect substitutes in production, ageing will affect the relative wages of younger and older workers. When young workers become scarcer, the relative wage of young workers should rise. Whether they actually do so depends on the degree of substitutability between different age groups in production and on the institutional framework of the labour market. Unfortunately, not much is known about labour demand substitutability between age groups. Therefore, it is difficult to draw straightforward conclusions except for the obvious conclusion that even if, at the individual level, productivity were to decline with age, there may be compensating effects at the aggregate level. Our study deals with the relationship between population ageing and productivity at the level of the individual and the level of the firm.

We contribute to the discussion on this relationship in two ways. First, we present a 'grand view', in which we discuss the various components of productivity in detail and look at long-term historical developments, where we take changing economic structures into account. Second, we present results from an empirical analysis in which we consider both the 'extensive margin' of productivity (absenteeism—at an individual level) and the 'intensive margin' of productivity (productivity conditional on being present at work—at group or firm level). Furthermore, we provide an empirical analysis of a subjective measure of productivity (working capacity). By its contents as well as by its empirical basis, the analysis of the relationship between ageing and group productivity is the most important, although the results are less conclusive. Nevertheless, the importance of the relationship between age and absenteeism should not be underestimated. Other than individual productivity, individual absence is easy to monitor and, in the perception of employers, absenteeism may be used as an indicator of individual productivity.

The main findings concerning the 'grand view' are the following. Productivity is multidimensional and age affects various skills differently. The productivity effects of ageing depend on the extent to which age-induced changes in cognitive and non-cognitive abilities are relevant for work performance. Concerning cognitive abilities, a distinction between crystallized and fluid abilities is important. The crystallized cognitive abilities increase to a relatively late age or remain stable throughout the working life; the fluid abilities deteriorate strongly with age. Different types of work will use different combinations of crystallized and fluid cognitive abilities and physical strength. In the past century, the structure of work has changed a lot and therefore the relationship between age and productivity is also changing. The fact that younger cohorts of older workers are healthier also affects the age-productivity relationship. The main findings concerning the relationship between ageing and the extensive margin of productivity (absenteeism) are the following. Younger workers tend to have a higher number of absences, while older workers are absent less often, but have longer durations of absence. The overall effect of age on absenteeism is concave. Sick leave increases with age up to age of 45 and flattens out afterwards. Age has an effect not only at the individual level. More age diversity within a group of workers leads to more individual absence. Concerning the subjective measure of productivity, we conclude the following. Age affects working capacity, at least to the extent that workers themselves think so. Rotation of older workers to tasks that are less physically demanding may improve perceived working capacity and may even improve actual productivity. The main findings concerning the intensive margin of productivity are the following. Productivity is monotonously decreasing with age, but this decline in productivity can be compensated if workers remain in the same plant and accumulate job-specific experience. So tenure is good for productivity (intensive margin), but not for absenteeism (extensive margin). From the point of view of the effect of ageing on firms' competitiveness, it is not only productivity that matters, but also the relationship of productivity and wage profiles by age.

From our analysis, we conclude that individual productivity deteriorates if no investments are made to keep human capital up-to-date. Nevertheless, drawing conclusions from this about the future relationship between ageing and productivity is not straightforward, that is, it is not clear how ageing at the level of the individual worker will affect productivity in the future. One of the reasons is that the age-productivity profile is changing over time. But, perhaps even more important is that the age-productivity profile is not exogenous to labour market institutions. If a worker anticipates early retirement, he will be less eager to invest in training to prevent his productivity from deteriorating. If an employer expects his worker to retire early, he will not have an incentive to invest in maintaining productivity. One of the main problems from a policy point of view is that population ageing requires changes in labour market institutions and social norms that are opposite to the changes that have been implemented in the recent past. Labour market institutions have been adjusted to facilitate early departure from the labour force. Social norms about when one should cease to participate in the workforce as a *social construct* do contain some truth. Age-norms and age-rules have come into existence as beliefs, norms, and ideological views on age and retirement have come about—and disappeared—as unions, leaders, and employer organizations change their beliefs. In art (Christian paintings in particular), poetry, and literature (ranging from Roman mythology to Norse folklore), older individuals represent wisdom, experience, calmness, and sound judgement; not withdrawal, sitting still, making demands, and dependence.

What does this all mean from a policy point of view? Well, let's first consider policy mistakes. In the past, based on the 'lump of labour fallacy', mistakes have been made that are partly irreversible. Early retirement has been used as an instrument to reduce unemployment, in particular youth unemployment. Current generations of older workers have been brainwashed to think that they can retire early. In the present, the relationship between ageing and productivity is partly a self-fulfilling prophecy. Because older workers anticipate retirement, they are not willing or able to invest in keeping their skills up-to-date. Therefore, the concave relationship between age and productivity is caused by the existence of mandatory retirement and not the other way around. A potential future mistake is to transfer the present skills of older workers and present job requirements into the future, ignoring the facts that future work will be less physical demanding and that future older workers will be healthier than current older workers, who in their turn are healthier than previous cohorts of older workers. Redefining age norms about when people should retire could be supported by changing personnel advertisements from being age-specific to being age-neutral. Age-discrimination legislation (job offers looking for *young*, dynamic workers being no longer allowed) may positively contribute to the employment of older individuals. Norms and attitudes often follow legislation, and the abolition of retirement ages and age-based pension allowance may have such effects on norms about retirement. 'Age-awareness' among employers (increasing training, giving health advice and preventive treatment such as gymnastics, installing technical equipment to ease the working life of senior employees) could further strengthen the relative health performance of older individuals. Allowing for more opportunities to combine work and leisure (as long as overall employment increases) could also be a possibility. How could one increase pension ages? To increase the amount of older individuals who would like to work, one needs to consider ways of increasing the incentives to work longer. First of all, a major reason why senior individuals choose to discontinue work is that by doing so, they expect to receive a pension that does not grow sufficiently to encourage postponing retirement. Increasing the amount of *actuarial neutrality*, keeping pension expenditure fixed and hence yearly pensions conditioned on age of retirement and expected remaining years of life, could increase the labour supply of seniors. Also other factors, such as employers encouraging older individuals to work for more years, increasing allowance for work-life balance or technical adjustments to ease the labour market situation of older individuals, could improve the labour market performance of senior employees.

The main lesson from our study is that labour market behaviour is more important than demographic changes. Age-productivity profiles will change in the future not because of demographics but because workers will behave differently. If their working life is expected to last longer, they will make the investments to keep their skills up-to-date and employers will find it beneficial to support these investments. Having a fixed retirement age for all workers introduces an unnecessary rigidity into the labour market. If some workers can retire later, it is likely that their productivity will start declining at a later age because they will find it worthwhile to

invest over a longer period of time. The retirement age could be individua-
lized by taking the effective number of years of labour market participation
as a measure on which the retirement age is based, that is, those who enter
the labour market at a higher age should also leave the labour market at a
higher age. Wage policies and human resource management concerning
older workers are also important. Seniority-based earnings systems, where
earnings peak relatively late in life, have a negative effect on the labour
force attachment of older individuals. Even when one maintains one's
performance level until late in life, when the learning pace is moderate
and management/communication skills are important, wages that increase
with age may weaken the labour force participation of older individuals.
Human resource management is related to the observation that older workers have a low probability of losing their job, but once they lose their job,
they often stay unemployed for a long time. Labour market institutions
prevent employers from hiring an older worker. Not only is this expensive,
because there is a strong relationship between age and wage, but it may also
be expensive to dismiss the worker if he does not live up to expectations. It
is probably much easier in many countries to prevent dismissals of older
workers than it is to encourage rehiring of older workers. When an older
worker is fired, the social costs are much higher than the private costs. This
is an argument for experience-rating of dismissal costs (severance payment
related to tenure). Wage subsidies could be provided for employers that
want to hire older workers. All in all, we think that the potential negative
effects of ageing on productivity should not be underestimated. Nevertheless, they should not be exaggerated either. The decline of productivity with
age is partly endogenous and subject to policy influence. The way productivity is affected by age is not just an exogenous phenomenon, but is also
influenced by choice.

APPENDIX III

Assembly Line Data

We make use of a unique data set that we have compiled from an assembly plant of a German car manufacturer. At this plant, work teams assemble cars on an assembly line. The quantity of output is determined by the speed of the assembly line. If work teams differ in productivity, this is not going to show up in differences in the quantity of output because the assembly line has the same speed for all teams. But production quality differs across work teams as they can make errors.

A 'quality inspector' at the end of the assembly line records these errors. The quality inspector is able to assign every error to the workplace where it happened. At any time, there is exactly one work team at any workplace. In addition, every error is given a weight (between 5 and 95) that specifies the severity of the error. From this data set, we know which team has made how many errors of which severity on any day between January 2003 and December 2004. We observe 100 work teams at 50 workplaces on roughly 500 days. The number of teams is double the number of workplaces because on every day, there is an early and a late shift. Our productivity measure is the sum of errors per team per day where the errors are rated with their respective weights. As larger teams work more and therefore make potentially more errors, we divide this sum by the number of workers in the team. For example, if a team with seven workers makes two errors on a day with weights 5 and 30, the sum of error weights is 35 in that team on that day. Our (inverse) productivity measure for this team for this day takes the value $35/7 = 5$.

The information on errors is matched with personnel data that inform us about the daily composition of the work teams, personal characteristics of the workers, such as age, sex, education, nationality, job tenure, and whether or not a worker is in her regular team.

The number of errors occurring in the plant is low. We observe 7,904 errors in 100 teams on 500 days. The probability that a random team on a random day makes an error is 15%. The distribution of error weights (only for those days and teams for which we observe errors) is given in Figure A.1.

The age composition in the plant is fairly representative of the German workforce in that workers older than 55 are rare. Figure A.2 shows the age distribution in the plant (black) in comparison with the age distribution of the whole population (grey). People younger than 20 are underrepresented because they are still in education or training. The share of workers aged 55 and over is low because many have

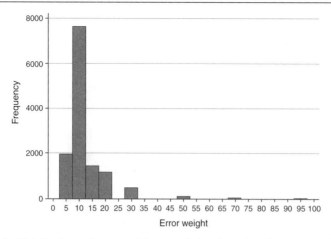

Figure A.1. Distribution of error weights conditional on the observation of errors

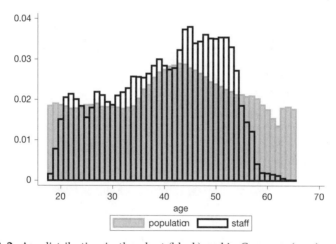

Figure A.2. Age distribution in the plant (black) and in Germany (grey)

already retired. Figure A.3 shows the distribution of average age of work teams, which constitute the observation unit in our regression analysis.

In addition to age, we have information on workers' job tenure. Job tenure increases with age but the two variables are not perfectly correlated as workers are hired at different ages. The distribution of job tenure in the plant is shown in Figure A.4. The spikes show hiring waves roughly every five to ten years, the most recent being just within the observation period (at job tenure = 0).

The distribution of average job tenure in work teams in Figure A.5 shows that at hiring waves, the new workers must have been spread evenly over existing work teams as the histogram does not exhibit any comparable spikes. Figure A.6 shows the

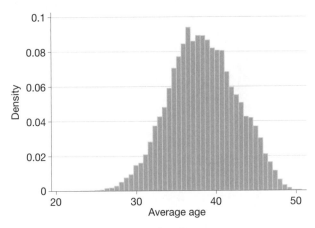

Figure A.3. Distribution of average age of work teams

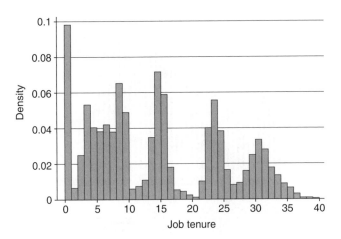

Figure A.4. Distribution of job tenure in the plant

relation between age and job tenure in the plant. For any individual worker, age and job tenure are perfectly correlated over time, but as workers are hired at different ages, the overall correlation (over time and across workers) is 'only' 0.79. Even though the relation is tighter at the team level (see Figure A.7), it is far from perfect so that (given the large number of observations) the effects of both variables on the number of errors can be identified separately in the regressions.

The size of work teams varies between four and 36 workers. Ninety per cent of work teams have between eight and 18 members (see Figure A.8).

The share of women in the plant is 3.2%. In 74% of all work teams, there are only men. In the other 26% of teams, women's share is about 12%.

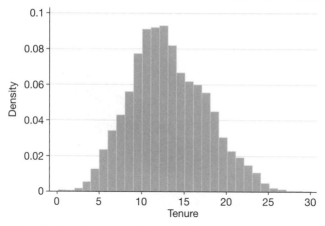

Figure A.5. Distribution of average job tenure of work teams

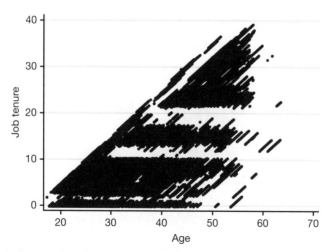

Figure A.6. Scatter plot of job tenure (vertical axis) vs. age (horizontal axis)

The composition of the personnel with respect to nationality is given in Table A.1.

We also have information on the education of workers. As a first attempt, we just calculated the total number of years of schooling for each worker. The distribution is shown in Figure A.9. Most workers went to school for nine years. Many of them completed an apprenticeship straight afterwards. We count this as 'schooling' as well, because in Germany, apprenticeships are very structured and for 50% of their time apprentices actually go to (vocational) school.

Table A.2 gives some descriptive statistics of all the variables used in the analysis of the assembly-line data.

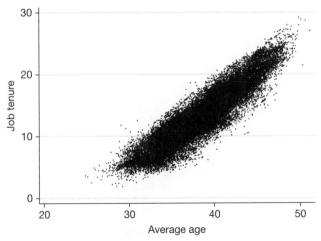

Figure A.7. Scatter plot of average job tenure (vertical axis) vs. average age (horizontal axis) of work teams

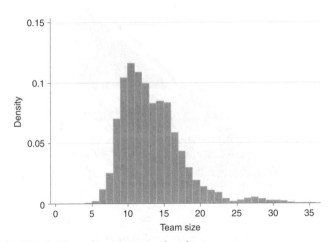

Figure A.8. Distribution of team size in the plant

Table A.1. Comoposition of work teams by nationality

Nationality	German	French	Turkish	other
Share	61.00%	31.20%	3.80%	4.00%

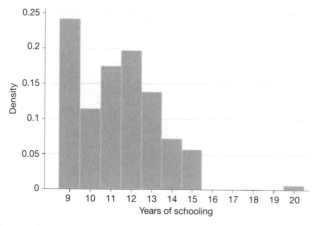

Figure A.9. Distribution of years of schooling

Table A.2. Descriptive statistics on assembly-line data

Variable	mean	median	minimum	maximum	Std. Dev.
Paid absence (dummy)	0.0556	0	0	1	0.229
Age	37.7	37.5	17.3	65.6	10.9
Tenure	12	9.05	0	41.7	9.74
schooling years	11.4	11.4	9	20	1.93
Female (dummy)	0.0367	0	0	1	0.188
Female share	0.367	0	0	0.667	0.059
External (dummy)	0.0623	0	0	1	0.242
Share of externals	0.0623	0	0	1	0.089
Early shift (dummy)	0.326	0	0	1	0.469
Excess work load	0.019	−0.015	0.441	−1.09	1.93
Team size	10.2	9.97	3	28	3.69

Quality of Work Life Survey

Statistics Finland (SF) conducts the Quality of Work Life Survey (QWLS) at irregular intervals. We use data from the year 2003. QWLS provides a representative sample of Finnish wage and salary earners, because the initial sample for QWLS is derived from a monthly Labour Force Survey (LFS), where a random sample of the working-age population is selected for a telephone interview. The 2003 QWLS is based on LFS respondents in October and November who are 15–64-year-old wage and salary earners with a normal weekly working time of at least five hours. 5,300 individuals were selected for the QWLS sample and invited to participate in a personal face-to-face interview. Out of this sample, 4,104 persons, or around 78%, participated (Lehto and Sutela, 2004). Owing to missing information on some explanatory

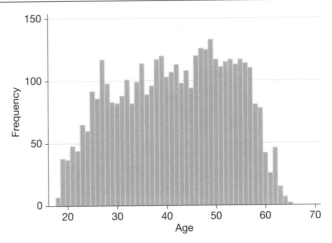

Figure A.10. Age distribution in the QWLS sample

variables for some workers, the sample size used in the estimations of this study is slightly under 4,000 observations. SF supplements QWLS with information from the LFS on, for example, working time and exact labour market status. Supplementary information on the industry and location of the employer, as well as on annual earnings and the level and field of education of the respondents, is gathered from various registers maintained by SF.

Many of the questions in the QWLS survey have alternatives, for example on a scale from 1 to 5. We have combined some questions to construct our indicators for harms, hazards, and uncertainty faced by the employees (see Böckerman and Ilmakunnas, 2006a).

Figure A.10 shows the age distribution in the QWLS sample. The lowest age groups, 25 or below, are relatively small, as many individuals are still studying at these ages. The lowest age in the survey is 16, but we restrict attention to those who are at least 18 years old, dropping the three youngest individuals. Among the older age groups, the number of individuals in their late fifties starts to fall and there are few who are over 60. This is related to the fact that the average effective retirement age in Finland is 59 years, as many take some form of early exit from the labour force.

Table A.3 shows descriptive statistics on the variables from QWLS that have been used in the analyses.

Finnish Longitudinal Employer-Employee Data (FLEED)

The FLEED data set merges the comprehensive administrative records of all labour force members in Finland as well as all employers/enterprises (also including information on their establishments) subject to value-added tax (VAT). A range of additional information from other sources complements it. Employment statistics,

Table A.3. Descriptive statistics on QWLS data

Variable	Observations	Mean	Std.dev.	Min.	Max.
Absences (dummy)	4,099	0.59	0.49	0	1
Number absences	4,095	1.33	1.88	0	25
Days of absence	4,092	8.34	20.93	0	365
Duration of absence	2,417	7.35	18.35	2	365
Accident	4,103	0.05	0.22	0	1
Working capacity	4,098	8.58	1.34	0	10
Chronic illness	4,097	0.31	0.46	0	1
Age	4,101	41.64	11.37	18	65
Age –20	4,101	0.02	0.14	0	1
Age 21–25	4,101	0.08	0.26	0	1
Age 26–30	4,101	0.11	0.32	0	1
Age 31–35	4,101	0.12	0.32	0	1
Age 36–40	4,101	0.13	0.33	0	1
Age 41–45	4,101	0.13	0.33	0	1
Age 46–50	4,101	0.15	0.36	0	1
Age 51–55	4,101	0.14	0.35	0	1
Age 56–60	4,101	0.10	0.30	0	1
Age 61–	4,101	0.02	0.15	0	1
Female	4,101	0.53	0.50	0	1
Comprehensive education	4,101	0.18	0.38	0	1
Lower secondary education	4,101	0.44	0.50	0	1
Upper secondary education	4,101	0.27	0.44	0	1
Higher university education	4,101	0.11	0.31	0	1
Log of monthly pay	4,073	7.51	0.47	6.21	8.52
Tenure 0–2 yrs.	4,098	0.30	0.46	0	1
Tenure 3–12 yrs.	4,098	0.35	0.48	0	1
Tenure 13–27 yrs.	4,098	0.26	0.44	0	1
Tenure 28– yrs.	4,098	0.09	0.28	0	1
Temporary	4,099	0.14	0.35	0	1
Part-time	4,095	0.12	0.32	0	1
Monthly hours	4,069	147.20	28.95	16	240
Blue-collar	4,101	0.35	0.48	0	1
White-collar	4,101	0.65	0.48	0	1
Industry	4,101	0.26	0.44	0	1
Services	4,101	0.67	0.47	0	1
Harms	4,101	0.26	0.44	0	1
Hazards	4,101	0.38	0.48	0	1
Uncertainty	4,101	0.68	0.47	0	1
Team work	4,090	0.27	0.45	0	1
Plant size –9	4,082	0.24	0.43	0	1
Plant size 10–49	4,082	0.37	0.48	0	1
Plant size 50–499	4,082	0.24	0.43	0	1
Plant size 500–	4,082	0.15	0.35	0	1

educational statistics, taxation records, business register, financial statement statistics, manufacturing census, as well as various surveys, are among the original sources of the FLEED variables. Data from Employment Statistics cover the whole working-age population and provide information (code) on the employer establishment and firm of the individuals at the end of the year. This allows linking of data on individuals to employers with near-perfect traceability of employers and employees over time. Ilmakunnas *et al.* (2001, 2004) describe the linking of the data sets. In our analysis, we use only industrial plants, which we define to include mining, manufacturing, energy, and construction.

The data on industrial plants come from a variety of data sources, including Industrial Statistics and the Business Register. The former is, for example, the data source that we used for calculating our productivity measure, total factor productivity (TFP). Changes in the coverage of Industrial Statistics change the number of plants in the data set. Until 1994, Industrial Statistics covered all plants with at least five employees. From 1995, the coverage is for all plants belonging to firms that have at least 20 employees. This means that, for example, small single-plant firms drop out of the data set, but on the other hand, very small plants belonging to large firms are now included. We therefore concentrate mostly on the period 1995–2002, but make the same estimations for the earlier period 1990–4.

The Business Register is more comprehensive, since it covers all establishments and firms in all industries. However, it has limited data content (number of employees, total sales, wage bill). The individuals can be linked both to the plants in Industrial Statistics and to plants and firms in the Business Register. When describing the age structure of plants we can therefore use the Business Register, but for the productivity analysis we use the Industrial Statistics.

Because of confidentiality, linked employer-employee data can be accessed only on site at the research laboratory of Statistics Finland (SF). To overcome the problems of using data at Statistics Finland, a sample has been formed from FLEED, with such information on firms and plants that guarantees that the employers cannot be identified. This data set has been obtained for use outside of SF. The sample data cover the years from 1990 to 2002. Every third individual in the 16–69 year-old age group is randomly included in the sample in the year 1990. This sample includes *c.*1 million individuals. For these individuals, all information from the subsequent years 1991–2002 is included. From 1991, in each year a third of all 16-year-old persons are selected for the sample and these individuals are included in the sample in all subsequent years. For each individual in each year, the data on the establishment and firm that she is working in is included. In addition, data on these establishments and firms are included for all years. Hence, even if an establishment appears only once as the employer of one worker, it is included in all the years 1990–2002. However, the public sector, agriculture, and some personal services are excluded. The establishment data cover all establishments in the business sector (NACE classes 10 to 75) that have at least one person in the data for individuals in at least one year. The company data include all companies that have at least one establishment or individual in the establishment or individual data, respectively. As a result, the plant and firm panels cover practically the whole populations of plants and firms for all years. The data set differs from FLEED in two respects. First, the number of variables has been slightly limited. Second, because of confidentiality, some of the data have been modified. Individual incomes are top-coded and only transformed variables for plants and firms are included. Basically, these variables are in the form of classified variables (e.g. size group dummies), ratios (productivity), or rates of change (e.g. rate of employment change). On the other hand, these modified variables still allow analysis of productivity, as in Daveri and Maliranta (2007). In our analyses, we use the data on the industry sector, which we define to comprise manufacturing, mining, energy, and construction.

Some variables that describe the characteristics of the workforce have been calculated from the original FLEED data, that is, the 'total' data. These include average age, seniority, and education years and their standard deviations. If at least one person from the Employment Statistics has been linked to a plant in the Business Register, we have information on these employee characteristics. To calculate additional employee characteristics, like diversity measures, we can use the sample data. The following figures illustrate the quality of the sample data. In Figure A.11, we plot average age of employees in plants from the sample data in the year 2002 against average age obtained from the FLEED data that covers all employees in each plant in 2002. We have selected those plants that have at least 20 employees in the sample data. In addition, we restrict attention to the industry sector and to plants for which the TFP measure is available. The figure shows that the sample data give a reasonably similar picture of the age of the workforce in the plants, at least for the larger plants.

Figure A.12 presents the evolution of the distribution of average age of employees across plants. The plants are those in the Business Register, so there is no change in the coverage over time. If at least one individual has been linked to a plant, we have information on the average age of the employees. In some very small plants, this may, however, lead to fairly extreme, very low or very high, values for the average age. They can, for example, have only a few teenagers or only a few employees close to (or even above) the retirement age. We therefore leave out the smallest size class,

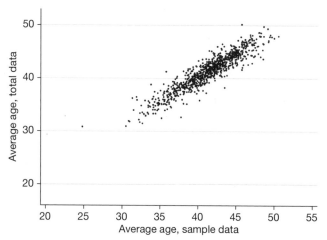

Figure A.11. Average age of employees from sample data and total data in 2002, plants with capital stock data and at least 20 linked employees

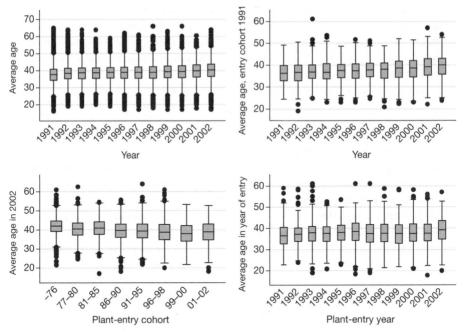

Figure A.12. Distribution of average age of employees

below five employees, in our analyses. This cuts the tails of the distribution of average ages. The graphs in the four panels of the figure are boxplots, where each box includes the middle 50% of the values and the line in the box depicts the median. The 'whiskers' show the range of the other 'non-outlier' observations[1] and observations classified as outliers are shown as dots.

The upper-left panel of Figure A.12 shows the distribution of average ages annually in 1990–2002. The figure reveals two interesting features. First, the plant average ages have increased over time. This is naturally connected to the increasing average age of the workforce. From 1991 to 2002, the median has increased from 37.7 to 40.3 and the mean from 37.6 to 40. Second, the distribution of average ages is relatively narrow, that is, the boxes that cover 50% of the observations are small. In all years, the middle 50% of the observations are within a range of clearly less than ten years.

To uncover the factors that lead to changes over time, we study the age distribution in alternative ways. In the lower-left panel of Figure A.12 we examine the cross-section of plants in year 2002 and plot the age distribution by the entry cohorts. The

---

[1] The end-points of the whiskers (so-called adjacent values) are defined as $x_{[75]} + 1.5(x_{[75]} - x_{[25]})$ for the upper one and $x_{[25]} - 1.5(x_{[75]} - x_{[25]})$ for the lower one; $x_{[25]}$ and $x_{[75]}$ are the 25th and 75th percentiles, respectively.

cohorts are defined as plants established in the periods 1976 or earlier, 1977–80, then five-year intervals 1981–5, 1986–90, and 1991–5, and finally slightly shorter intervals 1996–8, 1999–2000, and 2001–2. The intervals are dictated by the way the plant-age classes are defined in our data. The older plants clearly have an older workforce. The median of the average ages is 42 in the oldest and 38.8 in the youngest cohort (and the means are 41.9 and 38.5, respectively).

Yet another way of inspecting the age distribution is shown in the upper-right panel of Figure A.12, where we track the plants that entered in year 1991 over time by presenting the distribution of their average ages each year. We include only surviving plants, that is, those that are still in operation in the end year 2002. This shows the within-cohort change in the age structure. There is a slight upward shift over time in the age distribution. (The shift would be stronger if we had included the smallest plants.) Clearly, firms ageing together with their employees cause part of the increase in the age structure. If there were no turnover in the workforce, the increase in the age structure would coincide well with the increase in the age of the plant. Here the median has increased from 36.5 to 39.9 and the mean from 36.6 to 39.4 in the period 1991–2002. Since we include only surviving plants, this increase in average employee age is not caused by entry and exit of plants.

There is still one interesting phenomenon in the evolution of the age distribution that is revealed by the lower-right panel of Figure A.12. There we have plotted the distribution of plant-average employee ages for entering plants each year. For the plants entering in the period 1991–2002, we can determine the entry year from the appearance of the plants in the data set. There is an increase in the median from 36.5 in 1991 to 39.1 in 2002 (and the mean increases from 36.6 to 38.9). The increase may be related to an increase in the age of the available labour supply. Another explanation is that there has been an increase in the skill structure. If plants start with a more skilled workforce than the earlier entry cohorts, the workforce will also be older, since

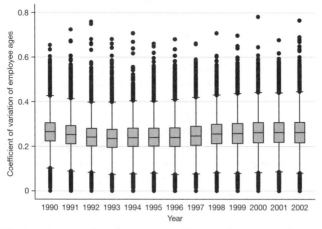

Figure A.13. Distribution of within-plant coefficient of variation of employee ages

231

Table A.4. Descriptive statistics on plant data

Variable	Observations	Mean	Std.dev.	Min.	Max.
log(TFP)	32,412	2.08	0.78	−8.15	7.48
Real log(TFP)	32,412	2.189	0.77	−8.04	7.61
Average age	32,412	39.24	4.18	17	60
Average age squared / 100	32,412	15.57	3.24	2.89	36
Average tenure	32,412	7.92	5.90	0	47.50
Average tenure squared / 100	32,412	0.975	1.25	0	22.56
Average education years	32,412	11.09	0.91	9	17
Share of females	32,412	0.33	0.24	0.01	1
Plant size 5–9	32,412	0.08	0.27	0	1
Plant size 10–19	32,412	0.14	0.35	0	1
Plant size 20–49	32,412	0.33	0.47	0	1
Plant size 50–99	32,412	0.20	0.40	0	1
Plant size 100–	32,412	0.25	0.43	0	1
Coefficient of variation of age	29,257	0.25	0.05	0	0.56
Coefficient of variation of tenure	29,257	0.95	0.43	0	4.65
Coefficient of variation of education	29,257	0.17	0.04	0	0.36
Age-tenure diversity (at least 20 linked employees)	12,523	0.55	0.18	0	0.99
Age-education diversity (at least 20 linked employees)	12,523	0.65	0.21	0	0.99
Age-tenure diversity (at least 10 linked employees)	20,345	0.52	0.19	0	0.99
Age-education diversity (at least 10 linked employees)	20,345	0.59	0.23	0	0.99
log(average monthly wage) (at least 20 linked employees)	7,578	7.71	0.23	6.46	8.66
log(average monthly wage) (at least 10 linked employees)	20,571	7.56	0.28	6.26	8.69

workers entering the labour market after education will be older than non-skilled workers. The distributions seem to vary more from year to year than the distributions in the other panels of Figure A.12. This is natural, since in different years the composition by size, industry, region, and so on, of the entering plants may vary quite a lot.

Figure A.13 shows how the distribution of within-plant age variability, measured by the coefficient of variation of employee ages, evolves over time. On average, the distribution of values has been relatively stable, but from the mid-1990s there has been a slight tendency for the median to increase.

Table A.4 shows descriptive statistics on the variables that have been used in the analyses. The information is shown for plants with at least five employees and information on all the variables. In some analyses, however, subsets of the data have been used. Measures for the diversity of workforce characteristics are available for a smaller number of plants.

References

Acemoglu, D. (2002), 'Technical Change, Inequality, and the Labor Market', *Journal of Economic Literature*, 40(1), 7–72.

Agell, J., and P. Lundborg (1995), 'Theories of Pay and Unemployment: Survey Evidence from Swedish Manufacturing Firms', *Scandinavian Journal of Economics*, 97, 295–307.

Ahituv, A., and J. Zeira (2000), 'Technical Progress and Early Retirement', CEPR Discussion Paper No. 2614, London: Centre for Economic Policy Research.

Allen, S. G. (1981a), 'Compensation, Safety, and Absenteeism: Evidence from the Paper Industry', *Industrial and Labor Relations Review*, 34(2), 207–18.

——(1981b), 'An Empirical Model of Work Attendance', *Review of Economics and Statistics*, 63(1), 77–87.

Andersson, F., and A. Vejsiu (2001), 'Determinants of Plant Closures in Swedish Manufacturing', IFAU Working Paper 2001:6.

Andrén, D. (2005), 'Never on a Sunday: Economic Incentives and Sick Leave in Sweden', *Applied Economics*, 37(3), 327–38.

Askildsen, J. E., E. Bratberg, and Ø. A. Nilsen (2000), 'Sickness Absence over the Business Cycle', Working Paper 4-2000, Department of Economics, University of Bergen.

Aubert, P., and B. Crépon (2003), 'La productivité des salariés âgés: Une tentative d'estimation', *Économie et Statistique*, No. 368, 2003, 95–119.

Ausubel, J. H., and A. Grubler (1995), 'Working Less and Living Longer: Long-Term Trends in Working Time and Time Budgets', *Technological Forecasting and Social Change*, 50(3), 113–31.

Barrington, L., and K. R. Troske (2001), 'Workforce Diversity and Productivity: An Analysis of Employer-Employee Matched Data', The Conference Board, Economics Program Working Paper Series, EPWP No. 01-02.

Barmby, T., M. G. Ercolani, and J. G. Treble (2002), 'Sickness Absence: An International Comparison', *Economic Journal*, 112, F315–31.

——C. D. Orme, and J. G. Treble (1991), 'Worker Absenteeism: An Analysis Using Microdata', *Economic Journal*, 101(405), 214–29.

————(1995), 'Worker Absence Histories: A Panel Data Study', *Labour Economics*, 2(1), 53–65.

Bartel, A. P., and N. Sicherman (1993), 'Technological Change and Retirement Decisions of Old Workers', *Journal of Labor Economics*, 11(1) (Jan.), 162–83.

Baumgartel, H., and R. Sobol (1959), 'Background and Organizational Factors in Absenteeism', *Personnel Psychology*, 12, 431–43.

Böckerman, P., and P. Ilmakunnas (2006a), 'Do Job Disamenities Raise Wages or Ruin Job Satisfaction?', *International Journal of Manpower*, 27, 290–302.

————(2006b), 'Interaction of Job Disamenities, Job Satisfaction, and Sickness Absences: Evidence From a Representative Sample of Finnish Workers', Labour Institute for Economic Research, Discussion Papers 224.

————(2007), 'Unemployment and Self-Assessed Health. Evidence from Panel Data', HECER Discussion Paper No. 148.

Boldrin, M., J. J. Dolado, J. F. Jimeno, and F. Peracchi (1999), 'The Future of Pension Systems in Europe: A Reappraisal', *Economic Policy*, 29, 289–323.

Boot, H. M. (1995), 'How Skilled were Lancashire Cotton Factory Workers in 1833?' *Economic History Review*, No. 2, 283–303.

Bosek, M., B. Grzegorzewski, A. Kowalczyk, and I. Lubinski (2005), 'Degradation of Postural Control System as a Consequence Of Parkinson's Disease and Ageing', *Neuroscience Letters*, 376, 215–20.

Börsch-Supan, A., I. Düzgün, and M. Weiss (2007), 'Age and Productivity in Work Teams: Evidence from the Assembly Line', MEA Discussion Paper 148-07, University of Mannheim.

——and Jürges, H. (eds.) (2005), SHARE, *The Survey of Health, Ageing and Retirement in Europe—Methodology*, Mannheim: MEA.

Bratsberg, B., J. F. Ragan, Jr., and J. T. Warren (2003), 'Negative Returns to Seniority: New Evidence in Academic Markets', *Industrial and Labor Relations Review*, 56(2) (Jan.), 306–23.

Bridges, S., and K. Mumford (2001), 'Absenteeism in the UK: A Comparison across Genders', *The Manchester School*, 69(3), 276–84.

Brown, S., and J. G. Sessions (1996), 'The Economics of Absence: Theory and Evidence', *Journal of Economic Surveys*, 10, 23–53.

Brugiavini, A., and F. Peracchi (2005), 'The Length of Working Lives in Europe, *Journal of the European Economic Association*, 3, 477–86.

Bull, H. H. (2006), 'Inntekts- og forsørgelsesforhold for eldre i Norge fra midten av 1700-tallet til midten av 1800-tallet' [The income and care situation for elderly in Norway from the mid-18th century to the mid-19th century], Dissertation Lecture, 14 Sept. 2006, University of Oslo, Norway.

Burnette, J. (2006), 'How Skilled were Agricultural Labourers in the Early Nineteenth Century?' *Economic History Review*, 59, 688–716.

Cameron, A. C., and P. K. Trivedi (2005), *Microeconometrics: Methods and Applications*, Cambridge: Cambridge University Press.

Carone, G., D. Costello, N. Diez Guardia, G. Mourre, B. Przywara, and A. Salomäki (2005), 'The Economic Impact of Ageing Populations in the EU25 Member States', *Economic Papers*, No. 236, European Commission.

Carroll, G. R., and J. R. Harrison (1998), 'Organizational Demography and Culture: Insights from a Formal Model and Simulations', *Administrative Sciences Quarterly*, 43, 637–67.

Cattell, R. B. (1963), 'Theory of Fluid and Crystallized Intelligence: A Critical Experiment', *Journal of Educational Psychology*, 54(1), 1–22.

CDC (2006), 'Health, United States, 2006', United States Centers for Disease Control and Prevention, available at <http://www.cdc.gov/nchs/data/hus/hus06.pdf#027>.

Costa, D. (2000), 'Understanding the Twentieth Century Decline in Chronic Conditions among Older Men', *Demography*, 37(1), 53–72.

Crimmins, E. M., Y. Saito, and S. L. Reynolds (1997), 'Further Evidence on Recent Trends in the Prevalence and Incidence of Disability among Older Americans from Two Sources: The LSOA and the NHIS', *Journal of Gerontology*, 52B(2), 59–71.

Dalton, G. W., and P. H. Thompson (1971), 'Accelerating Obsolescence of Older Engineers', *Harvard Business Review*, 49(5), 57–67.

Daveri, F., and M. Maliranta (2007), 'Age, Seniority and Labour Cost', *Economic Policy*, No. 49, January, 118–75.

Deary, I. J., L. J. Whalley, H. Lemmon, J. R. Crawford, and J. M. Starr (2000), 'The Stability of Individual Differences in Mental Ability from Childhood to Old Age: Follow-Up of the 1932 Scottish Mental Survey', *Intelligence*, 28(1), 49–55.

De la Mare, G. C., and R. D. Shepherd (1958), 'Aging: Changes in Speed and Quality of Work among Leather Cutters', *Occupational Psychology*, 32, 204–9.

de Zwart, B., M. Frings-Dresen, and F. van Dijk. (1995), 'Physical Workload and the Ageing Worker: A Review of the Literature', *International Archives of Occupational and Environmental Health*, 68, 1–12.

Digitalarkivet (2007), National Archives of Norway, available at <http://www.digitalarkivet.no/>.

Ericsson, K. A., and A. C. Lehmann (1996), 'Expert and Exceptional Performance: Evidence of Maximal Adaptation to Task Constraints', *Annual Review of Psychology*, 47, 273–305.

Eyal, A., R. S. Carel, and J. R. Goldsmith (1994), 'Factors Affecting Long-Term Sick Leave in an Industrial Population', *International Archives of Occupational and Environmental Health*, 66(4), 279–82.

Farrell, D., and C. L. Stamm (1988), 'Meta-analysis of the Correlates of Employee Absence', *Human Relations*, 41(3), 221–7.

Flabbi, L., and A. Ichino (2001), 'Productivity, Seniority and Wages: New Evidence from Personnel Data', *Labour Economics*, 8(3), 359–87.

Flynn, J. R. (1987), 'Massive IQ Gains in 14 Nations: What IQ Tests Really Measure', *Psychological Bulletin*, 101, 171–91.

Freeman, R. B. (1982), 'Union Wage Practices and Wage Dispersion within Establishments', *Industrial and Labor Relations Review*, 36, 3–21.

Gelderblom, A. (2006), 'The Relationship of Age with Productivity and Wages', in European Commission, *Ageing and Employment: Identification of Good Practice to*

Increase Job Opportunities and Maintain Older Workers in Employment, available at <http://ec.europa.eu/employment_social/emplweb/news/index_en>.

Griliches, Z., and J. Mairesse (1998), 'Production Functions: The Search for Identification', in S. Strøm (ed.), *Econometrics and Economic Theory in the Twentieth Century: The Ragnar Frisch Centennial Symposium*, Cambridge: Cambridge University Press.

Hægeland, T., and T. J. Klette (1999), 'Do Higher Wages Reflect Higher Productivity? Education, Gender, and Experience Premiums in a Matched Employer-Employee Data Set', in J. C. Haltiwanger, J. I. Lane, J. R. Spletzer, J. J. M. Theeuwes, and K. R. Troske (eds.), *The Creation and Analysis of Employer-Employee Matched Data*, Amsterdam: Elsevier, 231–59.

Haltiwanger, J. C., J. I. Lane, and J. R. Spletzer (1999), 'Productivity Differences across Employers: The Roles of Employer Size, Age, and Human Capital', *American Economic Review*, 89, Papers and Proceedings, 94–8.

————(2007), 'Wages, Productivity, and the Dynamic Interaction of Businesses and Workers', *Labour Economics*, 14, 575–602.

Hamilton, B. H., J. A. Nickerson, and H. Owan (2004), 'Diversity and Productivity in Work Teams', John M. Olin School of Business.

Harris, M., and B. Holmstrom (1982), 'A Theory of Wage Dynamics', *Review of Economic Studies*, 49, 316–33.

Harrison, D. A., and M. A. Shaffer (1994), 'Comparative Examinations of Self-Reports and Perceived Absenteeism Norms: Wading through Lake Wobegon', *Journal of Applied Psychology*, 79(2), 240–51.

Hedges, J. N. (1973), 'Absence from Work—a Look at some National Data', *Monthly Labor Review*, 96(7), 24–30.

Hellerstein, J. K., D. Neumark, and K. R. Troske (1999), 'Wages, Productivity, and Worker Characteristics: Evidence from Plant-Level Production Functions and Wage Equations', *Journal of Labor Economics*, 17, 409–46.

Hibbs, D. A., and H. Locking (2000), 'Wage Dispersion and Productive Efficiency: Evidence from Sweden', *Journal of Labor Economics*, 18, 755–82.

Horn, J. L., and R. Cattell (1967), 'Age Differences in Fluid and Crystallized Intelligence', *Acta Psychologica*, 26, 107–29.

Howell, D., and E. N. Wolff (1991), 'Trends in the Growth and Distribution of Skills in the U.S. Workplace, 1960–1985', *Industrial and Labour Relations Review*, 44(3), 486–502.

Hutchens, R. (1989), 'Seniority, Wages and Productivity: A Turbulent Decade', *Journal of Economic Perspectives*, 3(4), 49–64.

Ichino, A., and E. Moretti (2006), 'Biological Gender Differences, Absenteeism and the Earning Gap', mimeo, University of Bologna, available at <http://www2.dse.unibo.it/ichino/cycle28.pdf>.

——and R. Riphahn (2004), 'Absenteeism and Employment Protection: Three Case Studies', *Swedish Economic Policy Journal*, 11(1), 95–114.

————(2005), 'The Effect of Employment Protection on Worker Effort: A Comparison of Absenteeism during and after Probation', *Journal of the European Economic Association*, 3(1), 120–43.

Ilmakunnas, P., and S. Ilmakunnas (2006), 'Gradual Retirement and Lengthening of Working Life', HECER Discussion Paper 121.

——and M. Maliranta (2005), 'Technology, Worker Characteristics, and Wage-Productivity Gaps', *Oxford Bulletin of Economics and Statistics*, 67(5), 623–45.

————(2007), 'Aging, Worker Flows, and Firm Performance', HECER Discussion Paper 164.

————and J. Vainiomäki (2001), 'Linked Employer-Employee Data on Finnish Plants for the Analysis of Productivity, Wages, and Turnover', in T. Jensen and A. Holm (eds.), Nordic Labour Market Research on Register Data, TemaNord 593, Nordic Council of Ministers, 205–46.

—————(2004), 'The Roles of Employer and Employee Characteristics for Plant Productivity', *Journal of Productivity Analysis*, 21, 249–76.

Ilmarinen, J. (2001), 'Ageing Workers in Finland and in the European Union: Their Situation and the Promotion of their Working Ability, Employability, and Employment', *Geneva Papers on Risk and Insurance: Issues and Practice*, 26, 623–41.

Indik, B. P. (1965), 'Organization Size and Member Participation', *Human Relations*, 18, 339–50.

Iranzo, S., Schivardi, F., and Tosetti, E. (2006), 'Skill Dispersion and Firm Productivity: An Analysis with Employer-Employee Matched Data', Banca d'Italia, Temi di Discussione No. 577.

Juhn, C., K. M. Murphy, and B. Pierce (1993), 'Wage Inequality and the Rise in Returns to Skill', *Journal of Political Economy*, 101(3), 410–42.

Kohler, S. S., and J. E. Mathieu (1993), 'Individual Characteristics, Work Perceptions, and Affective Reactions Influences on Differentiated Absence Criteria', *Journal of Organizational Behavior*, 14(6), 515–30.

Kremer, M. (1993), 'The O-ring Theory of Economic Development', *Quarterly Journal of Economics*, 108, 551–75.

Kuhn, J. M. (2007), 'When Firms Get Old', in J. M. Kuhn, 'Firm-Employee Interdependencies: Four Empirical Analyses', Ph.D. thesis, Aarhus School of Business.

Kutscher, R. E., and J. F. Walker (1960), 'Comparative Job Performance of Office Workers by Age', *Monthly Labor Review*, 83(1), 39–43.

Lazear, E. and R. L. Moore (1984), 'Incentives, Productivity, and Labor Contracts', *Quarterly Journal of Economics*, 99, 275–96.

Lee, R. (2003), 'The Demographic Transition: Three Centuries of Fundamental Change', *Journal of Economic Perspectives*, 17, 167–90.

Leigh, J. P. (1981), 'The Effects of Union Membership on Absence from Work Due to Illness', *Journal of Labor Research*, 2(2), 329–36.

——(1983), 'Sex Differences in Absenteeism', *Industrial Relations*, 22(3), 349–61.

Lehman, H. (1953), *Age and Achievement*, Princeton: Princeton University Press.

Lehto, A.-M., and H. Sutela (2004), 'Uhkia ja mahdollisuuksia: Työolotutkimusten tuloksia 1977–2003' (in Finnish), Statistics Finland.

Leonard, J. S., D. I. Levine, and A. Joshi (2004), 'Do Birds of a Feather Shop Together? The Effects on Performance of Employees' Similarity with One Another and with Customers', *Journal of Organizational Behavior*, 25, 731–54.

Lesgold, A. (1984), 'Acquiring Expertise', in J. Anderson and S. Kosslyn (eds.), *Tutorials in Learning and Memory: Essays in Honor of Gordon Bower*, New York: Freeman, 31–60.

Levy, B. R. (2003), 'Mind Matters: Cognitive and Physical Effects of Aging Self-Stereotypes', *Journal of Gerontology: Psychological Sciences*, 58B(4), 203–11.

Lührmann, M., and M. Weiss (2007), 'Market Work, Home Production, Consumer Demand and Unemployed among the Unskilled', *MEA-Discussion Paper* 101-06, University of Mannheim.

Lutz, W., A. Goujon, K. C. Samir, and W. Sanderson (2007), 'Reconstruction of Populations by Age, Sex and Level of Educational Attainment for 120 Countries for 1970–2000', *Vienna Yearbook of Population Research*, 2007.

McEvoy, G. M., and W. F. Cascio (1989), 'Cumulative Evidence of the Relationship between Employee Age and Job Performance', *Journal of Applied Psychology*, 74(1), 11–17.

Maitland, S., R. C. Intrieri, W. K. Schaie, and S. L. Willis (2000), 'Gender Differences and Changes in Cognitive Abilities Across the Adult Life Span', *Aging, Neuropsychology, and Cognition*, No. 1, Mar., 32–53 available at <http://www.informaworld.com/smpp/title%7Econtent=t713657683%7Edb=all%7Etab=issueslist%7Ebranches=7-v77>.

Malmberg, B., T. Lindh, and M. Halvarsson (2005), 'Productivity Consequences of Workforce Ageing: Stagnation or a Horndal Effect?' Institute for Futures Studies, Discussion Paper 17.

Manton, K. G., L. Corder, and E. Stallard (1997), 'Chronic Disability Trends in Elderly United States Populations: 1982–1994', *Proceedings of the National Academy of Science*, 94, 2593–8.

Mathieu, J. E., and S. S. Kohler (1990), 'A Cross-Level Examination of Group Absence Influences on Individual Absence', *Journal of Applied Psychology*, 75(2), 217–20.

Medoff, J. L., and K. G. Abraham (1980), 'Experience, Performance, and Earnings', *Quarterly Journal of Economics*, 95(4), 703–36.

Miller, G. F. (1999), 'Sexual Selection for Cultural Displays', in Robin Dunbar, Chris Knight, and Camilla Power (eds.), *The Evolution of Culture*, Edinburgh: Edinburgh University Press, 71–91.

Neisser, U. (1997), 'Rising Scores on Intelligence Test', *American Scientist*, 85, 440–7.

Nicholson, N., T. Wall, and J. Lischeron (1977), 'The Predictability of Absence and Propensity to Leave from Employees' Job Satisfaction and Attitudes toward Influence in Decision Making', *Human Relations*, 30, 499–514.

Nurmi, S. (2004), 'Essays on Plant Size, Employment Dynamics and Survival', Helsinki School of Economics, A-230.

OECD (2006), *Live Longer, Work Longer*, Paris: OECD Publishing.

Oeppen, J., and J. Vaupel (2002), 'Broken Limits to Life Expectancy', *Science*, 296, 1029–31.

Olley, G. S., and A. Pakes (1996), 'The Dynamics of Productivity in the Telecommunications Equipment Industry', *Econometrica*, 64, 1263–97.

Park, D. C., G. Lautenschlager, T. Hedden, N. S. Davidson, and A. D. Smith (2002), 'Model of Visuospatial and Verbal Memory across the Adult Life Span', *Psychology and Aging*, 17(2), 299–320.

Paringer, L. (1983), 'Women and Absenteeism: Health or Economics', *American Economic Review*, 73(2), 123–7.

Phelps Brown, E. H., and S. V. Hopkins (1955), 'Seven Centuries of Building Wages', *Economica*, 195–206.

Phelps, R. H., and J. Shanteau (1978), 'Livestock Judges: How Much Information Can an Expert Use?' *Organizational Behavior and Human Performance*, 21, 209–19.

Porter, L. W., and E. E. Lawler (1965), 'Properties of Organization Structure in Relation to Job Attitudes and Job Behavior', *Psychological Bulletin*, 64, 23–51.

Quetelet, A. (1842), *A Treatise on Man and the Development of his Faculties*, Edinburgh: Chambers.

Raskin, E. (1936), 'Comparison of Scientific and Literary Ability: A Biographical Study of Eminent Scientists and Letters of the Nineteenth Century', *Journal of Abnormal and Social Psychology*, 31, 20–35.

Romeu Gordo, L. (2005), 'Compression of Morbidity and the Labor Supply of Older People', Working Paper, Berlin: Max Planck Institute for Human Development.

Salthouse, T. (1984), 'Effect of Age and Skill in Typing', *Journal of Experimental Psychology: General*, 113, 345–71.

——and T. J. Maurer (1996), 'Aging, Job Performance and Career Development', in J. E Birren and K. W. Schaie (eds.), *Handbook of the Psychology of Aging*, 4th edn., New York: Academic Press.

Schaie, K. W. (1996), *Intellectual Development in Adulthood: The Seattle Longitudinal Study*, New York: Cambridge University Press.

Schoeni, R. F., V. A. Freedman, and R. B. Wallace (2001), 'Persistent, Consistent, Widespread, and Robust? Another Look at Recent Trends in Old-Age Disability', *Journal of Gerontology: Social Sciences*, 56B, 206–18.

Scott, K., and G. S. Taylor (1985), 'An Examination of Conflicting Findings on the Relationship between Job Satisfaction and Absenteeism: A Meta-analysis', *Academy of Management Journal*, 28(3), 599–612.

Skirbekk, V. (2004), 'Age and Individual Productivity: A Literature Survey', in G. Feichtinger (ed.), *Vienna Yearbook of Population Research 2004*, Vienna: Verlag der Österreichischen Akademie der Wissenschaften, 133–53.

——(2008), 'Productivity Potential during the Life Cycle: The Changing Importance of Age-Specific Abilities', *Population and Development Review* (*Special Supplement*), 34, 191–207.

Smith, A. D. (1996), 'Memory', in J. E. Birren and K. W. Schaie (eds.), *Handbook of the Psychology of Aging*, 4th edn., New York: Academic Press, 236–47.

Spector, P. E. (1997), 'Job Satisfaction: Application, Assessment, Causes, and Consequences, Advanced Topics in Organizational Behavior', Thousand Oaks, Calif.: Sage Publications.

Spitz, A. (2004), 'Are Skill Requirements in the Workplace Rising? Stylized Facts and Evidence on Skill-Biased Technological Change', ZEW Discussion Paper No. 04-33, Mannheim, Germany: Zentrum für Europäische Wirtschaftsforschung.

Statistics Norway (2007), Census 2001, available at <http://www.ssb.no>.

Steers, R. M., and S. R. Rhodes (1978), 'Major Influences on Employee Attendance: A Process Model', *Journal of Applied Psychology*, 63(4), 391–407.

Stephan, P. E., and S. G. Levin (1988), 'Measures of Scientific Output and the Age-Productivity Relationship', in Anthony Van Raan (ed.), *Handbook of Quantitative Studies of Science and Technology*, Amsterdam: Elsevier Science Publishers, 31–80.

Tuomi, K., J. Ilmarinen, A. Jahkola, L. Katajarinne, and A. Tulkki, (1998), *Work Ability Index*, 2nd edn., Helsinki: Finnish Institute of Occupational Health.

UN (2005), *World Population Prospects: The 2004 Revision, Volume 1: Comprehensive Tables: United Nations World Population Estimates and Projections*, New York: United Nations.

US Department of Labor (1957), 'Comparative Job Performance by Age: Large Plants in the Men's Footwear and Household Furniture Industries', *Monthly Labor Review*, 80, 1468–71.

Vahtera, J., M. Kivimäki, and J. Pentti (2001), 'The Role of Extended Weekends in Sickness Absenteeism', *Occupational and Environmental Medicine*, 58, 818–22.

Waldman, D. A., and B. J. Avolio (1986), 'A Meta-analysis of Age Differences in Job Performance', *Journal of Applied Psychology*, 71, 33–8.

Warr, P. (1994), 'Age and Employment', in H. Triandis, M. Dunnette, and L. Hough (eds.), *Handbook of Industrial and Organizational Psychology*, 2nd edn., Palo Alto, Calif.: Consulting Psychologists Press, 485–550.

Weiss, M. (2007a), 'Are Age-Diverse Work Teams Better?', *MEA Discussion Paper* 150–07, University of Mannheim.

——(2007b), 'Sick Leave and the Composition of Work Teams', *MEA Discussion Paper*, 149-07, University of Mannheim.

Welford, A. T. (1958), *Ageing and Human Skill*, London: Oxford University Press.

Winter-Ebmer, R., and J. Zweimüller (1999), 'Intra-firm Wage Dispersion and Firm Performance', *Kyklos*, 52, 555–72.

Yatchew, A. (2003), *Semiparametric Regression for the Applied Econometrician*, Cambridge: Cambridge University Press.

Comments

Enrico Moretti

All industrialized countries are experiencing an unprecedented demographic shift. The demographic structure is flattening. Projections show that, for the first time in history, the demographic structure of European countries is expected to be almost flat by 2050. The main contribution of the report by Ilmakunnas *et al.* is to raise and address the following question: what is the effect of this demographic revolution on economic growth and productivity? Just based on the fact that it raises such pressing and extremely policy-relevant question, the report by Ilmakunnas *et al.* is well worth reading. Additionally, it presents some intriguing new evidence on the relationship between age and absenteeism and age and productivity. While the evidence is interesting in itself, more could be done on this topic in the future. The report is therefore the beginning of an ambitious research agenda and the authors deserve much credit for presenting such a comprehensive overview of the possible directions for research.

1. *The Question*

While very broad, the question addressed in the report can be further generalized along two dimensions. First, the report focuses on ageing and its effects on productivity and economic growth. There are different reasons why the population of industrialized counties is ageing. Specifically, the current demographic revolution is driven by two main forces. First, life expectancy is increasing, because of secular improvements in economic conditions and an acceleration in the technological progress in the pharmaceutical and medical industries. Second, fertility rates are declining. Fertility peaked during the baby-boom that took place in the late 1960s and early 1970s in Europe and a decade earlier in the US, and have been declining ever since.

These two forces have different effects on the demographic structure and therefore on productivity, and their effects on labour markets have different implications. For policy-makers, it may be important to distinguish between the effects of these different forces.

Taken in isolation, an increase in life expectancy affects the *relative* shares of young and old individuals, but does not imply that the *absolute* number of young individuals should necessarily decline. A relative increase in the share of the elderly population has tremendous implications for the sustainability of the social security system. However, as far as economic growth is concerned, an increase in health and life expectancy not accompanied by a decline in fertility can only be good news (or at least not bad news). The reason is that such an increase amounts to a potentially sizeable increase in labour supply. It is certainly possible that older individuals are relatively less productive and relatively more likely to be absent. But if individuals live longer, and are willing to work longer, the effect of economic growth can only be positive, or at least non-negative, even if older individuals are less productive. Lower productivity will presumably be reflected in lower wages.

The second force that is driving the demographic revolution is a decline in fertility rates. The effect on economic growth of the decline in fertility rates is potentially more problematic than the increase in life expectancy.

The reason is that, unlike an increase in life expectancy, a marked decline in fertility rates lowers not only the *relative* share of young individuals, but in some European countries it is expected to lower even the *absolute* number of young individuals. An absolute decline in the number of young individuals, accompanied by an increase in the absolute number of elderly individuals, poses a different set of problems. Such change can potentially result in a decline in quality-adjusted labour supply, if the productivity of older individuals is significantly lower than the productivity of younger individuals. It therefore becomes crucial to know how productivity varies over the life cycle, especially in the age range that seems the most likely to be affected by the demographic revolution: 65–75. The main focus of the report is indeed this very question.

For policy, the key point is that ageing is not the same everywhere. The relative importance of increases in life expectancy and declines in fertility varies tremendously across countries. Countries like Italy, where the decline in fertility rate has been particularly pronounced, may face marked *declines* in quality-adjusted labour supply in the coming decades, if indeed

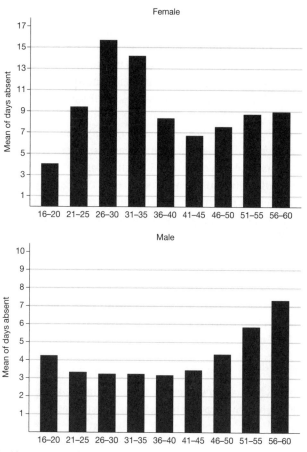

Figure C3.1. Absenteeism, by gender and age

the elderly are less productive than young individuals. Countries like the United States, that have experienced similar increases in life expectancy but much less pronounced declines in fertility rates, may actually be facing *increases* in quality-adjusted labour supply. This distinction is important and should be part of any analysis of the consequences of ageing.

A second dimension along which the focus of the report can be generalized has to do with *gender differences*. I think it would be worthwhile to explore in greater depth what increased female labour force participation at later ages may imply for productivity and economic growth.

The report distinguishes between the effect of ageing on productivity along the extensive margin (absenteeism) and along the intensive margin (decline in physical and mental ability). For the extensive margin, it is well

243

documented that women have a higher incidence of absenteeism than men, especially at earlier stages in their careers. But this gap tends to disappear later in life. Indeed, women are healthier at later ages (relative to men), and live significantly longer. This relatively slower decline in health could in principle affect the intensive margin as well. It would be interesting to compare empirical measures of physical and mental decline by gender.

For example, Figure C3.1, which is based on data from a large Italian bank, shows the incidence of absences for men and women, by age. The gender difference is remarkable. Women have high levels of absenteeism earlier in their life, especially between the ages of 20 and 35, arguably because of pregnancy and pregnancy-related reasons. However, after age 35 women's absenteeism declines, and then stays stable for the rest of their working lives. In contrast, men's absenteeism is flat until age 50, and then increases dramatically.

The two key questions in this respect are: (1) What does this gender difference imply for future productivity trends in countries where female labour force participation is increasing? (2) What would happen to productivity and economic growth if women's retirement age were raised to the level of men, or even higher?

2. Empirical Evidence

The empirical evidence presented by Ilmakunnas *et al.* aims at identifying the effect of ageing on productivity. Even before describing the evidence presented, it is always useful to ask ourselves the question: in an ideal world, with ideal data, what would be the ideal empirical analysis that we would like to see on this question? In this ideal case, we could measure individual-level output, irrespective of labour force participation, and we could easily see (a) whether output declines after a certain age; (b) by how much it declines; and (c) whether this declines varies by skill level.

The three main empirical challenges in answering these questions with real data are:

1. the fact that individual-level output is *rarely observed* and therefore we have to rely on proxies or aggregate data;
2. the fact that even those proxies are unobserved for individuals who are not in the labour force. Because selection in and out of the labour force is not random, but is presumably driven by potential wage, which is itself a function of individual output, there is the potential for a serious *sample selection* problem;

3. the likely presence of *non-linearities*. In particular, we are interested in learning how productivity varies over the life cycle in the age range that is most likely to be affected by the ongoing demographic revolution: 65–75.

The Ilmakunnas *et al.* report is a serious and convincing attempt to address these problems. However, I suspect that even more can be done on these three fronts.

The most interesting question that is addressed by the report focuses on the relationship between age and productivity. Here, of course, the main challenge is the fact that in most data sets, we do not observe an individual output. The authors begin looking at the relationship between age and a self-reported measure of working capacity. They then use two linked employer-employee data sets to estimate production functions, where the age of the workforce is the key variable of interest.

While this is potentially the most interesting contribution of the report, it is also the part that presents the most serious empirical challenges. First, I do not find the self-reported measure of working capacity particularly informative. They find that there is evidence that employees' own assessment of their working capacity falls with age, but that this decline is not very pronounced, because most older workers consider their working capacity to be still quite high.

Self-reported measures of output are notoriously noisy. While noise in the dependent variable is in theory less problematic than noise in the independent variable, I am not too sure how to interpret these estimates. How do we know that workers are not reporting their productivity relative to their age group? In this respect, I find it reassuring (and indeed quite interesting) that the self-reported productivity measure declines more for physical jobs than for non-physical jobs. The interpretation of these models is made more challenging because some of these models control for earnings. I am not sure that this is the correct specification. Earnings are indeed endogenous, because they are likely to be a function of working capacity.

The plant-level analysis is probably the most interesting empirical evidence presented in the report. The authors use a unique data set that they have compiled from an assembly plant of DaimlerChrysler. There is a clear output measure, which is the speed of the assembly line. Quality is also an important determinant of output, because workers can make errors, and a 'quality inspector' at the end of the assembly line identifies errors. The main finding is that the productivity of a team is decreasing with the average age of the team (although job tenure has the opposite effect).

This is interesting because it is a direct and easily interpretable measure of output decline.

The problem of non-linearities is particularly severe in this set of models. While the specifications adopted are non-linear, it is clear that variation in average team age is much less than variation in individual age. For example, average team age in the DaimlerChrysler sample varies between 26 and 50. What we are really interested in is how individual productivity varies in the range 65–75. It is difficult to take the estimate based on average age between 26 and 50 and draw inferences on the decline in individual productivity far from that range.

The other serious problem here is the endogeneity of team average age. What determines the variation in team composition? It would be important to determine whether there are differences in technology, incentives, or monitoring between teams with average age equal to 26 and teams with average age equal to 50.

3. *An Alternative Approach*

If the goal is to measure the decline in individual productivity, a possible alternative to measuring absenteeism and team-level output is to use wages. Wages have several advantages over the approach described above. First, wages are roughly equal to the marginal product of labour. Second, any decline in wages associated with age should in principle reflect any decline in productivity and any increase in absenteeism. Third, wages are measured at the individual level, and in many samples we observe individuals in the relevant age range (65–75). Of course, selection problems are particularly severe, especially in that range.

For the question addressed here, wages are a good measure only if there are reasons to believe that they are not very far from marginal product. The presence of union contracts makes ages harder to interpret. Furthermore, if nominal wages are rigid downward, we might not see significant nominal reductions for older workers, even if marginal product declines with age.

The ideal sample for this exercise is therefore a sample of workers who are not unionized and who are observed in a period of substantial inflation. In the presence of downward nominal wage rigidity, inflation allows employers to lower real wages.

To illustrate this point, I have used longitudinal data from the Panel Study of Income Dynamics (PSID), which follows about 10,000 US workers for 35 years. I began by estimating wage equations that only include a fourth-order polynomial in age and standard demographic controls. I then estimate a model that also includes individual fixed effects.

There are two types of sample selections in action in this exercise. First, workers who are observed in the labour force after age 65 may have a different set of skills, ability, and motivation than workers who retire at 65. Notably, the selection may be positive or negative, depending on whether income effects or price effects dominate in retirement decisions. Workers who have better skills (such as higher intellectual and physical ability, or lower cost of effort) have both higher permanent income and a higher hourly wage. If the price effect dominates, workers with better skills are more likely to keep working after 65. If income effects dominate, workers with better skills are more likely to retire earlier.

Second, given the set of skills of a given worker, an individual who happens to receive a particularly good draw in terms of wage after age 65 is more likely to be observed working. The line marked 'unconditional' in Figure C3.2 shows predicted log wages for each age, when no controls are included for all workers. Wages peak at 45–50. Between 50 and 60 log wages decline somewhat. By age 60, wages appear to be about 15% below their peak. After age 60, the decline is much more pronounced. In particular, between age 60 and age 80, wages decline by 60–70%.

The line marked 'conditional' in Figure C3.2 shows the predicted log wage for each age, after controlling for individual fixed effects. For ease of comparison, both lines have been renormalized so that they are equal to 1 at age 60 (before re-normalization, the conditional line is above the

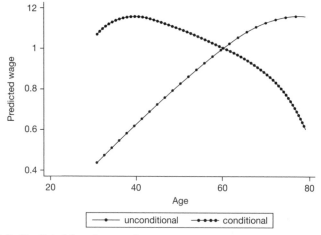

Figure C3.2. Predicted hourly wage by age

unconditional line). The conditional line shows that, relative to an individual mean, wages keep increasing at older ages.

I draw two conclusions. First, income effects seem to dominate price effects in retirement decisions. Second, after controlling for permanent unobserved heterogeneity, the amount of selection is still likely to be enormous. The fact that wages are observed to be increasing until age 70–5 is probably driven by the fact that workers who happen to receive a better draw *given their permanent income* delay retirement.

Comments

Etienne Wasmer

Introduction

This is a really interesting piece, which uses a general framework to analyse the relations between age and absenteeism, between age and working capacity, between age and productivity at the plant level, and which derives some policy implications.

The main findings can be summarized as follows. First, the productivity of workers is a multidimensional variable: health, cognitive skills, verbal skills among others. Second, the effect of age on those skills is complex, and in particular not monotonic. For instance, the frequency of absenteeism episodes is higher for younger workers than for older workers, but on the other hand, the duration of absenteeism is higher for older worker. Another example is that various cognitive and non-cognitive abilities vary differently with age: most skills tend to decline with age (the ability to learn, speed, memory), but some (e.g. verbal ability) increase. Finally, and this is very reassuring, overall, labour market behaviour is more important than age for productivity: *an individual's actions can partly or fully undo the biological effect of age and fatigue effects.*

Before making further remarks and suggestions, let us first ask why it is critically important to improve the state of our knowledge. In fact, there are several implications of the studies contained in the report:

(a) for reforms of pension systems, and notably to determine the optimal age of retirement, it is important to know whether senior workers can work efficiently after the age of say, 55, or whether one should instead optimally let them retire early if their productivity is declining fast;

(b) whether or not older workers' skills depreciate faster certainly matters for the design of training policies;

(c) the intensity of depreciation of skills matters for education policies too, notably whether education should be specific to a sector or to a type of job, but at the cost of future depreciation or whether it should be general at some possible short-run cost (less specialized workers).

In short, this type of work has implications for *most* aspects of labour economics. In this discussion, I will start with a couple of general remarks, then strengthen the conclusions and policy, and end up with two conjectures on the relation between age and productivity.

Before that, two concerns. First, there is very little in the report about the gender dimension. Are skills and productivity depreciating faster depending on gender or not? This question would be very interesting to address explicitly, at least to try to rationalize the observation that in most countries, the retirement age for female workers (both the effective retirement and the legal one) is lower than for male workers. This question may have deserved more emphasis since it has important implications for economic policy and the retirement age.

Second, a few dimensions of the relation between age and productivity are missing. In particular, very little is said about career mobility. This is an issue because arguably, most of the relations between age and productivity are driven by occupation changes or even sector changes. To see this, just consider a variant of the so-called Roy model, in which workers allocate themselves to sectors where they are more productive. If, as shown in the data, verbal skills improve over time, since they matter more at a higher level of hierarchy, an important dimension of the relation between age and productivity is access, over time, to jobs and occupations where those verbal skills are more rewarded. Symmetrically, learning skills is easier at a younger age and so younger workers are more likely to allocate themselves to occupations where learning is important. So, occupations are a first-order determinant of the age-productivity link, but little is said about occupations and occupation choices throughout the report.

Th second concern is: does the endogenous choice of occupations matter? Well, in works such as the one estimating the number of errors on the assembly line as a function of age, as in Chapter 11, there is potentially an upward bias: those older workers who make more mistakes may be more likely to miss out on promotion and hence to remain as an assembly-line worker. Alternatively, those who may end up staying on the assembly line may be there precisely because they are good at what they do; the other older workers who were less good at the task may have been kicked out or reshuffled to other activities.

An additional minor point here: there is a literature on peer effects showing that the fewer mistakes are committed by co-workers, the more costly it is to commit an error. This means that the 'error' terms in the regressions (error in the econometric sense!) are likely to be correlated between individuals, and thus that the variance-covariance matrix may be more efficiently estimated with a particular structure.

Now, in a more general set-up, where one is interested in the late career productivity profile, another endogeneity concern may be raised. This is essentially a similar issue to the previous one, if one simply reinterprets occupation choice as participation (vs. non-participation) decisions. And one can very easily see that participation decisions are elastic, depending on the individuals and their environment.

For instance, the figures that follow indicate that institutions affect participation choices. In particular, the implicit tax rate of continuing to work between the age of 55 and 59 years is negatively associated with the change in the participation rate between the early and the late fifties, across countries. Given this and the position of Italy and more generally continental European countries as regards implicit tax rates, the participation/age profile as indicated in Figure 7.1. (see Chapter 7) is not too surprising.

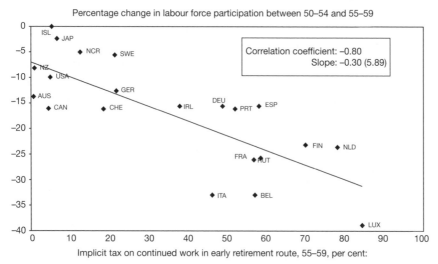

Figure C4.1. Change in labour force participation and tax on continuing work

Source: OECD (2005), 'Economic Policy Reforms: Going for Growth 2005', OECD Publishing, available at <http://www.oecd.org/document/4/0,3343,en_2649_34325_34429380_1_1_1_1,00.html>. Reproduced by kind permission of OECD Publishing.

Beyond the skills question, the incentives to retire or not matter a lot, as convincingly argued in the report. Notice that given what we said above, namely that skill maintenance decisions also depend on the time horizon, the effect of tax incentives is multiplied: the higher the implicit tax rate, the lower the skill investments by individuals in their early fifties, and thus ex post the lower the optimal retirement age.

Human capital theory explains why and how most skills are maintained as long as they are useful and necessary. Going one step further, since the time horizon matters a lot, one might have wanted to address life expectancy in this chapter and its role in shaping the structure of human capital investments and reciprocally, how cognitive ability impacts on life expectancy. Since statistics on life expectancy are relatively easy to find, it might have been possible to draw inferences about the end of careers of senior workers by sector, education, country, gender... (this is why older persons should play Scrabble as long as they can, why their skills deteriorate fast when their spouse dies, why older heads of states often die one or two years after they resign, etc.).

What does the Age-Productivity Profile Mean?

A typical finding of the human capital literature is that productivity first grows with age, reaches a peak (empirically, estimated to be in a worker's fifties in cross-section data,[1] and finally declines over time. Do wages follow productivity? This is unclear. Two arguments run here against the view that both are equal at any point in the life cycle. First, human capital must be accumulated, and in the 'learning-or-doing' view of the world, a worker cannot be full-time productive and learn. So her wages will equal her potential productivity (that is, human capital), net of the time spent learning, at least over the periods where she learns. Second, there are incentive effects: for workers to stay in the firm and learn, that is, to sacrifice the short-run gains of working full-time instead of learning, they must have incentives, and in particular, get a higher wage at a later stage of their career. Lazear (1979) made this point in a famous paper: either by contract or by implicit agreement, workers receive compensation above their productivity after some point. To avoid workers exploiting this rent, it must be compulsory to end the career at some point known in advance.

These arguments, illustrated for the career path of a random researcher in Figure C4.2, would indicate that it is difficult to measure productivity with

---

[1] Works based on longitudinal data are less clear about the existence of this hump-shaped curve.

Productivity

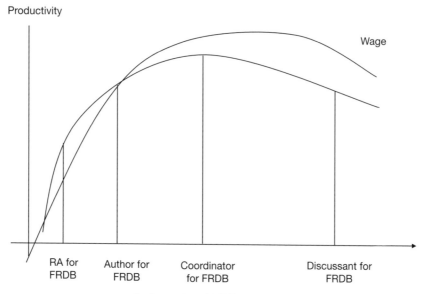

Ageing and productivity: comment

Figure C4.2. Labour market theory of this curve

Source: N. Lepage-Saucier and E. Wasmer (2007), 'Cross-Country Regressions of Stress and EPL' mimeo, Sciences PO-Paris.

wages (hence the study based on errors at the assembly line is a particularly valuable one).

Another remark on this type of figure linking age and productivity is that age and cohorts are typically confounded. However, as regards 'crystallized abilities', education policies may have had a large impact on cohorts, affecting the interpretation of such non-linear relationships. The generation before us makes no grammatical mistakes and remembers much poetry, but often cannot plug in a PC and is bemused by the 'trial and error' process of the internet. This would suggest that the construction of skills is as much a collective effort as an individual one.

Finally, what would really improve the work, and this is the first conjecture of this discussion, is the missing link between technology and ageing. This link has only been briefly mentioned in the introduction to the report, but more precise answers to the following two questions would be very important: (a) is IT youth-friendly relative to older workers and does this explain the declining productivity of older workers relative to younger workers? And (b),

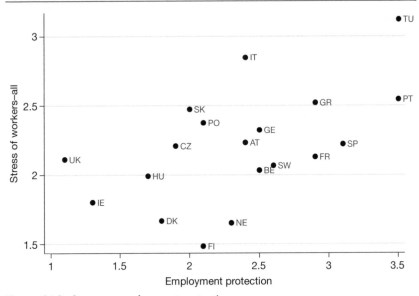

Figure C4.3. Stress vs. employment protection

Source: N. Lepage-Saucier and E. Wasmer (2007), 'Cross-Country Regressions of Stress and EPL', mimeo, Sciences PO-Park.

can we think of ITs that would instead raise the relative productivity of senior workers? If so, what are they and would it be socially optimal to subsidy them?

A last issue and the second conjecture of this discussion is that the amount of stress experienced by individuals in the workplace is different between countries; it even seems to vary enormously. In Figure C4.3, taken from Lepage-Saucier and Wasmer (2007), it appears that countries where workers report more stress (Greece, Italy, Portugal) tend also to be those where retirement occurs earlier. To the extent that older workers suffer more from stress and that various workplace organizations generate more or less stress (as suggested by the positive correlation with Employment Protection Legislation), this suggests that one major improvement in the employability of senior workers may be to favour 'cooler' workplace organization where the amount of stress is less important.

References

Lazear, Edward P. (1979), 'Why Is There Mandatory Retirement?' *Journal of Political Economy*, 87(6), 1261–84.

Lepage-Saucier, N., and Wasmer, E. (2007), 'Cross-Country Regressions of Stress and EPL', mimeo, Sciences Po-Paris.

OECD (2005), 'Economic Policy Reforms: Going for Growth 2005', OECD Publishing, available at ⟨http://www.oecd.org/document/4/0,3343,en_2649_34325_34429380_1_1_1_1,00.html⟩.

Index

Index

Index